MANUS DAYS

The Untold Story of Manus Island

MANUS DAYS
The Untold Story of Manus Island

Michael Coates
Foreword by Miranda Devine

Published in 2018 by Connor Court Publishing Pty Ltd

Connor Court Publishing Pty Ltd
PO Box 7257
Redland Bay QLD 4165

sales@connorcourt.com
www.connorcourt.com
Phone 0497 900 685

ISBN: 9781925501735

Front Cover Design: Maria Giordano

Front Cover Picture: Rich Froning

Printed in Australia

CONTENTS

FOREWORD

To refugee activists, Greens and assorted other "compassionistas", Manus Island is a "gulag", a "concentration camp", a shameful moral stain on Australia's character.

But this beautiful tropical island off the coast of New Guinea also has been a crucial element of Australia's successful border protection policies, which, in turn, have ensured public acceptance of the world's most generous per capita refugee resettlement program.

Manus has been a political pawn in Australia's culture wars since August 2001, when the MV Tampa sailed into view.

Australia's then-Prime Minister John Howard refused to allow the Norwegian freighter to unload 438 Afghan asylum seekers rescued in international waters from a sinking people smuggler's boat.

The Afghans eventually were taken to a detention centre hastily set up on the small Pacific country of Nauru. Another offshore processing centre followed on Manus Island, and the "Pacific Solution" was born.

In an election that November, in the aftermath of the September 11 terrorist attacks on the United States, Howard summed up his tough border protection policies with the immortal line: "We decide who comes into this country and the circumstances in which they come."

His government won an increased majority.

Business soon dried up for people smugglers and, by 2004, the Manus Regional Processing Centre was empty.

But the Rudd Labor government, elected in 2007, dismantled Howard's border protections on the urging of refugee activists, and the boats started flooding back, bringing 50,000 "illegal maritime arrivals" over the next six years and the tragedy of 1200 asylum seekers drowned at sea.

In July, 2013, months before an election he would lose, then Prime Minister Kevin Rudd announced his own hardline border protections, jointly with PNG Prime Minister Peter O'Neill. All new asylum-seekers would be sent to Manus and would have "no chance of being settled in Australia as refugees".

Thus began phase 2 of the Manus story.

The Abbott government – was elected in 2013 with the mandate to "stop the boats".

Manus Regional Processing Centre soon was full and recruiting security personnel from the ranks of ex-soldiers recently returned from the war in Afghanistan.

Among them was Michael Coates, a 27 yearold ex-soldier who arrived on Manus just after the much publicised 2014 riots in which Iranian asylum seeker Reza Barati was killed.

His book humanises the fraught joint history of Manus and Australia.

For the first time, he has told the story of Manus from the point of view of an Australian without an axe to grind. He had no view on the government's policies. He was there to do a job, to provide security for local staff and asylum seekers.

His keen observations of daily life on Manus and his insights into the characters of diverse groups of asylum seekers paints a far more nuanced picture than either side of the refugee debate has provided thus far.

It is not the picture of persecuted innocents, as painted by refugee activists, but nor is it a picture of con-artists scamming our immigration laws. The truth lies somewhere in between.

Coates has a gift for drawing pen portraits of asylum seekers.

There was the Iranian pickpocket "Captain Jack", named because of his resemblance to Johnny Depp in Pirates of the Caribbean.

> "He would later go on to tell me of his illustrious career as a heroin addict, proudly displaying the track marks along his arms and between his fingers and toes. He also spoke of the sugardaddy he had lived with in Thailand before boarding the boat to Australia, who supplied him with a never-ending stream of drugs in exchange for sex."

Coates writes with compassion about the Tamil, Rohingya and Hazara asylum seekers, who were "a pleasure to be around. They were respectful and cooperative – none of the yelling and abuse that came from their Iranian neighbours".

He also gives a brutally frank assessment of the middle-class Iranian "party boys" who were "fleeing from prosecution, not persecution", and who led riots and stood over other groups on the island.

> "They had a more respectful but still strained relationship with the centre's Arab community, which was mainly made up of Iraqi and Lebanese. The only group they didn't seem to want to antagonise was the Africans."

The Iranians told him how they had spent months in Thailand before buying passage to Australia with people smugglers, "drinking and womanising and [indulging in] vices that had not been so easily available back in Iran ... That is the freedom they want."

He describes how the peaceful Manus locals grew increasingly hostile towards badly behaved asylum seekers, mainly Iranians, who they were paid to wait on hand and foot, but who returned the favour with racist insults.

"They are rude! They call us animals, they mock our country," the locals told Coates. "They yell 'Fuck Australia! Fuck PNG!' They flash their cocks to the women walking by on the road! They yelled at us that they would kill us and rape our wives."

In the end, Coates grew suspicious of case managers on Manus, who he came to believe were "actively encouraging unrest amongst the transferees" along with refugee activists back in Australia.

He was disillusioned about "the violence, the sexual assaults, the treatment of the locals – but also the manipulation of well-meaning but naïve people back in Australia who seemed so desperate to believe what they were being told."

Coates's book is a valuable contribution to one of the most contentious debates in Australia's history.

Miranda Devine, December 2017

PROLOGUE

My armour stank.

That's a weird thing to be noticing when you are about to head into an all-in brawl, but it was pungent. The Scorpion body armour that adorned me and sixty-five other men shoulder-to-shoulder reeked to high heaven.

This was to be expected – I had lost count of the amount of times we had kitted up in the last three days. In the equatorial heat of Papua New Guinea it would take just seconds for the sweat to be flowing and soaking into every crevice of you and anything you were wearing.

It wasn't like training. There was no spraying down of kit, drying it in the sun and then carefully packing it away in your kitbag like after an exercise. Every time we had de-kitted it had been straight back in the bag, ensuring the flavour was sealed in for the next inevitable call-up. But this time was no call-up.

The deadline had passed.

It had been nearly seventy-two hours to the minute since everything had started to go to shit at the Manus Regional Processing Centre (MRPC). Seventy-two hours since the transferees in Delta compound had made good on their threats to attack the local and ex-pat staff working there and driven them out. Seventy-two hours since those same transferees had then barricaded the entrances to the compound, effectively countering the initial attempt by our Emergency Response Team (ERT) to gain entry and restore order.

The last time the MRPC had experienced disorder on this level had been eleven months prior, when rioting transferees had overwhelmed staff and necessitated the intervention of the much-feared PNG Police Mobile Squad. That had resulted in one death and dozens of serious injuries not to mention a full-scale political incident.

A lot had changed at the MRPC since then. Physically the place was almost unrecognisable, and the ERT (now heavily-reinforced from off-island) had spent many a long hot hour over the last year preparing for scenarios just like this one. We knew that we were a lot more prepared this time. But we still didn't know what we would encounter inside, and there was a lot riding on how the next hour played out – not just the government's policy of offshore processing, but the safety of our lives and our jobs.

The last three days had not been kind to anyone at the MRPC. For those on our side of the fence, it had been three days of little sleep and even less concrete information. For the two compounds under barricade (Delta's neighbour Oscar had also joined in after seeing their mates getting the better of the ERT) it had been three days since any food or fresh water had gotten in.

This was not due to some sort of sadistic medieval siege tactic as some elements of the media were already suggesting, but more to do with fact that with all the gates barricaded the caterers could not physically get the food in. Any attempts were met by either a barrage of rocks or threats of mass suicide. In essence it was simply a more directly confrontational version of the non-violent hunger strikes that were occurring concurrently in the adjoining Foxtrot and Mike compounds.

Even Oscar, who had removed the barricades during the subsequent days and allowed some staff to return was still refusing the delivery of food under the usual tactic of threatening violence and self-harm. It wasn't the majority of course – just the highly-vocal and troublesome core group. They influenced by intimidation – mainly of their own people, but they were trying their best on us as well. Like always, the many were paying for the actions of a few.

It wasn't as if those who were enforcing these hunger strikes were going hungry themselves. In the moments following the initial barricading the canteens and their plentiful supplies of chocolate and two-minute noodles had been forced open and looted, the contents no doubt in the hands of the enforcers. You can't run a hunger strike on an empty stomach.

There was still running water for ablutions, but the thousands of bottles of drinking water that are usually delivered every day had not been getting in. The bottles that had already been inside the compounds beforehand could provide a sizable stockpile to anybody with any discipline. But seeing the wasteful manner in which many transferees treated life's most precious resource led us to believe that by this time the water situation inside Delta would be dire.

But the food and water situation was not our greatest concern. What worried us the most were the threats coming from inside the compound that would force our hand – of mass self-harm, or more likely, the deliberate injury or murder of an innocent victim by the ringleaders orchestrating the siege from within. After all, why hurt yourself when you can hurt somebody smaller and weaker and still achieve the same goal?

If people inside were being physically harmed, we would be compelled to go in. But breaching a barricaded compound when you are heavily outnumbered and hamstrung by political considerations that dictate how you undertake such a task... you can see why we wanted it done on our terms and not a moment before we were ready.

For the last three days whilst the plan for exactly how we would get in there had been thrown back and forth, volatile Oscar had kept us on our toes with incidents and threats of just about every scenario you could imagine. Most had turned out to be false alarms, but every call to kit up, followed by the waiting for information that seemed painfully slow in coming, then the inevitable call to stand down, was beginning to take it's toll.

Every time that call comes you begin to psych yourself up, mentally preparing yourself to charge head first into whatever situation might be waiting. The crash from that adrenaline build-up when the signal to stand-down comes was absolutely draining, and this was happening around the clock.

So as I stood there, in the blazing afternoon sun, sweating my arse off and trying to ignore the nervous butterflies doing hot laps around the pit of my stomach, I just wanted it to be over. Not just because I wanted to do what we had trained to do for so long and because I wanted some consequences to finally come the way of those that had caused this whole mess, but because I wanted to sleep.

We began to hear a commotion in the distance. That sound and the situation updates making their way across the radio net told us that the diversionary breach teams were beginning to have the desired effect. After what seemed like an eternity but was probably only half a minute, the call crackled from the net that we had all been waiting for.

"Ranger One, Ranger One – Go! Go! Go!"

CHAPTER 1

INTERESTING WORK IN THE SOUTH PACIFIC

Just about everybody in Australia has an opinion about this country's policy of offshore immigration processing. It may not be a strong opinion, and most won't even articulate it unless asked. A lot of them also won't have it based on any hard facts, and even fewer on genuine first-hand experience.

For an issue that has such little impact on the lives of everyday Australians, it certainly is a divisive one. Perhaps that is the reason in itself – it's a far away issue, snippets on the news or social media. It's easy to have an opinion on something when it doesn't directly affect you and when the consequences are not yours to deal with. It's part of our modern society, where the information age has led us to be better informed than ever before, though not always as much as we might like to think.

To some, it is a deeply moral and emotional issue. To others, it is simply pragmatic and practical. It appeals to our innate sense of what is right – compassion to all and the notion of a "fair go" versus the need for security and due diligence. The one thing that almost everyone has in common, be they an activist or a supporter, is that their view is largely academic. Until the day I first set foot on the humid Pacific Ocean outpost that was Manus Island, I was exactly the same as all of them.

So how had I come to be a part of this whole mess? How had I ended up on the literal front-line of the so-called Pacific Solution? For me, just like so many of my friends and colleagues sweating it out in high-order under the blazing equatorial sun, it had begun almost eleven months earlier with us feeling much the same way — tired and completely unsure of what we were about to walk into.

My reason for wanting to work in the centres had nothing to do with politics, and certainly nothing to do with my own thoughts on their morality. My motivation for signing up to Operation Sovereign Borders was perhaps the most basic of motivations — money. That and the desire to be doing something out-of-the-ordinary. But I think deep down, what I wanted most of all was to escape my current situation.

It was the closing months of 2013, and I was amid a quarter-life crisis. I was twenty-seven, going on twenty-eight. In the year since discharging from the Australian Army, I had had my share of highs and lows. Things had started off very high, I had spent three months road tripping across America, then cruising the Caribbean with rock-stars. Following a quick visit home for Christmas I jetted off again — this time to South Africa.

I had originally intended to pursue work in anti-poaching, something that would allow me to apply the skills I had to a worthy cause, as well as live the life-less-ordinary I desired. It was not to be. South African visa issues notwithstanding, I was still receiving a salary from the army in lieu of unclaimed leave, and spent the next few months in the loving embrace of the bars and beaches of Cape Town, sharing a beach house with Scandinavian backpackers and generally having the gap year that most young Australians these days seem to have a decade earlier in life.

But coming home, the reality of having to start from scratch was a harsh reminder that the real world was not going away. My preparation for transition to civilian life was woefully inadequate and I had not really given any serious thought to anything beyond travelling. I had made enquiries into the police and fire services, but nothing had come of it. I even tried my hand at working at a travel agency, but I found the office-bound minimum-wage existence depressing.

There were far lower points than my lack of direction, however. Just over a year previously, my mother had been diagnosed with cervical cancer. I had been staying with my sister in Melbourne since my return from Africa and was painfully aware of the fact that time was not on anyone's side. With my foray into the travel industry a dismal failure and conscious of the fact that my mother was in her last days, I packed up and returned to my hometown of Bundaberg in regional Queensland.

As well as trying to spend some quality time with my Mum (if you can call the final months of terminal cancer quality time) I set about trying to find work in a town which I was now discovering had one of the highest unemployment rates in the state. This was a real eye-opener for me, something that was both frustrating and humbling. I had always taken a rather dim view of the chronically unemployed but now I was starting to see the other side of the equation.

I was keen, motivated, and well-presented. I must have applied for literally dozens of jobs. I cold-called. I went door-to-door. I applied for almost every advertised position, drafting elaborate cover letters explaining how my skills and experience could be utilised to fit the vacancy. Most went unanswered. The few interviews I did manage to secure led to nothing. Maybe they sensed that I didn't really want to be there, or maybe they just had better qualified applicants. Either way, it wasn't happening for me.

I would have been in real trouble if it wasn't for my father and stepmother, who were supportive of me throughout the whole situation and let me stay with them rent-free. The situation was really getting to me. It was about this time that I discovered my application to the police service had been rejected. Admitting that I had been involved in a bar fight in Florida had apparently horrified the psychologist. When the horrible day finally came, and cancer took my mother, it's fair to say I was at a low point.

With my savings dwindling and a burning desire to get out of town, I needed something quick. The highly-lucrative but competitive Middle East security circuit was out of my reach, due to the conventional nature of my army time as well as my lack of industry contacts in what is very much a "who you know" game. Not knowing what else to do, I enrolled in a course to obtain my security licence. It was due to run for two whole days.

The course was an eye-opener, and not in a good way. The security industry in Australia is not a respected one, and is anything but lucrative, especially for those at the bottom. Perhaps this is a testament to the relatively safe lifestyle we are fortunate to experience in this country. But I was still disappointed and disheartened by the calibre of the folks attending the course.

In an industry which really only exists as a means of keeping insurance premiums down, the old saying that you pay peanuts and get monkeys was ringing true. I was shocked when I learnt that a security licence was one of the government-funded training courses offered by Centrelink to the long-term unemployed. Despite my recent brush with joblessness, I couldn't see how that in addition to the already laughably low entry requirements could assist an industry already seen by many as a joke.

Things did not start well. We were half an hour late in starting as one of the students – a kid who was at least 50kg overweight and had trouble navigating the stairs – arrived at the grand hour of 9a.m. with two jumbo sized McDonald's meals for breakfast. It then took us another hour for him and some of the other students to complete the enrolment forms.

The course instructor, a former police officer and private investigator, could clearly sense my frustration and asked me to join him for a coffee during the morning break. He told me that there was no way he was going to have me sit through the course and that he would submit my certification and licensing through Recognition of Prior Learning. I was eternally grateful. We had plenty of time to discuss this and many other things – the fifteen-minute break stretched out to forty-five as many of the students forgot how to look at their watches when having a cigarette.

After filling out a few RPL forms I knocked off for the day – all I had to do was return the following afternoon and complete the Basic First Aid component. Having been a Combat First Aider, the instructor simply had me demonstrate the techniques for the class and then signed me off. Before leaving, I asked him whether the other students on the course were going to pass.

"They already have, because they have already been paid for. Nobody has to give them jobs though."

That stinging indictment of our industry's future delivered, we shook hands and parted ways.

* * *

I quickly secured a job with a company that claimed to be the primary security provider for some major Brisbane infrastructure. As soon as I started work however I saw that this was not exactly the case. My views on the industry were quickly proving to be correct. They did work for the corporation, but they were hardly the primary provider.

The corporation actually had its own in-house security department which was quite well looked after – we were simply hired as an outsourcing of all the crappy and menial tasks that they didn't want to do. Not only that, those tasks were often erratic and last minute, leading to uncertain and unreliable rostering. Poor pay and uncertainty about whether you would have any shifts from week to week led to a very high turnover and the quality of staff they attracted was low.

Many of the in-house staff encouraged me to cross over and I gave it serious thought. But I was my own worst enemy. I was unenthusiastic and frankly embarrassed about the work and it showed in my increasingly bad attitude. The office politics were out of control and I whilst I did my best to stay out of it all, they seemed to still find me. I began clashing with both the in-house and contract staff. One colleague even started taking it upon himself to make notes on everything I said or did, trying to make me out to be either rogue or negligent. I confronted him about it and made my feelings clear.

"You think I'm not taking this job seriously? You're right! This job is a joke. Unlocking doors and disarming alarms just so you can turn them back on and re-lock them? A monkey would be embarrassed to be doing it!"

Somehow, I kept my job. The writing was on the wall though, and you can imagine my relief when a phone call came during my shift one Saturday evening...

* * *

As the soul-crushing monotony of checking locks and jiggling keys wore on, I had been actively looking for new opportunities. Still keen to escape the mundane, I had been applying for security jobs aboard cruise ships and at remote tropical resorts, everywhere from the Whitsundays to the Maldives. Anything to escape my current situation.

Who would have ever thought that Julia Gillard's revamp of the Pacific Solution would have come knocking?

In the later months of 2012, Gillard's Labor government announced the recommencement of offshore immigration processing on the tiny Pacific island nation of Nauru and on Papua New Guinea's Manus Island province. Ironically, its abandonment had been one of the key policies in her Labor Party's election campaign of 2007 – something they followed through with the following year when the centres on Nauru and Manus were closed.

Just as many suspected, the flow of seaborne illegal immigration – which had all but halted under Howard's original Pacific Solution – was soon back in full swing, with boats arriving almost daily. Not only that, the increased number of boats was leading to the inevitable increase of at-sea tragedies, with many of the overcrowded and under-maintained vessels sinking or running aground and hundreds of lives being lost.

In one of those policy back flips that politics is famous for, Labor had been forced to reintroduce offshore processing to deal with the influx. On the 19th of July 2013, Kevin Rudd said something that would change the game completely, especially for the people smugglers who relied on Australia's treatment of unauthorised boat arrivals as an indicator of how their business would fare:

"From now on, any asylum seeker who arrives in Australia by boat will have no chance of being settled in Australia as refugees. Asylum seekers taken to Christmas Island will be sent to Manus and elsewhere in Papua New Guinea for assessment of their refugee status. If they are found to be genuine refugees, they will be resettled in Papua New Guinea... If they are found not to be genuine refugees they may be repatriated to their country of origin or be sent to a safe third country other than Australia."

The date and content of that quote would come to live on in infamy for these asylum seekers and their advocates. I would be constantly reminded of it too for the duration of my working life on Manus, as those same voices sought to somehow use it to draw parallels between that statement and the speeches of Adolf Hitler. Incomparable and ridiculous of course, but emotive.

I often wondered if the same fixation was placed on John Howard's famous choice of words during the original incarnation of the policy:

"We are a generous open-hearted people taking more refugees on a per capita basis than any nation except Canada, we have a proud record of welcoming people from 140 different nations.

"But we will decide who comes to this country and the circumstances in which they come... We will be compassionate, we will save lives, we will care for people, but we will decide and nobody else who comes to this country."

Critics and the left-leaning in the media always got a lot of mileage out of that one. I always shook my head as to how they made it sound as if it was the most diabolical and grotesque statement imaginable. I always thought it was a fair point. Would people not expect the same say into choosing the guests entering their own home? Besides, it never said anything about *not* helping those who were genuinely in need. It was all about due diligence. That's how I saw it anyway.

The reopened Nauru and Manus Island centres started to come onto my radar personally in late 2013, in the time leading up to my mother's death. I came across it through Facebook of all places, where suddenly a lot of my old army mates were checking in more than usual at the Brisbane International Airport, as well as other exotic-sounding locations like Meneng and Yaren.

I knew from news reports that the Army had a construction unit on Nauru to begin resurrecting the facilities that had fallen into disrepair after the centre's abandonment back in 2008. But there was no way these guys were heading over there in uniform. Something else was happening.

Just as it had occurred with the Pacific Solution's original incarnation in 2001, the military had been involved in the initial start-up of the centres, but only briefly. It wasn't a traditional military task, but the military just happens to have the self-contained and rapidly-deployable ability to move into a remote area and basically create something from nothing. They don't complain as much about the lack of comfort either. (Actually, that's a lie. Soldiers do complain and complain hard, it's just that nobody really listens.)

Once that initial groundwork is done, the military packs up and goes home. At that point the Pacific Solutions true overlord, the Department of Immigration and Citizenship (DIAC) comes in and gets down to business doing what they do. At some point around this time, DIAC changed it's name to DIBP (Department of Immigration and Border Protection).

Whatever its acronym, the department needed people to run the nuts and bolts of the centre and its supporting infrastructure. Stuff like construction, transport and logistics, medical and catering services and, of course, security. To do this, the government did exactly what has become expected of governments in these modern times – they outsourced.

It didn't take too many e-mails to find out who the head of this big outsourcing animal was, and it was a name that was very familiar to me. Anybody who has spent time in the defence forces in this country would be familiar with Transfield and other similar logistics conglomerates to who the Department of Defence outsources a lot of its day-to-day garrison operations to. Cleaning, catering, accommodation services, even firefighting on some bases. It came as no surprise that a massive jack-of-all-trades organisation such as them would get the call to take on the task of running this new take on offshore processing.

To take care of security at the centre Transfield had subcontracted Wilson Security via a new PNG-registered sub-arm, and appeared to be recruiting almost exclusively from Brisbane's sizable community of former defence and law-enforcement members. This was the first thing that appealed to me. I had had my fill of the Paul Blart Mall Cop wannabes that inhabited the security industry and desired to again be amongst like-minded people – the sort of people whose abilities you could trust and who most of all, you could take seriously. But mostly I just missed the mateship. The prospect of good money and plenty of time off on a fly-in fly-out roster was the icing on the cake.

Nothing was being advertised publicly, but the boys hooked me up with an e-mail address and within days I had received a reply. The e-mail contained some extra information about the contract but also advised that they currently had plenty of inducted candidates on the books awaiting deployment. It didn't look like there would be any South Pacific adventures for me just yet.

Nauru wasn't the only offshore processing centre being given a new lease of life by this policy back flip of course – word had already begun to spread along the grapevine about the reopening of the facilities on Manus Island and the subsequent recruitment drive in place for that. The company looking to fill this contract was none other than G4S – a major multinational with a dubious reputation following its very public failure to fulfil the staffing requirements of its London Olympics contract the year before.

I started the online application process but before I had the chance to complete it real life got in the way. My mother's already rapidly deteriorating health took a nosedive and I missed the cut-off date. Not that I really cared at that point. A few months later though, it was a very different story. Returning from another night shift on a job I hated, I was understandably enthused to open my e-mail to find that Wilson had remembered me after all. In fact, they were seeking "security specialists" with a background in defence or law enforcement who were comfortable with remote deployment. Nothing more was said except that it was an "exciting offshore opportunity".

Despite coming off a mind-numbing graveyard shift, I was suddenly wide awake. I completed the attached paperwork and sent it off before crashing out. I woke to find a reply containing a link to further online testing and reference checks which I promptly completed. The next time I heard from them was the following night when they asked if I would be available to come in for an interview. I suggested the following afternoon to which they readily agreed.

The fact that they were ringing on a Saturday night and agreeing to an interview on Sunday afternoon told me that this was all cylinders firing. I had just one final question to ask before we signed off:

"Where exactly is this job?"

"Manus Island," the young woman on the other end of the line replied against a background of what sounded like a crescendo of ringing telephones. "We're taking over the contract at the MRPC."

The office was a hive of activity, but I managed to source some information from a guy who appeared to be in charge in some way. The tender for the Manus Island contract had just been awarded to Transfield (with Wilson on board as per Nauru) and they were due to take over all operations from G4S by mid-to-late March. It was already the first week of February.

I was ushered upstairs for an alarmingly brief interview. The young woman barely glanced over my resume before asking me about the status of my passport and vaccinations and my availability for deployment. I was given an appointment for a chest x-ray to check for tuberculosis and an application for a Papua New Guinea work VISA.

"Does this mean I have the job?" I asked.

"Pretty much," she replied.

As soon as I got home, I told my flatmate Gloves about how things had gone. A New Zealand Army veteran, Gloves was a qualified tradesman, but like me was also having trouble finding his feet. I had clued him in to the original Nauru gig and like me he had an interview scheduled for the following day.

The next few weeks proved frustrating. The administration staff at Wilson were overwhelmed by the sudden task of recruiting a large workforce from scratch and were really showing the strain due to the pressure. Paperwork was misplaced and at one point I brought some documents into the office to replace those that had disappeared only to find the originals lying on the floor next to the water cooler. Meanwhile the administration staff where running around like the sky was falling, trying to juggle a million different things at once. It was chaos.

The PNG Consulate did nothing to assist with the smooth running of the transition. Due to constantly shifting goalposts, most of us had to complete our visa applications two or three times. They couldn't seem to decide whether they wanted them in black and white or in colour, or the documentation to be copies or originals. But as I entered the office one morning in late February, bearing a folder containing replacements for my twice-lost passport ID photos, one of the offshore operations coordinators hit me with a proposition that I was not expecting.

"Can you deploy tonight?"

"Of course," I laughed, thinking it was a joke referring to the chaotic state of affairs in the office. It turned out though, that he was completely serious.

"No doubt you have seen the media reports about the current situation on the island. We are looking to get some guys on a plane late tonight, or early tomorrow morning at the latest."

I had seen the news. Although the early reports were sketchy, there had been some sort of disturbance at the centre overnight. The scale of things and what exactly had occurred were still unknown, but it was becoming clear that Manus Island was now experiencing the same sort of unrest and violence that had plagued Australia's other immigration processing and detention centres.

It had caught my attention, not only because I had a number of mates working there with G4S, but because I wondered how this all would affect the contract. Hardly altruistic I know, but a concern none the less. I certainly wasn't expecting to be asked to head out *sooner*. It was still over a month until Wilson was due to assume responsibility.

> "This request has come directly from DIBP," the coordinator explained, "G4S is still in charge on the ground, but we are looking to have at least fifty reinforcements on-island by this time tomorrow."

I wondered if this was simply a case of the job taking priority over company boundaries, or whether Wilson just wanted to be being able to handle anything and everything, even if they weren't running the show yet. Whatever the reason, I wasn't about to let this opportunity pass me by. I agreed on the spot.

> "Keep your phone on you, we'll let you know what's going on as soon as we know more ourselves."

Returning home, I turned on the TV to try and catch any more information about the situation on Manus. I called Gloves, who had also received a request for immediate deployment. It really was looking to be a case of all hands on deck. A few hours later I received a phone call. They wanted to know if I was still keen to go. I told them I was, and it seemed like I was not the only one.

> "We are easily filling our request for fifty personnel, so it's

basically going to be first-come-first-served. Can we get you to drop by the office in a few hours for some final paperwork and equipment issue? We are having to stagger it throughout the evening otherwise everybody will be here at once!"

I could only imagine how the situation in that office would be now that this whole emergency deployment was going on. If it was crazy before, it must have been absolute bedlam now. My predictions were readily confirmed when I returned a few hours later. The smell of coffee was thick in the air – it didn't look like anybody would be going home any time soon.

I immediately saw a group of guys gaggling around in the waiting room, not an unusual sight in that office. What did make it unusual was that they were in uniform. Not an army uniform either. Upon closer inspection I saw that they were members of the RAAF Airfield Defence Guards – the ground defence unit of the air force. It turned out these guys had all recently finished their stints in the full-time force but were still in the reserves, hence the uniforms – they had literally come into the office straight from their weekly parade night.

ADG's (or "Adgies") have always had a difficult relationship with the army. There is always a lot of friendly and not-so-friendly banter regarding their abilities and their perceived high opinions of themselves (the derogatory term "RAAFSAS" gets thrown around a bit) but these guys would prove themselves over my time on Manus to be a credit to their service. Not only were they great blokes, they were highly-professional and would go on to have a big hand in many of the capabilities we developed on the emergency response side of things.

The Adgies weren't the only group to have rocked up straight from another job. A few guys that were already working for Wilson on Nauru had answered the call and were there trying to navigate their way through the paperwork required to enter PNG. Many of these guys had only just returned from Nauru for a couple-of-weeks break and were basically doing overtime, whilst others had already been tapped weeks ago to move over to Manus to help facilitate the contract transition there and introduce the facility to the new provider's way of doing business. Many of them had been on duty on Nauru during that centre's own riots the previous year and their experience in this environment would be invaluable when we finally arrived on Manus.

We filed through the storeroom to receive our uniform and equipment issue. But the thing that interested most of us by far was finally getting our contracts. Some poor soul had had to quickly redraft them all due to the changed circumstances of the emergency deployment, but all the big-ticket info was there.

We were to be working on a fly-in fly-out roster of three weeks on, three weeks off for an initial contract of six months from the date of changeover (giving those of us flying out immediately an extra month by default) and a salary that was roughly twice what most of us had been making in the forces, and certainly a lot more secure than the unpredictable week-to-week roster I had been receiving in my current employment. The moment I signed my copy, I texted my old job to let them know that I was done. Somebody else would have to check the locks and rattle the keys.

Outside, I called my Dad and let him know that I would be heading over a lot sooner than expected. He wished me luck and told me to take care of myself. He had been watching developments on the news as well. I then called Gloves, who told me he would not be joining me on the late-notice flight due to commitments he had in Brisbane, but Wilson was already preparing for a second deployment in a few days' time and that he would try and get onto that.

As I began the drive home, I received a text message from my Dad:

"I know you're up to this job, mate. But be careful. Keep your head down and don't do anything stupid over there."

With only a few hours in which to pack and try and get some sleep before heading to the airport for a long day's flying into a possible riot situation, it seemed like getting my head down would be one of the last things I would be doing for a while.

CHAPTER 2

NO TIME LIKE ISLAND TIME

My first impression of Papua New Guinea as I descended the aircraft off-ramp at Port Moresby's Jackson International Airport was the humidity. But it didn't take long for the oppressive temperatures to be joined by a second and far more unpleasant addition – inefficiency. It was a stark reminder that despite our shared histories and our coastlines being only five kilometres apart at the closest point, our two countries are about as far apart as any could be.

Don't get me wrong – going through international terminals sucks in Australia too. The endless lines made seemingly longer by fellow passengers who don't have their shit together combine to make the process even more painful. But it had been a very long day, and the absolute last thing any of us needed at this point was an introduction to that Pacific phenomenon known as "Island time".

After having arrived home and packed the night before – everything I would wear and use for the next three weeks crammed into my trusty old 511 backpack – I had found it impossible to get to sleep. Gloves had dropped me off at the airport hours before I needed to be, and I attempted to grab some shut-eye on one of the surprisingly comfortable airport couches. I had been spectacularly unsuccessful.

With only about fifty of us on-board the specially charted Air Niugini flight, things had been mercifully uncrowded, and we managed to stretch out and get a little rest during the three-hour journey. But it felt like I had only just dozed off when I was awoken, and we began our descent in Port Moresby. I got the first glance of the country that was to become my working home.

Papua New Guinea's capital is built on a natural harbour, surrounded by the lush, jungle-filled Owen Stanley mountain range. Its beauty from the sky however does not completely disguise the fact that it is still very much a developing nation with one of the world's highest crime rates. The modern skyscrapers in the city-centre give way to sprawling suburbs and industrial areas, and as the plane descended I could make out many of the houses – ramshackle Queenslander-style dwellings packed haphazard around the teeming arteries of roads that followed no noticeable system.

As we made our way into the arrivals hall, the heat was replaced by a thick wall of stale air. There were three lines at immigration control – one for returning PNG residents, another for expatriate workers and tourists, and one for diplomats and aircrew. Unfortunately, as we had left before our permanent PNG work visas had been secured, we had to apply for a "visa-on-arrival" (I would have to do this for another four rotations, as it would take several months for the permanent visa to be processed. For some guys it took five or six rotations.)

Unfortunately, the visa-on-arrival desk was manned by a single person who had to process all fifty of us. Even more frustrating was that after processing two or three people, the clock struck twelve and he promptly knocked off for lunch! After fifteen minutes it was clear that he was not being replaced, and after much running around by our minders we were finally able to secure some staff to get us through the process.

After strolling through customs with barely a second glance from the customs officers we made our way towards the domestic terminal. I immediately noticed the number of security guards around the place. You might think that in a city with a crime-rate like Port Moresby that this would be understandable. But none of them seemed to be securing anything, and there certainly didn't seem to be any sort of overarching security effort. In fact, it was hard to spot two guards who wore the same company uniform.

They stood on the side of each doorway, and in the corner of almost every room. Then there were the checkpoints. You were screened to walk into a room, then screened again to walk out the exit on the other side (the room being little more than a corridor with nowhere to actually pick up or drop anything). Often the guards were asleep at their post or might as well have been, given the level of interest shown.

The reason for this was clear, as I had seen the same sort of thing in Africa – creating extra jobs that served no real purpose other than to employ people. Of particular note were the guards wearing G4S uniforms – we were later to learn that the company's large footprint in PNG was a big factor in it being awarded its initial no-bid tender. Our favourite however was the unfortunate acronym ASS Security whose logo was nothing other than a clenched fist. With the tired state that many of us were in, we found this hilarious.

Finally, we made our way back onto the tarmac and boarded the small Fokker turboprop that would take us over the Bismarck Sea to Manus Island within 90 minutes. Manus Island is the largest of over a dozen islands that make up PNG's Manus Province. Situated about 300km north of the mainland and just under the equator, the islands form part of a larger archipelago known as the Admiralty Islands.

My first impression of Manus Island as it came into sight was its size. I don't know why, perhaps it was due to its media depiction as a harsh island outpost, but I guess I was expecting a small rocky outcrop. But Manus Island was in fact over 2100 square kilometres in size, with a population at last count of over fifty thousand. The second thing that stood out as the plane began to descend was the physical beauty of the place.

The water sparkled radiantly blue in the afternoon sun, where every cove and inlet seemed to be filled with reefs and small islands. Excited talk began to make its way around the cabin of the fishing and diving opportunities that could be on offer – if we ever had the time. The island itself appeared relatively flat, but covered in lush tropical rainforest. We could not see any large settlements, but as we got lower I could start to make out small huts and dwellings in clearings below the jungle canopy.

As we rounded the island, some noticeable infrastructure began to appear in the form of a port. Manus Province was the northern outpost of the PNG Navy and its patrol boats could be seen tied up alongside at the wharves. Numerous container ships that served as the island's main supply link to the outside world snaked their way out to sea from the natural harbour. But the thing that really grabbed my attention was the huge blue-and-white box-like structure floating alongside the largest of the wharves. It was called the Bibby Progress, and we would all become well acquainted with her over the next few months.

I got my first real sense of the media's misrepresentation of Manus Island as soon as we got off the plane. The runway at Momote Airport sits in a clearing on a narrow peninsula that sticks out into to the sea. I couldn't even see it from my seat as we came into land, and it felt as if we were going to put down in the water. The equatorial humidity hit us hard as we stepped off the plane and into the corrugated-iron shack that was the arrivals and departures terminal.

The sign that greeted us at the entry gate caught my attention:

MANUS ISLAND LIONS CLUB
WELCOMES YOU TO OUR BEAUTIFUL ISLAND
PARADISE IN THE SUN.
WE HOPE YOU ENJOY YOUR STAY

It took me a moment, but I remembered where I had seen that sign. The previous night, whilst trawling the internet for news on the

current situation, I had seen a picture of that very sign at the head of
the article. Its caption had seemed to imply that it was a sign at the
gate of the actual MRPC – like it was supposed to be some sort of
ill-humoured joke. Score one for journalism right there.

Once we collected our bags we boarded a couple of mini-buses
that looked (and sounded) as if they had seen better days. They were
accompanied by a couple of G4S transport officers, who we later
learned were there less as a welcoming party but an assurance that
the local bus drivers would drive to their intended destination and not
just disappear to do their own thing. Eager for news, we immediately
pressed them for information.

> "Shit really hit the fan last night. We're glad you fellas are
> here – but don't expect much sleep tonight."

The drive from the airport took about twenty minutes. The roads
were unpaved, and in some parts near washed-out and cratered with
potholes. It was bumpy and uncomfortable, but the scenery was
stunning. Beautiful beaches on one side and lush rainforest on the
other. We passed dozens of small thatched-roof dwellings, some
little-more than open-walled huts. Smiling locals, some barely clothed
but seeming not to care, would run out to the road to wave. It really
did seem like an island paradise, and even more than that it felt as if
we had gone back in time.

Finally, we arrived at the wharf and got our first close-up look
at what was to become our home-away-from-home. Known in the
maritime construction industry as a "coastal" the Bibby Progress
was effectively a floating hotel, over a hundred metres long and four
storeys high. As the buses pulled in, I noticed several G4S guards
milling around the walkway connecting the Bibby to the wharf. I
recognised one of them as my old army mate Zack.

"Wow mate, you look like shit." I had never seen him

looking so exhausted, but he was smiling.

"It's been a big couple of nights bro," he croaked, his voice so hoarse it caught me off-guard "I'm definitely keen for some sleep."

MRPC had other ideas though, and as we unloaded our bags Zack and his colleagues headed off for their afternoon shift. (We later learnt that in the last 24-hour period G4S had been running shifts of six-hours on, six-hours off to fight fatigue. By the looks of Zack and the others it wasn't working.)

The air-conditioning hit us like a welcome glacier as we entered the Bibby's foyer, but what hit me even more was the contrast. We had left behind the jungle-covered humidity of Manus and stepped into the lobby of a western-style hotel. The next thing to hit us was a tirade of hysterical ranting by a strange red-faced man who looked as if he'd never left the climate-controlled paradise over which he was presiding.

"Take your shoes off! Take your shoes off when you enter the Bibby!"

We had just met the "Bibby Master"– the closest thing this floating hotel had to a ship's captain.

"At least somebody here knows what the big issues are," muttered somebody behind me, eliciting a chorus of laughter.

We didn't get much time to revel in the splendour of our new surroundings, as we were quickly ushered into a briefing room that was clearly designed for far less than our number. Three G4S officers greeted us. They were trainers, usually tasked with delivering the on-island inductions to incoming staff but for now their job was giving us unexpected new arrivals the run-down on what was going.

The first to speak to us was Max. Tall and athletic, he had been a soldier and police officer back home in New Zealand before doing a stint as a private contractor in Iraq. Somehow, he wound up coming to Manus. Max was a born-again Christian and when not delivering training packages he could often be found strumming his guitar and chatting to everybody in sight. To this day he is one of the most positive and cheerful people I have ever met.

> "First up guys I want to make one thing clear. I reckon I speak for everyone one here at G4S when I say we are glad to see you all. The last couple of days have been nothing short of crazy and it's probably not over yet."

Solemn nods and excited glances made their way around the room. Everybody was keen to get into it. It was the reason we were here.

> "A lot of shit is going to be said between G4S and Wilson over this whole contract thing. But I want you to know that it won't be coming from us or anybody who has been on the ground here the last few days. I will say though that we expect the same from you guys – as you can no doubt appreciate there is going to be some grievances about the whole situation and the stress of the last week won't have helped that."

This was a good point – as we were to soon learn, G4S had been less than honest with its staff about the contract coming to an end and a lot of people were soon going to be out of work. It certainly wasn't a good time to be having a riot, especially when it transpired that many of those who had expected to simply walk into a position with Wilson were to be sorely disappointed. Thankfully that didn't include Max and his fellow trainer, Kelly.

Kelly was tiny, almost pixie-like. She looked out-of-place addressing a group of brawny ex-soldiers, but she was more than capable of navigating that world having spent years as an undercover officer with the Australian Federal Police.

> "The situation at the MRPC right now is tense but calm. We've got one dead transferee and about eighty wounded. Things were such a mess after the PNG Police became involved last night that the entire wharf area alongside the Bibby was transformed into an emergency-triage area last night. The badly injured were medevac'd to Port Moresby early this morning."

Until now we had only heard rumours, but it was clear that this had been more than a run-of-the-mill protest. We were all keen to see the situation for ourselves and were keen to get going when Kelly informed us that we were going to be heading over to the centre shortly, although not to take up duty just yet.

> "It'll be a lot easier to explain what has happened over the last few days when we are actually at the MRPC and you can see the layout of the ground."

Before we could go however, there was something we had to get out of the way.

When the trainers had said we were going to the theatre, we all thought it had been a joke. It turned out that was the name of the tin-roof-covered concrete slab at the top of the hill behind the wharf, across the road from a well-ventilated (i.e. no walls) Seventh-Day Adventist Church and a derelict concrete structure which we later learnt was the morgue for the naval base's medical centre.

It turned out that the structure was once a reel-to-reel projection theatre, during World War II when Allied forces had used Manus Island as a staging post for air and naval forces heading north from Papua New Guinea.

By the time we made it to the theatre, we were all covered in sweat and gulping down bottled water to acclimatise. Right now, the centre was quiet, but as it was possible that we could be called in to assist at any moment, we first had to be signed off on G4S's defensive tactics package. Or at least what some bureaucrat in an air-conditioned office back in Canberra had deemed to be tactics we should use to defend ourselves should the need arise.

> "Don't have it in your head for a minute that the guys down in the centre are all starving refugees who just stumbled off a boat. There are guys in there who can bench 200kg and have muscles in their piss. There are ex-boxers and wrestlers and Revolutionary Guards. There is a shitload of testosterone flying around down there, and the first thing those guys want to do given half the chance is have a crack at one of you."

We formed a circle around Max and continued to smash down water.

> "The last thing we want to be telling you guys to do here is suck eggs. I know that there is a massive amount of experience amongst you guys and at the end of the day you're going to revert to what you know. DIBP has signed off on this being the self-defence package, so just bear with us."

Bear with him we did. For the next couple of hours, we ran through some of the most hopeless self-defence techniques many of us had ever encountered. Max and the other trainers looked embarrassed. A lot of the content was familiar to the group, having been cobbled together from various military, police and corrective services DT packages. Unfortunately, however, it seemed to consist of the most ineffective and needlessly complicated techniques.

God help anybody who didn't know any better who tried to rely on this stuff in a real situation. It seemed like it had been designed more for political considerations than any genuine concerns for self-defence.

The trainers convinced that they could tick off the boxes, we made our way back down towards the Bibby and its welcoming air-conditioned embrace. I asked Max what he thought the chances were of things kicking off-again that evening.

> "Bro, just wait until you get down there and see the state of Mike compound. Then tell me if you think any of them will be gutsy or stupid enough to make another go of it tonight."

There was no sign of bravado in his voice, he was genuinely concerned. The occupants of Mike compound had learnt a harsh lesson first hand – it was one thing to protest the Australian government and its policies, it was another thing when you turned your anger against the people of Manus Island.

* * *

It was about a half kilometre walk from the Bibby to MRPC, along a sealed dirt track cut straight through the thick Manusian jungle. It was late afternoon, but the blazing equatorial sun showed no signs of setting. As we walked, Kelly began to fill us in on what had gone down to the centre. Even before she began talking, it was clear that things had been a lot more full-on than initially reported.

"Don't get the impression that things just suddenly kicked off on the first night. Things had been slowly building up for a few weeks. Fights and self-harm incidents had been increasing, but they were occurring simultaneously on opposite sides of the centre. It was pretty clear that things were being coordinated to test and stretch our reaction capabilities."

We exchanged greetings with a group of locals passing us on the road, no doubt amused by the large unfamiliar group of white men sweating it out in a furious attempt to acclimatise. Before long though, we found ourselves on the main road adjacent to the magnetic beacon of controversy that was the Manus Regional Processing Centre.

It didn't look like a maximum-security prison. In fact, it didn't look like much of anything. The buildings were large prefabricated bungalows, coloured a brilliant white which reflected brightly in the sun. The compound itself appeared to be almost deserted – apparently the occupants chose to spend most of the daylight hours indoors in the air-conditioning to escape from the harsh humidity, something I could totally understand.

The fence, far from being imposing and topped with razor-wire, was thin and low – the kind you would find around a warehouse in an industrial neighbourhood back in Australia. It didn't look like it could survive a harsh gust of wind. A few transferees (due to the unique legal status of those asylum-seekers being processed offshore, they were not to be referred to as detainees as they would if they were being housed on Australian territory) sat across the fence on plastic chairs, chatting and smoking and hardly giving us a second glance. One section of the fence was collapsed and mangled – clearly something had gone down here:

"This is Oscar compound. This is where the disturbance
kicked off on the first night, although the seeds were
definitely sown at the *other* side of the centre at Mike
compound."

Sown *and* reaped, as it had turned out. We were already aware that
Mike compound had been the site of the previous night's fatality. We
made our way along the road, past the main entry-gate, and along
the fence-line of another compound known as Foxtrot. In contrast
to Oscar's white bungalows, Foxtrot appeared to be row-upon-row
of squat wooden demountables painted a jungle-green. Like Oscar,
small gaggles of transferees were moving around outside, but most
remained out of sight.

Compared to Oscar and Foxtrot, Mike was quite a sight. By far the
most sizable of the compounds, the accommodation blocks consisted
of a series of two-storey modularised buildings, giving the appearance
of apartment blocks in a housing-estate. I wasn't surprised when I
later learnt that Mike compound had originally been constructed as
accommodation for MRPC staff, before an influx of boat arrivals and
the subsequent transfers from Christmas Island had forced its use for
the transferees. It was a far-cry from the leaky tents the media seemed
happy to imply made up the bulk of the accommodation.

In fact, I never once saw the rows of tents often pictured in media
pieces written on the MRPC. Either they were using pictures of the
Nauru centre (where transferees had been housed in tents by necessity
after the hard-standing accommodation had been burnt down by
rioters) or more likely they were using the years-old photographs of
the tents used to accommodate the military engineers that had been
sent in to get the centre up and running. Not exactly lying, but not
exactly honest either. Score another one for journalism.

The size of the accommodation however was not the only thing
that set Mike apart from the other compounds. In its centre was a

large covered area, and it was teeming with dozens of transferees camped out on stretchers. G4S officers mingled amongst them, giving us our first close look at the kind of interaction we could expect on the other side of the fence.

> "That's the Mike mess hall." Kelly pointed towards the single-storey building adjacent to the covered area. "Two nights ago the community leaders from each of the compounds gathered there for a meeting with DIBP. They were told that they would never be settled in Australia. As I said before things were already tense at the time in the lead-up to this meeting, and we believe that they knew exactly what they were going to be told. But once the community leaders had moved back in to their respective compounds, that was when the mood really began to change."

We gathered in the shade of a giant Manusian palm as Kelly began to explain how the first disturbances had occurred not at Mike compound, but in Oscar. A crowd of nearly seventy transferees had gathered and began to march en-masse within the perimeter, chanting loudly. The mood in the compound began to take on a dark atmosphere, and the decision had been made to evacuate all non-essential staff.

> "At this stage all off-duty security staff were reacted back on the Bibby. By the time they arrived however, the protest had petered out and some of us thought we may have dodged a bullet. Unfortunately, that wasn't the case, because at that point Mike began kicking off. They took it a step further though, and started directing the chants over the fence."

We listened as Kelly explained how the mostly Iranian transferees within Mike began chanting "FUCK PNG!" Which understandably attracted the attention of the locals (both staff and residents) as well as the PNG Police Mobile Squad who was stationed across the road from the centre. In later days I would hear PNG colleagues recount how the Iranian transferees had threatened to "rape their mothers". A vile yet empty threat no doubt, but one that was soon to raise the ire of these seemingly laid-back island folk.

CHAPTER 3

THE PRINCES OF PERSIA

Tired as we were, we had all been expecting to begin working in the centre that very night. As it turned out though it would be 48-hour period before we would be in there on the floor. The reason was one that was very unwelcome for us but even more so for the exhausted G4S guys whose burden we were there to ease – bureaucracy.

Despite having been flown in as emergency reinforcements, red tape prevented us from entering the compounds without first completing the mandatory three-day classroom induction. We would have completed an induction with Wilson back in Brisbane had the deployment kept to its original timeline, but as G4S were still running the show we would be doing their version. So, after a welcome feed in the Bibby dining hall, we filed back into the briefing room ready to consume a lot of coffee and even more power-point slides.

Most of it was watch-and-forget, but there definitely was some important stuff there – such as learning the G4S radio-procedures and our legal rights and obligations advising us of just what we could and couldn't do. We also got our first introduction to the Hoffman Rescue Knife and the procedure for "cutting-down," a hanging victim. I'm sure I wasn't the only person wondering if self-harm and suicide attempts would be as rampant as the media and refugee advocates claimed.

After a few hours we called it a night, but we were advised to wait just that little bit longer before heading to bed in case things kicked off again at the MRPC. Following the events of the previous evening this was considered unlikely, and in any case, most the G4S guys told us that if it didn't happen by 10p.m. it probably wouldn't happen at all. So, with a couple of hours to kill we all started doing something we hadn't really had a chance to do in the last 24 hours – get to know each other.

I knew a few guys in the group from my old regiment – there was Cal, a Toowoomba boy and the owner of two of the cutest blue-eyed Staffie pups I had ever seen. There was Brock, a Brisbane native and drift-driving enthusiast who was the biggest anti-establishment advocate I had ever met for somebody who made a career in the military-industrial complex. Then there was Watto, who had been my crew-commander for a brief period a few years earlier. Watto had always been a relaxed NCO, but it was still funny to see how previous rank seemed to disappear into the wind in this new environment. It reminded me that I wasn't the only one for whom this gig was a fresh start.

One group I got to know were the Adgies, who quickly began to break down the barriers between themselves and the army guys. Proving how small the world was, one of their boys, Ben, was an old school friend of a mate I had travelled through America with.

There was Carlos, a giant of a guy despite being the youngest in the group (who also shared my fondness for heavy metal) and Hanno, the group's token ranga who had a young son back home. There was Rusty, who was heading down the family path and trying to plan his upcoming wedding whilst on Manus. Rounding out the group was Bodhi, a wild-looking specimen if ever there was one. His fellow Adgies would often joke that he had a few extra chromosomes and it didn't take long to see why. He was a real character however and was somebody you would want beside you in a scrap.

We finally got to bed and after becoming reacquainted with the joys of sleeping within a moving structure, we rose early to smash our way through the remaining induction material. The previous night had passed quietly, but we still needed to get in there to give the G4S crews some much-needed relief. Having completed and signed off in just a day and a half, we were deemed ready to join the workforce at MRPC. Only we wouldn't be going inside just yet.

One of the consequences of the riots had been the complete removal of local staff from within the compounds at the MRPC. Not only had this left the ex-pat G4S officers undermanned at a time when they needed to be anything but, it also raised the dilemma of what do with all the local guards, who local sub-contracts and government-to-government agreements stated they had to be employed.

The result turned out to be the creation of many external posts located on the roads surrounding the centre, and us lucky guys with Wilson were to be the ex-pat liaison and de-facto supervisors. As our contracts stipulated that we were employed as "Safety and Security Advisors" it was as good a time as any to get out there amongst the locally-employed guards that we were to be mentoring.

The W's contingent were split in half between day and night shifts, and I was assigned to nights. I had no problem with this, as I was keen to escape the heat. I was surprised to learn when I arrived at the MRPC for my first shift that rather than being farmed out amongst the external posts, I had been assigned to ride shotgun with the external shift supervisor. Not that this was any reflection on any perceived leadership experience on my part however – they had simply missed my name off the roster on the first run through and had tacked it on later when they realised.

It was a lucky mistake to come my way though. It would give me a chance to get out and see the surrounds of the centre and how everything fits into place, rather than being stuck in a static position willing the night away. I was introduced to Bart, a former Tasmanian policeman and army reservist who led me to a beat-up Land Cruiser that had definitely seen better days – much like every vehicle on Manus Island.

"None of the guys out there really need any coordinating, so we are basically just a taxi and courier service. We pretty much just do the rounds, delivering radio batteries and water or whatever else the guys need as well as bringing them back to the centre for breaks. We don't usually have any problems out here, but we are pretty much the external guys' first back-up if anything ever does happen."

"When was the last time anything did happen outside?" I asked. Given the stories we had heard so far, I half expected every tree-line and shadow to conceal a machete-wielding local high on betelnut and ready to pounce.

"Not for a couple of months really. The navy and the local police had a drunken shoot-out up the road from the centre a while back, but that was over local women. So, unless you want to get involved in that I wouldn't be too worried."

The external posts mainly consisted of a series of vehicle-check points, situated on every intersection between the MRPC and the Bibby, as well as at each end of the road along the centres front. Each of these was manned by two Wilson SSAs and a dozen or so local guards. Officially, the VCPs were there to screen traffic and prevent unwelcome guests like journalists coming in for a sticky-beak. They were little more than a couple of plastic chairs and the only vehicle traffic, as far as I could see, was *our* vehicle.

The local guards didn't seem too interested and before the night was half-gone many of the VCPs had only a handful of the Papuans still on post. By the early hours of the morning the Wilson SSAs were pretty much alone. They must not have gone far though, as leading up to shift-change come morning most of them had miraculously returned.

As we drove around, we could see small camp-fires just inside the tree-line. When I saw Carlos at one of the VCPs later that night, he told me of how he had found many of his local guards sleeping on makeshift beds just off the road. I guess the concept of round-the-clock shift work had not really caught hold in sleepy Manus Island.

I couldn't help but laugh when Bart told me that usually he had a representative from the local labour-hire company riding with him to make sure the local guards were manning their posts. Tonight however, he hadn't turned up to work. Despite all this, it was clear that Bart had a genuine respect for the Manusians, if not affection.

> "A lot of guys here say that the locals are scum, but I don't get into that. If the shit kicks off again they will be there for you to back you up, and things would have gone a lot worse for us the other night if they hadn't been there."

The VCPs weren't the only external posts. The warehouse that housed the stores bound for the Bibby and MRPC was situated within the former allied airbase adjacent to the PNG Navy yard, now serving as storage for the mountains of cargo that were unloaded from the wharf almost daily. It was impressive how the old corrugated iron hangars had survived the decades of neglect and I wondered how much of the structures had been reclaimed from the jungle.

Backing onto the warehouse was 'The Swamp'. Despite what its name suggested, The Swamp was a hard-standing area that hosted a village of Connex accommodation units. These were mainly used to house local guards flown in from Port Moresby on a FIFO arrangement like ours (it turned out that just like at the airport, the contract for local security at the MRPC was shared by many different companies). It was also the quarantine area for ex-pats struck down by gastroenteritis.

"The Swamp is not a place you want to end up. On the upside though, it's got the best WiFi on the island."

At around midnight, we became the "food van" Under G4S the staff mess at the MRPC was not a 24-hour operation. The mid-shift meal for the night crew thus came in the form of a "shitwich" — two pieces of slimy bread and some foul-smelling and unidentifiable meat. No SSA I knew ever ate one (except as part of a bet) but the locals couldn't get enough of them. In fact, by the time we finished our delivery at the second VCP we had pretty much been fleeced.

It's always good to get some perspective. I will always be grateful for living in a country where we can turn up our nose at food. That's not a luxury most of the world has.

The next night I wouldn't be quite so mobile. I would be getting to experience the (lack of) excitement of the VCPs first hand – or so I thought. We had all been wondering what the local people must have thought of the centre being on their land. We were technically within the boundaries on the Manus Island naval base, but we hadn't seen any signs of any real military activity. I was about to get two answers for the price of one.

It was still early evening but most of the local guards on the post with me had long since abandoned it. I was fighting to stay awake and alert myself when I heard a massive crash. I leapt out of my chair to see the handful of locals scattering in all directions.

"GET THE FUCK OUT HERE! FUCK OFF!"

A trio of large Papua New Guineans dressed in dark-blue naval overalls were rampaging through the checkpoint. The plastic fold up table and chairs went flying, as did the water cooler.

"FUCK OFF! THIS IS NAVY LAND!"

The local guards had all vanished into the tree line, and I was alone. As the biggest and loudest of the three turned to face me, liquor bottle in hand, I was convinced I was about to be beaten to within an inch of my life. But before I could decide whether to fight or fly, his eyes widened.

"Australia!"

I didn't know if this was a good thing or not, but as he stepped towards me the mood started to change.

"I am a PNG Naval Officer! I trained in Australia with the Australian Navy!"

Having done a training exercise at Creswell, the Royal Australian Navy's officer training school, I saw an opportunity that I seized immediately.

"You went to Jervis Bay?"
"Jervis Bay! Yes, Jervis Bay!"

I introduced myself, shaking hands with the three sailors and briefly swapping stories about our military backgrounds. Soon they wandered off, happily swigging from their bottles and leaving me standing alone amid my destroyed checkpoint in the jungle.

I jumped on the radio and advised control of what had happened. Bart and some other SSAs arrived soon after to take me back to the centre to make a report.

* * *

After a few nights on the peripherals we were finally doing what we had come here to do – getting inside the compounds amongst the transferees. At last we were going to get up close and interact with these people whom a decade's worth of political policies had been based around. I wondered if they were as keen as me.

As it turned out, we were a bit of a novelty. Thanks to internet access and regular communication with refugee advocates at home, the transferees were quite well-informed. They knew about the upcoming change in contract and were no doubt curious to see how that would affect them. In our khaki shirts and black cargo pants we couldn't have contrasted more against the blue polos and trousers of G4S. It didn't take long for transferees to strike up conversations with us, and whilst most of it seemed to be a genuine curiosity of new faces, it was obvious that many of them were also trying to size-up the new guys.

Many were still stand-offish however, and we soon learnt why. When we had moved through the centre on our day of arrival, the rumour had spread through the compounds that we were the Australian military (which, we joked, was pretty much true!). The second part of that rumour was far less helpful, however. Word was that it was *us* that had been doing the shooting in Mike. Not only that, we had been firing from sniper hides in the tree-line across the road!

This was our introduction to the wild rumour mills that would engulf the transferees. Despite the word of the street regarding our supposed itchy trigger-fingers (and it wasn't confined to the compounds – I'm regularly asked back home if I carry a gun at work on Manus) many of them were getting in early to suck up to the new guys. Comments along the lines of "Wilson good! G4S no good!" were offered up. Funny how things would change in the months to come.

* * *

I was assigned to Delta compound for my first few nights. Unlike the other three compounds, Delta didn't face out onto the main road (known as Route Pugwash) at the front of the MRPC. It did however, back onto the beach front. It was quite relaxing in fact to sit at the compound's rear fence on a quite night, listening to the waves gently break on the sand.

Perhaps this was a calming affect that had led to Delta being dubbed "The Happy Boys". (Manus Island was a single-male only facility. Families were housed on Nauru – something the Nauru hands told us to be grateful for. After hearing the stories of what they had to deal with, I'm inclined to agree.)

The "Happy Boys" of Delta had a reputation as the least troublesome of all the compounds, and during the riots of the previous week it had been the only compound not to produce a significant disturbance. In fact, the morning after the riot the community leaders within Delta had presented the G4S staff with a haul of makeshift weapons. These had been fashioned they said, not for use against security staff, but to protect themselves from the transferees in Foxtrot compound, who had threatened to breach the internal perimeter and attack them if they did not join in the action.

Despite Delta's reputation, tension was still heavy in the air throughout the centre and we were instructed to exercise caution within the compound – always travel in pairs and in sight of other staff, as well as having a clear path to the front gate should a rapid exit be required. Just like the other compounds, Delta's design and layout was completely unique. The accommodation comprised a grid-pattern of small and cramped shipping-containers each converted into a four-man room, very similar to what staff were being housed in at 'The Swamp'.

I was paired up with Cam – a baby-faced G4S officer who had spent eight years in the navy before going to work the prisons in North Queensland. As a crewman on the navy's patrol boats, he had been many asylum-seekers' first point of contact with Australia's illegal immigration policy. It was completely possible that's Cam's ship had intercepted the boats that had carried some of the guys in Delta. If any remembered him, they weren't saying.

Cam introduced me to a few of the more talkative personalities in Delta. First up the Iranian Captain Jack – so named for his resemblance to the Johnny Depp character, in both appearance and manner. Although our first conversation didn't really progress past his complaints of a tooth ache (dental care at MRPC was poor at this stage, and many transferees apparently refused treatment when they saw the state of the medical and dental facilities in the provincial capital Lorengau) he did show me a magic trick that displayed some impressive sleight-of-hand. When Cam advised me that Captain Jack was an accomplished pickpocket, the Iranian just smiled.

Captain Jack would later go on to tell me of his illustrious career as a heroin addict, proudly displaying his track marks along his arms and between his fingers and toes. He also spoke of the sugardaddy he had lived with in Thailand before boarding the boat to Australia, who supplied him with a never-ending stream of drugs in exchange for sex. Before that he had spent five years in the Iranian Army, about half of which was in military prison. Cam let me in on another interesting fact.

> "Captain Jack was actually the only guy in Delta who tried to join in the other night. He actually climbed the fence over onto Route Charlie, but jumped back over when the locals started streaming down the road looking for a fight."

Another interesting character was a kid we nicknamed Breaks. Born to a wealthy family in Dubai, his moniker stemmed from his being a world-champion break dancer (a fact verified by YouTube). Breaks spoke perfect English, was very well-educated and it baffled me as to why a young man like him was in this situation. I was even more incredulous when I learnt that his father was a high-ranking official in his home country – in their *immigration* department, no less!

"I got into a fight." Breaks explained matter-of-factly, adding that it had been a drink-and-drug fuelled encounter in one of Dubai's underground nightclubs. "The other guy died. My father would not clear it up. So, I got on a plane to Indonesia and went to stay with a friend in Bali. I met a guy in a nightclub there who told me he could get me on a boat into Australia, and now I'm here!"

Breaks smiled throughout the entire story. The flippant manner of his telling led me to think there simply *had* to be more to it, but it also led to another question dawning on me. How many guys were here because they were trying to escape *prosecution*, not *persecution*?

* * *

Despite such pleasant introductions, it didn't take long for me to have my first hostile interaction with a transferee. It was nothing serious, but it was my first direct experience of some of the attitudes we were going encounter.

After a few days treading the floor in Delta, I was rostered onto a shift with the escort team. This was great again, as it gave me the chance to move around the MRPC and see how things operated. With more guys from Wilson on the ground, G4S were finally able to start rotating their staff through rest days, and this night the escort's tasks were an all-Wilson affair. Ben had emerged as a natural leader the last few nights and was running our call-sign that night as "Echo One."

In the days immediately following the riots, telephone time for transferees had been severely curtailed. This was not due to an attempt at censorship but the fact that most of the telephone facilities had been damaged. As an interim measure, we were given a bag of pre-paid mobile phones and an even-bigger bag of recharge-vouchers and left with the task of making sure every man in the MRPC could call home.

It was clear straight away that not every transferee was going to be cooperative with this less than ideal situation. The SSAs would recharge each phone using a pre-paid voucher before handing it over to the transferee, meaning that the length of a call would be determined by the destination they were calling. When a call cut out, those who felt hard done by would turn their frustration on us.

> "You've rigged this, so I can't speak to my family!" was one such accusation.
>
> "This is only temporary until the landlines are fixed. It is not a time for long conversations, just to tell your friends and family you are safe."
>
> "Fuck you!" He spat, storming away. The dust had barely settled from this tantrum when a tall Somali man hurled his phone at the wall and got in my face.
>
> "You sabotaged my phone, so it would not connect!"
>
> Ben picked up the phone and examined the number.
>
> "Mate you've called an American number. You're lucky it even connected. There is only ten kinas on the voucher."
>
> "You're a liar, you did this! On my phone I got three hours phone call to America on five American dollars!"

Not interested in arguing the unlikely merits of his previous phone plan, I politely asked him to move along and let the next person make a call, assuring him that the landlines would soon be repaired. Instead he sat back down and crossed his arms. Without the authority to remove him, we simply placed all the phones back in the bag. The queue to use them was getting longer and longer, and many of those lining up were becoming increasingly agitated about what was holding things up.

"We cannot continue until your friend leaves," I explained to the growing crowd.

Ben was trying to negotiate, but the Somali was not responding. It was a complete farce – we were supposed to be maintaining order but did not have the authority to remove a grown man who was sulking like a child. All the while, the waiting transferees were becoming increasingly worked up. Then the Somali threw out an ultimatum:

"Give me another call or YOU will be responsible for my self-harm."

I wasn't about to be drawn into this. I made a note of the man's individual boat number (the identification number each transferee was assigned) for the inevitable report, then removed all traces of negotiation from my voice.

"Get up. Move away. Let your friends make a call."

Neither of us broke eye contact. Eventually, some of the Somali's friends made their way to the front of the line and managed to move him away, but not without a liberal sprinkling of what I can only assume was a thank you directed towards me.

Thankfully, most transferees were far more understanding of the situation. I noticed a quiet little man waiting nearby, smiling sheepishly. He had been the next in line and had been standing there patiently throughout the whole performance. Taking a phone that had been hung up halfway through its recharge, I topped it up with a fresh voucher so that the patient little guy could have a few extra minutes.

* * *

After a few nights on escorts, I was rotated into Mike compound. I was paired with H, a former infantry corporal who just prior to jumping on the Manus bandwagon had been a recruit instructor at the Army Recruit Training Centre at Kapooka. Kelly was also supposed to be in there with us, but due to the threats against female staff G4S had decided not to take any chances.

By now most of the bedrooms had been reopened after the PNG Police investigation had been concluded but the outdoor covered area that many of them had been sleeping under when we first arrived was still a hive of social activity. H and I quickly got drawn into an animated and high-stakes game of dominoes with a group of Sudanese. Despite not knowing what I was doing I managed to pull off a brief winning streak before crashing out, much to the Africans' amusement.

Later we shared coffee with a trio of Iranians who told us more about the logistics of their travels which led them to the MRPC. They explained that there were three countries that Iranian citizens could travel to without a visa – Indonesia, Malaysia and Turkey. From there, it was a matter of getting in touch with the people smugglers who promised them passage to the west. Malaysia and Indonesia made sense when considering a seaborne voyage to Australia, but Turkey shared a much safer-to-attempt land border with the European Union.

Wouldn't this have been the easier route?

"It was. I did that, and I stayed in Turkey for three years. But then my friends contacted me and said to join them in Indonesia and we would go to Australia together. Now we are here."

His two friends nodded and smiled sheepishly. Fascinated by the insight to be gained, H asked a pointed question.

> "Do you think it's fair that you are here on Manus?"
>
> "NO!" They all declared emphatically.
>
> "What would happen to me though if I tried to enter Iran illegally?"
>
> "You would be shot on sight or hanged as a spy."
>
> "Then why did you think it would be any easier to enter Australia in this way?"
>
> "Most of the men here already have friends and family in Australia who have entered in that way. They knew that they would be caught and would spend some time in detention, but that eventually they would be allowed in. But after July 19 that changed."

They recounted tales of excitement and excess in Thailand, of drinking and womanising and vices that had not been so easily available back in Iran.

> "Many Iranians want to come to the west because they can drink and smoke and fuck whores. Back in Iran you can do this too but not as easily. That is the freedom they want."

It was a scathing indictment of their fellow countrymen, but the trio seemed unwilling to disclose their own reasons for making the journey. This seemed to be a running theme the more transferees we spoke to. Maybe it wasn't a purely Iranian phenomenon, but as they seemed to be the most able to communicate it was Iranian stories we were hearing. They seemed adamant in reinforcing the fact that they *had* to leave Iran, but when asked the reason the conversation would grind to a halt.

I wasn't alone in seeing the contrast between the Iranians and the other groups. One night I found myself at one of Mike compound's external posts manned by local guards. Relations between the locals and transferees were still tense, and whilst those employed by the MRPC remained professional, the same could not be said for the (usually intoxicated) local men who would saunter past the front of the centre, often making cut-throat gestures if not openly brandishing machetes. The local guards on this check-point were invaluable in trying to keep this provocation at bay – far more effective than some white boy trying to tell a few drunken locals not to walk down a road in their own land.

After getting over the fact that I lived in the same city as the Brisbane Broncos and had a similar-sounding name to one of their star alumni (rugby-league is akin to a religion in PNG) the local lads wasted no time in sharing with me their opinions on the Iranians.

> "They are rude! They call us animals, they mock our country. They yell Fuck PNG!"

> "They get given everything! Free food, free cigarettes. They don't have to work for anything, but they complain all the time!"

Similar sentiments had already been voiced by many of us, but hearing it from the locals gave it a whole other perspective. Watching the transferees behave in this manner whilst being given all the things that the locals couldn't hope to buy on their pittance of a wage... Add to that the contempt with which the Iranians seemed to speak to them, it was little wonder the pot had boiled over.

> "What was their behaviour like leading up to the riots?"

"They yell Fuck Australia! Fuck PNG! They flash their cocks to the women walking by on the road! They yelled at us that they would kill us and rape our wives."

"What about the others? The Afghanis and the Burmese?"

"They are much better. I feel sorry for them. Some of them got hurt in the riot, even though it was the Iranians that caused it all."

"The others smile, they say thank you. They come from a bad place, they are just glad to have food and be safe. Not the Iranians though, they ruin it for everyone!"

* * *

"We have been here six months, and the PNG Government are accepting this shameful agreement! We entered Australian territory, not PNG! They took us by force to this country that is fifty-percent HIV-positive, sixty percent TB and malaria. The capital is the second most unsafe city in the word! How can we be safe here?"

Wushu was Mike compound's resident shadow boxer. Every compound had them – groups of guys who would make a big show of their sparring prowess, always out in the open and always ramping things up whenever SSAs came into view. It was supposed to be intimidating, but we found it more amusing. The centre was festering with pent-up testosterone, and the injection of dozens of fresh military-aged men from Australia was cause for some serious pea-cocking behaviour.

But despite the concerted display of his fighting skills, the Iranian was keen to describe the terror of an unprovoked and savage attack at the hands of the Manusians.

"We were peacefully protesting, none of us were being violent at all! They came over the fence and attacked us! They set dogs on us, they shot us and stabbed us and beat us with sticks! They dragged people from their beds. My friend lost an eye, and another in Oscar compound had his throat cut with a machete!"

"Hold on a minute, Wushu!" Cam had been listening patiently to this diatribe but had clearly had enough. "I was here too, remember? There was nothing peaceful at all about the behaviour in here. And the guy in Oscar with the neck injury caught himself on the wire when he tried to jump the fence. You know as well as I do that if a local with a machete had done that he wouldn't have a head anymore."

"Where were *you* during the riots, Wushu?" H asked.

"I was hiding in my room. They were trying to kill us all!"

"Wushu," Cam interjected, again. "I saw you throwing rocks at the locals. I saw you yelling at them and agitating everyone. You only ran and hid when they came in looking for you. A lot of bad things happened that night, but it wasn't all one sided."

Wushu of course was adamant that this was incorrect, but seeing as I had seen video footage from that night that featured him front and centre, I was inclined to believe Cam's version of events. Just like people back-home, it seemed like even the people on the ground at the MRPC couldn't agree on what was really going on.

It wasn't long before I had another encounter with Wushu, this one far more telling for his actions rather than words. I was assigned to Mike's internet room – effectively an internet cafe with several rows of desktop computers. On the other side of a dividing wall was a similar set up with telephones. The roster system assigned each transferee an hour every day or two, and it was our job to supervise it.

The roster was written up by the Salvation Army case-workers assigned to look after the transferees' welfare. The Salvation Army only worked during the day however, so we were left to deal with the fallout of some questionable decisions. For one thing, the phone roster was compiled by alphabetical order, with no consideration giving to the time-zone in which the transferee was calling. They would complain about this during the day, and the Salvos who wrote the roster in the first place would simply tell the transferees to come back at night and that we (the security) would let them on at a more convenient time. The fact that the roster ran 24/7 made that flippant promise a little difficult to keep on our end, and as we hadn't made it we weren't inclined to anyway. The transferees would then complain to the Salvos that we had broken the rules that *they* had created in the first place.

The computers were not dependent on the time-zone however so proved a little easier to manage. Transferees would wait patiently outside in groups of ten and change over on the hour. As with almost everything we were seeing however, the Iranians seemed intent to make this difficult. Whilst the Afghanis and Rohingyas would arrive early and wait patiently for their turn, the Iranians would push their way to the front of the line and bang on the door, demanding to be let in. Rarely if ever was it their time on the roster.

Tempers soon began to fray on both sides. I would ignore the banging and yelling until it became disruptive to those inside, then I would stick my head out the door to face the indignant Iranian causing the commotion.

> "It's still fifteen minutes till change-over. You are disturbing your friends. Be patient."
>
> "I missed my time. I want to go now."

This was a common occurrence. Somebody would miss their

allocated time for whatever reason then expect to be let in when it suited them. We could use some discretion with this – if somebody else had not shown up, we would sometimes let latecomers in on the proviso that they would vacate it if the originally rostered person showed up within their allocation. But almost every time we did this the original would then show up and the ring-in would refuse to leave as agreed, and so yet another argument would kick off. You just couldn't win.

> "Why did you miss your slot?" I asked. Transferees could come up with some elaborate and entertaining excuses, and often helped to pass the time. Not this one, however.
>
> "I went to dinner, then I had a sleep."
>
> "Are you *serious*?" I snapped. "How do you guys keep doing this? You don't have to work, you have everything provided for you. You have no responsibility all day except to be prepared for this very moment!"

I slammed the door, leading to the resumption of loud banging and abuse mixing English swear words with what I could only assume were similar endearments in Farsi. I felt like a nightclub bouncer denying entry to a stroppy patron after lock-out. It might sound harsh, but the attitude and conduct of the Iranians were continually adding to my increasingly poor impression of them. Were they really that institutionalised? Had the time they spent here left them so incapable of managing their own time?

The Afghans and Tamils and Rohingyas seemed to manage just fine, and were a pleasure to be around. They were respectful and cooperative – unlike the yelling and abuse that came from their Iranian neighbours. It was as if they realised that we were all in the situation together and that whilst it was not ideal, if we all worked together things would run smoother. They conducted themselves with a quiet dignity and seemed to genuinely appreciate everything that was provided for them – simple things like food and shelter that we in the west – and Iran, apparently – took far too much for granted. I was beginning to see the Iranians as nothing more than middle-class party boys who were unwilling to accept the consequences of their actions and expected us to wait on them hand and foot.

I noticed that Wushu was on one of the computers, as he always was. In fact, he was a near constant presence in the internet room. Usually he was a "helper" – he would come in with a "friend" who was rostered on but had trouble using the computer. Invariably that "help" would consist of Wushu using the time-slot for his own business whilst his "friend" sat in the corner. It was a blatant stand-over, but one of the outgoing G4S guards explained why nobody was doing anything about it.

> "It's not worth the hassle. He's a serial agitator, and he'll start writing up statements and complaints the moment he feels hard done-by. The Salvos will side with him, so if none of the transferees are complaining why bother? No point putting yourself on the line to help them when they won't help themselves."

Change-over time arrived, but as usual a problem arose. One of the Iranians was refusing to log off.

> "Time to get off mate, you've had your hour. Now you are holding up your friends."

The Iranian refused to acknowledge me and kept on typing away at his screen. I glanced at his Facebook page – pictures of fast cars and nightclubs with Iranians adorned in gold chains. Still he refused to move. I tapped the desk.

"I don't want to have to ask you again. Please log off and let your friends have their turn. They have been waiting."

I didn't have the authority to physically remove him, and he knew it. I tapped the desk harder, repeated myself louder. That was when Wushu intervened.

"He needs to speak to his family. He cannot call them, and the internet is very slow!"

"Other people are waiting, Wushu. It's not fair on them if he stays. You know that. He will have to come back later."

Ben and Bodhi had entered the room behind me, and it felt good to have some back-up. Not just physically, but materially as witnesses. I could hear the beginnings of a commotion outside, as waiting transferees grew impatient at the delay.

"Please help us to keep things running smoothly Wushu," Ben reasoned. "People listen to you, so we would appreciate your help."

Ben's diplomacy failed to appeal to Wushu's ego, and the Iranian continued to insert himself into the situation. All the while his friend was typing away, smirking. As the negotiations continued, Bodhi took a novel approach. He reached over the typing Iranian's shoulder and switched off the monitor. The typist then made his exit, but in his haste brushed against Wushu's back. Then Wushu just lost it.

"HE PUSHED ME!" Wushu screamed hysterically and spun around, pointing an accusatory finger at Bodhi.

"He didn't push you mate, your friend just bumped you, that's all."

"HE PUSHED ME! YOU CANNOT DO THIS TO ME!

WE ARE PEACEFUL PEOPLE! YOU'VE ALREADY
KILLED ONE OF US AND NOW YOU WANT TO
SILENCE US!"

"What the fuck?" Bodhi pretty much summed up what we
were all thinking.

"I WILL GO OUTSIDE AND TELL THE IRANIAN
COMMUNITY WHAT YOU HAVE DONE. I WILL
MAKE PROTEST!"

Bodhi locked the door. None of us wanted Wushu's wild histrionics
to attract any more attention, especially with the tension still hanging
over the compound. And we didn't want to be trapped inside with an
angry mob. But the precaution just set him off even more.

"WHY ARE YOU LOCKING THE DOOR, WHAT
ARE YOU GOING TO DO TO ME?"

Did he really feel threatened, or was he trying to create a scene?
Either way, Ben was somehow able to convince Wushu that he in fact
had not been assaulted and we were finally able to let the next group
through. Cam joined us as the crowd outside began to disperse.

"You know that he is the advocates main source, right?
He runs the main social media page for the transferees
too. No doubt by morning there will be a story posted
about how he was bashed for trying to use the internet.
Get used to that."

CHAPTER 4

BAD MEDICINE

It had been seven days since the death of Reza Barati in Mike compound, and in line with Islamic mourning periods several memorial services were to be held around the different compounds. Tension was still high, and expectations were that there was a possibility of a disturbance in line with this.

The potential threat was brought home by the discovery of a "snatch kit" in Foxtrot. That morning, the PNG Police supported by Wilson and G4S had executed a search warrant on the compound. Incredibly, we didn't have the legal authority to conduct regular searches of transferees' accommodation without the local constabulary, so the boys on day shift had been expecting some interesting finds. The discovery of a garrotte – a hollow pipe with wires going through to make a noose – dispelled any remaining doubt that there wasn't a hostile, calculating element amongst the population of the MRPC.

Foxtrot's memorial was held in the "holy tent" – a prayer-matted area of the compound used by the Muslim transferees for their daily prayers. We kept a respectful distance, but kept a close note of the footwear of the mourners. Transferees usually wore flip-flops day-to-day, and the wearing of shoes (except when playing sports or exercises) was considered an indicator for potential trouble. G4S guards described hundreds of transferees emerging in shoes in the hours leading up to the riot.

Pictures of Barati adorned every public space throughout Foxtrot in an almost shrine-like fashion, but the service was pretty much an all-Iranian affair. The dynamics between the different ethnic groups in the MRPC was anything but equal, and it was no surprise that the

Iranians used their larger physical statures to stand over the Afghanis, Tamils and Rohingyas. They had a more respectful but still strained relationship with the centre's Arab community, which was mainly made up of Iraqi and Lebanese. The only group they didn't seem to want to antagonise was the Africans.

> "Barati was a bully. He was a standover man for the Iranians in Foxtrot. That's why you won't see anyone else shedding a tear for him"

Anders was another soldier-turned-screw who had traded the prisons of North Queensland for Manus Island. He had been barely able to conceal his disgust at the news of candlelight vigils being held across Australia in memory of Barati.

> "Bunch of do-gooders jumping on a bandwagon. Would they have been attending these vigils if they saw him flashing his cock at the local coppers and threatening to kill their families? What about if they had seen the way he used to rape the little Burmese guys in the shower block? Do they think it's just a coincidence that he was the one the locals targeted when they came into the compound? He was one of the main instigators of this whole thing!"

The transferees saw things differently, as demonstrated by the inscription above a well-painted mural that had appeared on one of the walls:

REZA BARATI: WHAT WAS HIS FAULT?

* * *

Despite these warnings, the mourning period passed without incident. I suspected, as did many others, that the memories were still too raw and the wounds still too sore. Nobody wanted another riot just yet – especially not with the PNG Mobile Squad still camped on the road outside, itching to finish the job.

I rotated out of Foxtrot for a stint in X-Ray compound – otherwise known as the medical centre, operated under contract by the International Health and Medical Service. It basically provided GP and minor outpatient services for both staff and transferees. We were there to maintain safety as well as to ensure the smooth running of medication timings – which once again seemed to mean stopping the Iranians from disrupting things for everybody else.

I was partnered with Dorn, an ex-paratrooper who had spent the better part of the last decade on the private security circuit in Iraq and Afghanistan. Manus Island was almost a retirement gig for Dorn, family reasons having led him to trade the motorways of Baghdad and Kabul for the shorter rotations closer to home. The language skills and cultural awareness he had picked up over his years in the Middle East would assist us greatly.

It seemed like nearly every transferee in the MRPC was on some form of medication. In a three-hour block each morning and evening, they would file through IHMS to receive their pills or to attend appointments with the doctors. Afterwards thing quietened down considerably – the doctors clocked off and X-Ray was left in the hands of security and a couple of paramedics to respond to any medical emergencies that occurred throughout the night.

Medication time was another telling insight into the group dynamics and behaviours of the transferees. Each compound would send patients to IHMS in groups of ten, and before long the waiting areas would be full. Dorn and I would call the arrivals forward in manageable numbers to see the medical staff. Whilst we were left to tend to the waiting areas, doctors and nurses interacting with the transferees were left under the watchful eye of local PNG security guards.

Whilst the rest of the MRPC had ceded to the transferees demands that PNG staff be removed, X-Ray was different. The message seemed to be that if you want your drugs, you will work with the locals. The transferees seemed quite happy to abide by this compromise, although later we discovered the real reason was one that made my assessment even more apt – the local-transferee interaction there was the conduit for a booming marijuana trade.

Marijuana literally grew on trees on Manus, but tailored cigarettes were another story. With the transferees being provided a free and nearly unlimited supply of smokes courtesy of the Australian government, they were the obvious choice of currency for trade with the cash-strapped Papuans. It wasn't just drugs either – weapons and sexual favours were other big sellers. A quick chat with some transferees gave me a basic run-down of the going market rate.

> "Five cigarettes for a blow job, and for one packet she will back up to the fence for fucking!", a grinning Iraqi declared. He was there to restock his syphilis medication.

By the time med-time was over, it was obvious that a lot more transferees had passed through than had seen the medical staff. It appeared that most of them were just using the waiting room as a chance to socialise with friends from other compounds. Inside, it was much the same story as always – the Iranians would complain about everything from the waiting times to the quality of the doctors, whilst the Rohingyas, Afghans and Tamils would sit quietly, thanking everyone with a smile. They had probably never experienced this level of care and seemed truly grateful.

Many of the Iranians that did attend appointments seemed to be under the impression that they could only see the doctor if they were showing dramatic – if not contradictory – symptoms. I watched one guy make his way from the waiting area, completely fine and walking unaided. But as soon as he came within view of the medical bay he started limping, then stopped to steady himself against the wall. He held his head and moaned throughout his consultation. He had come to complain about dirt in his eyes.

One older Iraqi gentleman came in complaining of a headache. This was by far the most common ailment, and when I suggested this could be due to their habit of drinking cup after cup of coffee all day without any water, I got a less than appreciative response:

"YOU STUPID YOUNG MAN, YOU KNOW NOTHING!"

He demanded everything from valium to morphine, and when the doctor's examination confirmed it was dehydration and he was offered two Panadol and a bottle of water, he flipped his chair and screamed.

"YOU CANNOT TREAT ME LIKE THIS! I WILL GO BACK TO OSCAR AND MAKE PROTEST! YOU ALL WILL BE RESPONSIBLE FOR THIS!"

It was all very dramatic and hard to take seriously. But a few minutes after he left we started to hear a commotion in neighbouring Oscar compound. Hoping I hadn't misjudged the situation, Dorn and I jogged around to Oscar's front gate to check it out. Headache man was making quite the scene, and the crowd around him was growing larger. But after a few moments they began to disperse, and many appeared to be laughing. His moment in the spotlight gone, headache man disappeared into the compound, presumably to sulk.

"Nobody listens to him, he's crazy," a transferee explained to me. "When I saw who it was I just came to look!"

* * *

Despite the dramatic hypochondria on show in IHMS, I did get to see first-hand some serious medical distress. G4S had set up a special area called D-Block for those transferees in need of round-the-clock monitoring. And it was there I met the Syrians.

Despite the brutal war occurring in that country between rebel groups and the Assad Government regime, there were only two Syrians at the MRPC. Perhaps most of the refugees from that conflict were stuck in the overcrowded UN camps just over the Syrian border, struggling to survive. The other unusual thing about these two men was that they wanted to go home. This was not as unusual an occurrence at the MRPC as you might think. Many did take the opportunity to be repatriated to their home countries, courtesy of the Australian Government and the International Organisation for Migration. In doing so they received a considerable cash payment – roughly equal to what they paid the people smugglers – and most stated openly that they would attempt the journey again once the government's policy changed. Good luck to them.

But due to Syria's status as an all-out war zone and its regime's international isolation, repatriation was not an option for these men due to political and legal reasons. Afghanistan, Burma, Sri Lanka and Iraq may have had their own civil conflicts and oppressive regimes, but those dodgy governments were still somewhat legitimate, and had diplomatic relations with Australia. Syria had none of these, so these two guys were stuck here. In response to this, they had decided to starve themselves to death.

This wasn't the attention-seeking, but superficial hunger strikes we would become so familiar with, these guys were in a bad way. When I had first arrived in D-Block, the G4S guard I was replacing showed me one of the bedrooms. It appeared to hold nothing but an empty bed with a blanket thrown over the top.

"Where is he?" I asked.

"He's *under* it," the G4S guard whispered.

At first, I thought me meant under the bed, but then it dawned on me – *he was under the blanket!* I could see his hair sticking out from the far end. He was so thin it appeared as if there was nobody under the blanket. His mate in the next room wasn't much better. He was rail-thin – like a cancer or AIDS patient in their final days. His eyes were sunken into his skull and he gave off a distinctive odour – I later learnt it was the result of his organs beginning to shut down.

I sat down outside their rooms with my partner for the shift. Geoff was yet-another ex-soldier, and his baby-face masked a history with some serious combat action. Eventually the other Syrian awoke and the two of them sat together speaking quietly. They never once engaged with us, nor did they touch the apples, bread or meal-replacement shakes that had been provided to encourage them to eat. They drank water though, and smoked cigarettes. Cigarette after cigarette after cigarette.

"I don't understand what they are trying to do", Geoff whispered, "I mean, they are hunger-striking because they want to go home, but then why did they flee their homes in the first place? I wonder what's changed?"

"Maybe they left before the war started? They might have been hanging out in Indonesia or Thailand for a few years? Now that there is a rebellion on they might have decided they want to actually go back and fight instead of running away?"

I looked at the pictures above their beds – young children, presumably theirs.

"I don't understand how they could leave their kids over there,"

Geoff said. I was inclined to agree. Neither of us were fathers, but the guys who were would often express the same sentiment. Both of us had been soldiers though, and I'd like to think that if something was threatening my home and family that I would fight to protect them, not pay a people-smuggler to whisk me halfway around the world.

> "Do you think they were separated and he has only just learnt where they are, or that they are dead? Maybe now he wants to go back to find or avenge them?"
>
> "I don't know, but wouldn't you want to stay close by if you thought they were still alive? There are hundreds of camps just over the border, why travel to Indonesia then try and jump on a boat to Australia?"

There was little chance the Syrians themselves would tell us their stories, but in any case, the speculation kept us from having to focus too much on the third resident of D-Block – he was known as 'The Pacer'.

'The Pacer' had been moved from Foxtrot at the request of the psychologists. For days he had done nothing but shuffle back and forth from one end of the compound to another. Now he was doing that here with us. Although he only had a few metres either way, he would pace back and forth, looking at the ground and rubbing his fingers together, always whispering quietly to himself never to us. This went on for hours. It was all a bit much, but whether it was a legitimate psychological problem or a ploy, he was committed. Finally he sat down.

Then I saw Geoff's eyes widen. I looked over my shoulder. 'The Pacer' was sitting cross-legged, staring right at the two of us and masturbating furiously. It was going to be a long night.

* * *

After three weeks we were all exhausted. Some guys signed on to do a fourth, but I was ready to head home. Our flight out was just as sudden as the one in – we didn't even know if we would be going until the evening before. We drove to the airport straight off a night shift and spent several uncomfortable hours in the unventilated terminal waiting for our plane to arrive. Finally, that familiar Air Niugini turboprop touched down and offloaded our replacements. I didn't see Gloves, but did recognise a few old mates from the army. One of them, Roger, grabbed my arm as we passed each other on the tarmac.

"Shit mate, you look like a vampire!"

It was the first time I had been out in sunlight for three weeks. As our plane left the ground and rounded the island, we got a last look at the tropical island that had become our de-facto home. I even managed to catch a glimpse of the centre in the far-ground – I wondered if anything would change whilst we were away. I also wondered what I would tell people. I was now one of the very few to have seen and experienced the issue first-hand. Would people care? Would I even care to tell them?

As I dozed off to sleep, I put Manus Island out of my mind.

CHAPTER 5

SAME SHIT, DIFFERENT SHIRT

I only ended up having two weeks back home. I had barely had a chance to unpack and readjust to the normality of daylight living when I received the e-mail. The change-over between G4S and Transfield was fast approaching, and management needed as many boots on the ground as possible for when they took up the reins.

Being on a non-charter flight, we couldn't transit straight from Port Moresby to Manus. Instead we were to spend the night at Transfield's Port Moresby base, otherwise known as the Lamada Hotel. Once we got past the rolling gates and shotgun toting security-guards at the front entrance, we found ourselves amongst colonial style splendour complete with valets and posters advertising performances by Shaggy and UB40 in the hotel nightclub. I guess no matter where you are in your career, you're still the biggest deal in town somewhere.

I met Gloves as I checked into my room. He had spent the last fortnight living at the Lamada and spending his day shifts at Port Moresby's private hospital, where those transferees medevac'd in the wake of the riots were being treated. Night shifts were spent at a nearby resort, where those same transferees were being accommodated. He shook my hand and reminded me of something that the long day had caused me to forget – it was my birthday.

My team-mates jumped upon this news and a night on the town was soon in the planning. After lunch and a swim in the hotel's lagoon pool we headed out against better advice to sample the nightlife in what was statistically the third most violent capital in the world. With me were Bodhi and Rusty the Adgies, plus Manly and Soap – two ex-infantrymen that I had met on the first rotation. Joining us on his visit to PNG was Rich. Rich was one of the nicest and most subdued guys you will ever meet – probably some useful attributes in his former career as a sniper.

After an interesting cab ride which involved the vehicle's front right wheel coming off as it crossed a roundabout, we eventually found ourselves at a local dive that went by the name Chilly Peppers. Inside it was hot, smelly and the jukebox played nothing but Midnight Oil. The beer was also lukewarm. The local women took an immediate shine to the six out-of-place expats, which immediately drew a less-than-welcoming reception from the local men. Not being interested in either scenario, we quickly bailed and made our way to what the cab driver promised was Port Moresby's most up-market nightclub.

Situated on the top floor of the city's largest shopping mall, the Cosmopolitan sure looked the part. The bouncers wore suits and you had to ride an elevator up to get in. They weren't going to let us in at first because we apparently weren't dressed-up enough, but after Bodhi greased their palms we were soon on our way.

Imagine our surprise when we entered to see the club's splendid interior – and that we were the only people there apart from the staff. Realising that we had been had, we caught another cab back to the hotel, expecting to have a few quiet drinks at the hotel bar before heading to bed.

As it turned out, the Lamada Hotel nightclub was the most happening place in town that evening. The atmosphere was great, and it was packed wall-to-wall with expats and well-to-do locals. We wasted no time catching up on my birthday drinks, and wondered what Manus Island would have in store for us this time.

* * *

They had not been exaggerating when they said they needed us on the ground. No sooner had we checked in to the Bibby we were asked if we were able to start a shift that very night. We all agreed. We regretted it straight away.

Still hungover and having spent a long painful day in the embrace of Air Niugini, the compounds were really the last place we should have been. The supervisor realised this and was grateful for our help. Once the tempo had died down after midnight, he discreetly arranged for us to knock off early and head back to the Bibby for some much-needed sleep.

Rich and I were crammed into a five-man room built for two, and the other three guys were all assigned to day shift. Not wanting to wake them but knowing they would be up and about in a few hours anyway, we decided to bed down on the couches in the Bibby's TV lounge for a nap. I woke about an hour later to Rich pacing around the room, a pissed off look on his face.

"My wallet and phone are gone!"

Rich had fallen asleep with both in his pockets, and somehow, they had both been spirited away. It was quite a welcome. The poor guy had been on the island less than twenty-four hours and he had already been fleeced. I had no doubts about what had happened and immediately headed for the lobby.

Danger Dave was an Akubra-wearing ex-Federal copper who rubbed a lot of people the wrong way with his gruff demeanour, but I had a lot of time for him. On this particular evening he was responsible for coordinating the security of the Bibby. To this he had a small army of local guards, which was part of the problem. When you add the dozens of night cleaners, laundry staff and others hired from the local community what you basically had was an unchecked mob roaming the corridors of our accommodation every night.

It was impossible for Danger Dave to keep track of them all, and in any case due to local sensitivities he was in no position to tell them off if he felt that they were doing the wrong thing. These "midnight wanderers" would be a constant headache for the rest of our time on the Bibby, and a big part of the break-down in trust between the ex-pat and local communities. Stuff was always going missing. Guys would often wake up in the night to find silhouettes creeping around inside their rooms, and others heading to the laundry to investigate why their laundry bags had come back to them so much lighter would be greeted by local staff wearing the very clothes that had gone missing.

Dave was furious when I informed him of what had happened, and it was obvious that he already had some suspects in mind from amongst his workforce. Still a copper by habit, he took a statement from Rich in his notebook, recording descriptions and contents of everything that had gone missing. A thorough search later turned up the phone and wallet in the hands of one of the cleaners, minus the cash of course.

The cleaner claimed that he had simply found them and had no idea about who they had belonged to, and he kept his job. Relieved to have found his property but understandably pissed off about having to have gone through it at all in the first place, I reminded Rich how important it was to lock your belongings down whilst on the Bibby.

"It doesn't matter anyway," Danger Dave said. "The cleaners have all got master keys to the rooms anyway, as well as the master codes to the in-room safes. They'll get in if they want to."

It's true that poverty breeds opportunism, but it was sad and infuriating to see it demonstrated so blatantly. The centre and our presence here was bringing unimagined employment and business opportunities for the local community, but even those lucky enough to score jobs here were still stealing from us. I wondered if we would ever be able to trust them.

* * *

The date of the change-over finally arrived. I was assigned front-gate duties that night, and was lucky enough to be on the receiving end of many a dirty look from departing G4S staff who had failed to secure employment with Wilson. At midnight the passing of the torch formally occurred, and from now on anybody wearing a G4S uniform was not authorised to enter the MRPC. I guess this memo hadn't filtered out to the local nationals.

For hours after the change-over, locals in G4S shirts continued to wander up to the front gate, reacting with a mixture of surprise and indifference when I informed them of the new policy and quizzed them about their employment at the centre.

> "You need to be wearing your Wilson uniform to come into the centre, brother. Where's yours?"
>
> "Um, I didn't get one."
>
> "Do you have your Wilson ID card.?"
>
> "Um, I left it at home."

I wondered if G4S had simply not bothered to inform their local staff that they were no longer employed, and given the way they had treated a lot of the ex-pats workforce, I wouldn't have been surprised. But according to my partner on the gate, an ex-G4S officer who had been brought across to the new contract, there was another explanation.

> "A lot of the locals when they went home would just give their uniforms to their friends or family. The locals and ex-pats who work the gate usually let in anybody wearing a G4S shirt. They raid the staff canteen, watch a bit of TV in the staff mess and head off again. It's pretty much the local pastime."

This continued for the rest of the night and into the next, but soon word must have made its way around the island that things down at the centre had changed. The model of operations Wilson began to implement was transplanted from Nauru, and I could immediately see that it was superior to the style G4S had been running with. This was immediately apparent at the front gate, where electronic ID scanners replaced manual sign-in books. It was the front gates of the compounds themselves that was the biggest difference between G4S and Wilson. However under the new management, the gates would be open.

With G4S, the compound gates had always remained padlocked with only the compound supervisor carrying a key. This would have been fine if we had been in an onshore *detention* centre, but as this was an offshore *processing* centre, things had to run a little differently. People often saw them as one and the same, but there were legal differences. I wasn't sure if G4S had been illegally locking down the compounds or if Wilson were simply importing the open-camp concept from Nauru, but from that moment on the gates would always remain open unless the security situation dictated otherwise.

It may seem funny given the prison-camp moniker the centres were tagged with, but we had no legal authority to stop the transferees from simply walking out. All we would be able to do in that situation is try and convince them not to do so. It wasn't a hard argument really – the centre being where their beds and food were, and we couldn't guarantee their safety beyond the front gate. As the transferees were still technically wards of the Australian government and didn't hold PNG entry visas, they were liable for arrest by the local police once they stepped outside, but the biggest deterrent was the roaming local drunks that seemed to fill the roads surrounding the MRPC, few if any being likely to have much sympathy for an absconding transferee in the wake of the riots.

Rather than a great rushing of the gates, the first night of this new policy actually had the opposite effect. As I walked past Foxtrot I noticed that instead of being its usual hive of activity, the grounds of the compound were eerily quiet. Everybody seemed to be inside. I saw Roger sitting in the guard-hut outside the compound – he seemed as unsettled by the strange atmosphere as I was.

"None of them have come out of their rooms since the gates went open. I don't think anybody has told them what's going on."

This wasn't surprising – nobody had told us either. We had been vaguely aware it was going to happen but there hadn't been any real explanation of how to handle it when it did. Who knows what the transferees thought was going on? Eventually one of them was brave enough to leave his room and slowly approach the box. It was like watching the family dog who knew he wasn't allowed into the house but who was coming in anyway.

"Are we allowed to come out," he asked meekly. Roger and I exchanged a look and shrugged.

"I don't know mate. Are you?"

* * *

G4S and Wilson weren't the only workers to change shirts when the contract changed hands. Transfield took over the case management duties from the Salvation Army. These case managers were each assigned a portfolio of transferees, and were responsible for assisting them to coordinate appointments with the various other stakeholders at the MRPC. As well as the case managers, Transfield employed a recreation team (responsible for sports and exercise) and education teams (providing classes in everything from English and PNG culture to business and economics)

Relations on the ground between SSAs and the case workers was always going to be interesting. At its best we were on friendly terms, seeing our roles as different sides of the same job. At its worst they saw us as a bunch of reactionary thugs and meat heads, whilst to us they were nothing more than a collection of bleeding heart do-gooders.

There was another side to the relationship, which flipped it from professional to personal. The case-workers were predominately female, whilst security was pretty much an all-male workforce. More than a few hook-ups occurred, but none that I knew of that continued when off-island. Many of us suspected though – and we often saw evidence – that security workers weren't the only ones to be receiving this sort of attention.

I think in the end you could put it down to optimism vs pessimism in how we viewed our interaction with the transferees. As social workers, they were naturally inclined to see the best in people. As the people employed to deal with threat, we were inclined to see the worst. The more manipulative of the transferees took full advantage of this difference in viewpoints and tailored their interactions accordingly. They would act tough and aggressive around us (mainly piss and wind, of course), but sweet and vulnerable around the case workers. It was painfully transparent, but as far as I could see it was also working. The case managers fell for it hook, line and sinker.

* * *

"Wilson good! G4S no good!"

Despite such amusing brown-nosing, for most of the transferees life continued as normal. A few of them even pointed out to me aspects of the Wilson's operation that were more efficient and made their lives easier. We very still very much in the honeymoon phase but there certainly was an element that were keen to push the boundaries.

One of the first changes Wilson implemented was the closure

of the "crazy box" in D-Block, replacing it with another initiative imported from Nauru (the soon-to-be-dreaded Whiskey Watch) or as many were soon to dub it, Wanker Watch.

Mental illness and self-harm have become by-words when outsiders talk about offshore processing. I won't claim to be an expert on mental health, but I always have subscribed to the theory that when it comes to suicide it is always the quiet ones you have to watch out for. The noisy ones always get the most attention, but they usually stay alive as well. If somebody truly has reached the stage where they don't see another option, the first you may know about it is when you walk into a room one day and find them hanging.

Who knows if somebody may have picked up on the signs, no matter how subtle, if their time and focus hadn't been taken up by the attention-seekers? Those who abuse this attention for non-genuine purposes are putting those legitimate cases at risk of slipping through the cracks. I have no respect for them, nor any sympathy.

Wilson set up a dedicated welfare team, going by the call-sign Whiskey (hence the name). SSAs were selected for their demeanour and ability to build rapport amongst the transferees. Whiskeys were supposed to be a voluntary assignment, but before long what can only be described as a piss-taking element within the compounds necessitated a draft.

Acting on the reporting of Psycare (the agency contracted to provide mental health services for both transferees and stakeholders) transferees deemed to be at risk of self-harm were placed on a Whiskey watch-list. The level of risk determined the level of watch. I don't know who decided which transferee was supposed to be at which level, but it seemed that making the threat of self-harm resulted in a higher at-risk level than actual acts of self-harm. This led to the whole thing being open to serious abuse by the very people it was supposed to be looking out for.

Unlike the old D-Block days when those deemed to be suicidal where locked away for their own safety, the at-risk would remain in their compounds. The watchers would come to them. For those at the lower end of the scale, these watches could be as simply as a welfare check every half-hour or the hour round the clock. For those on high watch, however, it was a very different story. High-watch meant two SSAs at arm-reach 24/7. They were with you while you ate, while you slept and while you showered.

It was not an enjoyable experience for anybody involved. For the SSAs, it was mind-numbing and mentally draining, not to mention manpower-intensive. For those being watched, it could be either infuriating or amusing. This was where the problem began. Transferees could see how many staff were being tied down by the high-watch, and the effect it was having on the SSAs. Overnight, requests for Psycare appointments came flooding in. Transferees were parading through the psychologist's office, all expressing thoughts of self-harm. All were placed on high-risk.

To cover this ballooning workload, SSAs from all over the MRPC were being drafted onto Whiskey watch. Within a few days, the number of SSAs assigned to this task overtook every other post in the centre combined. It had become a joke. Everywhere you looked, supposedly high-risk transferees barely able to hide the grins on their faces were leading their less-than-enthusiastic watchers on merry laps of the compound, seeing just how far they could take things. At one point I saw two high-risk transferees pass each other in the middle of the compound and exchange a high-five, laughing as their Whiskey tag-alongs could do nothing but shake their heads.

"This is bullshit," Manly grumbled as he followed his ward on yet another lap of the accommodation. Obviously not expecting the unfunny comedy road-show it had become, he had volunteered for the welfare team when it had first been announced. His partner however, had not. Roger was clearly not impressed with his imposed duty as hand-holder for this joker.

> "The worst thing I thought I was going to have to deal with doing this would be listening to some sook cry. It's worse. I've had to watch this guy take a dump. They're just laughing at us. Some poor guy has probably legit strung himself up in the toilets whilst we are following these fuckwits around."

This continued for another week. As well as the frustration of knowing we were being taken for a ride but were powerless to do anything about it, we began to consider more serious possibilities. With the coordinated violence of the February riots still fresh in our minds, the scenario where this was all part of something far more sinister than a massive piss-take had to be taken seriously. With such a massive chunk of our manpower now devoted to 24/7 observation of just a few individuals, who knew what else could be going on behind the scenes?

The case managers were naturally appalled by this suggestion. To them there was nothing premeditated about any of this – it was completely genuine, a desperate cry for help from desperate men in a desperate situation. I could understand that it was their jobs to support the transferees, and that we were in effect there to support them in doing this. I found them incredibly frustrating to deal with.

There was no doubt a lot of men in the MRPC who were genuinely suffering, but these pricks skipping around grinning whilst SSAs followed them because they were apparently suicidal were not them. Once again, the perpetrators were mainly Iranian. Thankfully, the problem largely sorted itself out in time, once the novelty factor wore off. Apparently having two guys shadowing you every hour of the days watching you whilst you showered or used the toilet wasn't all that fun in the long run.

It also turned out that the piss-takers now found company was having a disruptive effect on their room-mates, and they had not been shy on expressing it. Transferees sharing rooms with high-watches would complain about SSAs sitting in their rooms all night, their radios at full volume and crackling with traffic. Once this started, the number of transferees on high-watch returned to a more manageable level.

A lot of people breathed sighs of relief, and it wasn't just the guards.

* * *

It wasn't just self-harmers that occupied the Whiskey's time. Mental illness can manifest itself in many ways, some far more dramatic than others. Whether or not it was genuine or not was beyond me, but it certainly wasn't dull. If the belief remained that being certified crazy was a ticket into Australia (even if it was just for admittance to a psychiatric hospital) then people would continue to try to push it as far as they could. Some kept it along similar lines to the suicide threats and did stuff like drinking shampoo and laundry detergent. While some took it way further. That's how I met Cat-Boy.

Cat-Boy got his nickname in rather obvious manner – he thought (or at least acted like he thought) he was a cat. I had to see it for myself one night as I made my way through Foxtrot compound. Manly was coming the other way, having just completed his half-hourly check on our feline-feeling friend. The look on his face said it.

"This guy is a fucking fruit-bat!"

As I approached the doorway to the accommodation block, many frustrated Somalis began to bombard me with complaints about their unusual room-mate.

"We cannot sleep with him in there! He makes animal noises all night, and he shits in the corner!"

I stuck my head in the room. The light was off, and I decided to leave it that way. I didn't see him at first, but there he was – perched on the edge of the top-bunk furthest from the door. He was hunched over, licking the top of his hand like it was a paw. He looked straight at me.

"Meow."

I looked back at the Somalis. They motioned towards the door, as if to say "You've seen it now. Do something about it."

I reached for the light switch, but my sudden movement seemed to startle him.

"Hssssssssssssssssss!"

The Somalis motioned towards something in the corner. As my night-vision adjusted, I could see it was a tray. I could also see many suspicious lumps in the tray. This guy was really taking it all the way.

Cat-Boy would eventually leave the MRPC, but not to go to Australia. In time he recovered from his condition and arranged to return to his home in Iraq via the IOM repatriation service. The day the vehicle arrived at the compound gate to take him to the airport, a large crowd gathered to see him off. As the vehicle drove away, spontaneous cheers and applause broke out. Manly and Cat-Boy's room-mates high-fived.

"Finally, he is gone!" The Somali cheered. "Now we can sleep!"

* * *

The misconception that mental illness was a ticket into Australia continued to hold sway amongst the transferees, despite constant reassertions from Immigration that this would not influence their situation. Much of this could be blamed on the internet. The numerous social media groups set up by asylum seeker advocacy groups were heavily trafficked during internet times, and in many ways, gave them an unrealistic impression of how their plight was being viewed by the public back in Australia. At best this was well-meaning but naive. At worst it was irresponsible in that it encouraged potentially dangerous behaviour.

I had a conversation about this in the internet room one night with a young Iranian man. Unlike the armchair activists and hash-tag warriors, I wasn't going to bullshit him.

> "To be honest mate, most people don't care. There are a lot of people who are your supporters, but just because they have Facebook groups and organise rallies in the Queen Street mall in Brisbane doesn't mean that they are the majority or that they can influence government policy. People have enough going on in their own lives, and this situation doesn't affect them personally. It also has to be said, when people in Australia see stuff like transferees rioting and damaging property and trying to hurt people, it actually makes a lot of people more hostile towards your cause."

We didn't have to look as far as the internet however, to see examples of irresponsible influence. Suspicions began to grow that many case managers, rather than being simply well-meaning if gullible supporters, were actively encouraging unrest amongst the transferees. One case worker was even overheard telling an influential transferee that they should be capitalising on the unprecedented media coverage the riots had given the MRPC back in Australia.

She called it civil disobedience – as if giving it a name like that covered up the fact that she was advocating further rioting. The SSAs who overheard this conversation reported it immediately. Nothing ever came of it though, and she continued to be employed as a case manager. A few guys were keen to confront her about it. I didn't blame them – she was putting our safety at risk. The case managers were never shy to lodge complaints about *us* when they felt the transferees were hard done by.

Thankfully wiser heads prevailed, and it was decided to just shut up and smile. We had done the right thing and followed procedure. All we could do now was keep our wits about us. Transfield was still our boss and it was easy to see how any such confrontation would end – not to mention when the inevitable bullying or intimidation claim was made because of being so upfront.

* * *

The next couple of weeks quickly fell into the same grinding routine as my first rotation. I was keen to escape the monotony of working the compounds, and enquired about the specialist capabilities Wilson was looking to implement. There was talk of an aviation escort-security team being raised, to deal with the inevitable involuntary repatriations once the double-negatives started rolling in (double-negative being a preliminary and final negative refugee-status assessment of a transferee's refugee claim to the PNG Immigration department).

Teams dealing with intelligence, investigations, behavioural management and even fire-fighting were also being stood up. I was keen to be involved in everything, but understandably Wilson needed to have people with experience in those disciplines – of which there was plenty to choose from. When talk began circulating about a team, I felt it had my name all over it. I was on my way towards getting my very own riot shield.

CHAPTER 6

REFUGEES AND RIOT SHIELDS

Public Order Management is a fancy way of saying riot control, but it is so much more than that. When somebody says riot squad images come to mind of giant black-clad thugs, drumming their batons upon their shields and savagely beating disobedient crowds into submission. Now whilst the protective gear and the show-of-force and intimidation factors are obviously a big part of what goes on, to characterise a professional public order management team as nothing more than a dim-witted and blood-thirsty pack shows a lack of understanding of what that team would likely face in a large-scale public-disorder situation.

If you are afraid of a good stoush and averse to loud noises, a public order management team is probably not the place for you. It's hard to describe the complete sensory overload that is a riot unless you have been close to one. While the word may imply anarchy and disarray, an undercurrent of coordination and not to be discounted mob mentality can see a charged-up crowd take on an almost singular mindset intent on overrunning everything in its path.

To stand in front of this beast, to overcome tunnel vision in the face of multiple threats and to ignore the natural desire to move anywhere but *towards* the danger requires a team to be well-trained, well-drilled and well-led, complete with a repertoire of tactics and procedures able to be called upon at a moment's notice to counter whatever the rampaging mob decided to throw at them.

As much as the helmets, shields and body-armour play their part, what happens before they go on is just as important, if not more. The best way to control a riot is to prevent it when it is still just a disturbance. An understanding of crowd psychology, tactical communication and negotiation skills are essential. You have to be able to outsmart the angry beast as well as outfight it. And when you looked at the numbers game at the MRPC between potential rioters and responders, it was clear that odds in a fight were not on our side.

As soon as Wilson announced the formation of a full-time Emergency Response Team I knew I wanted to be a part of it. I remembered the footage I had seen from the riots – transferees with their faces covered by masks, hurling rocks and swinging poles and other makeshift weapons. The MRPC being the powder-keg that it was, it was just a matter of time until it happened again. When it did happen, I wanted to be there on the front-line to confront it.

G4S had maintained a similar but less capable group known as the Incident Response Team, which had been comprised of local guards with ex-pat team leaders. With a complete lack of training and resources, it had only been the bravery and skills of the team leaders that had held things together on the night of the riots. Wilson was not going to make the same mistakes. Working off the system in Nauru, the ERT was to be predominantly ex-pats, with selected locals trained up to supplement rather than dominate the manning.

A preference was expressed for candidates with previous public-order training from the military or police. A training package for a professional POM team is four weeks. That is just the entry-level, not considering the constant on-line training required to prevent skills fading. We had three days. It was more of a refresher to consolidate what had been learnt at other organisations and get everyone on board with the Wilson way of running things. What made it even more imperative was the fact the contract had changed over before Wilson had gotten the ERT up, so now things were in a mad rush.

Courses were being run back to back, and it was the last week of the rotation before I finally saw my name on the list. The trainees met at first light the next morning at the end of the Bibby wharf for our first training session – Indian-file runs around the potholed back roads of Manus Island.

After a welcome shower and breakfast, we filed into the briefing room where we were addressed by Zane, the on-island Wilson ERT Manager. A former police tactical operator back in South Australia, Zane had been G4S's liaison to the PNG Police before changing shirt.

I recognised Dyson and Tom – the head trainers of the course – from our walk through of the MRPC on that very first day. Both ex-AFP, I learnt that they weren't employed by Wilson, but were specialist contractors who provided niche capability training to government and non-government organisations. Private-sector riot squads weren't exactly commonplace, and they had been brought in to get the capability up and running until our own trainers could be signed off.

The Wilson trainers-in-training who were assisting with the course included 'H' and three of the Adgie boys – Ben, Hanno, and Carlos. They would go on to become the ERT's permanent training cadre once Dyson and Tom handed over. We were also joined by half a dozen local guards who were to complete the course with us. After an hour of presentations on the theory of public order management, we headed outside and were immediately mustered into a mock scenario. We began running up the hill towards the old theatre, the trainers giving us a running brief of the situation at hand as we pushed ourselves up the broken track. We got to the theatre and were thrown straight into the deep end.

There was a small but angry crowd. There was a bus with a half-naked man jumping manically on the roof – quite distracting given the hostage situation going on inside involving a case manager and a knife wielding transferee. All the parts were played brilliantly by the already-qualified ERT members currently on-team. We trainees *didn't* perform quiet so well. That was the whole idea – throw us into a situation where we are overwhelmed and didn't know what to do. It would then make things much clearer when we *did* know.

Next up we went into Level 1 tactics. This is essentially cleanskin work – no armour, no shields. Advanced crowd control techniques for use against an unruly or violent gathering that has not yet resorted to weapons or projectiles. The basis of all this was teamwork. The only way to hold or recapture ground from an aggressive mass is to work as a single, united front at all times. If the integrity of the line was breached, things could go downhill quickly.

Level 2 was a step up from that. The basics are the same, but everything is hardened and a lot more aggressive. We began the first of many rehearsals in kitting up into "high-order". We worked from the ground up. First were the toe guards, followed by the shin-to-knee and quad pads. This was considered "low-order", for when action was imminent but not immediate enough for high-order. To complete that picture, you added the breast and back plates, followed by upper and forearm protectors. Once you had secured your helmet and completed the checks requiring dexterity, you pulled on your gloves and were good to go. In the thick Manusian humidity, it would take all of twenty seconds before you were absolutely drenched in sweat.

We practised kitting up again and again until we could be ready in just over a minute. Once you were finished, you immediately turned to your battle-buddy to see if he needed any help. As we were each teamed up with a local guard for these exercises, things quickly began to get frustrating. These overly-relaxed island boys didn't have the ingrained sense-of-urgency that the rest of us had drilled into us over the years, and the ex-pats would often turn after having gotten fully kitted-up to find their buddy having barely applied his toe and shin protectors. We were really going to have to earn our stripes as mentors.

* * *

Having mastered the basics of getting dressed, we began to move onto Level 2 tactics. When broken down to its most basic, the role of any riot squad is to control ground. When moving as or holding a formation, the constant struggle is maintaining a wide enough frontage whilst still maintaining the integrity of the line. Holding the line against a hostile crowd is one thing – it's all about discipline. When it came to retake ground, a lot more moving parts began to present themselves. It all came down to listening out for commands and knowing your position in the formation.

We drilled constantly, stopping every half hour or so to replenish our fluids and remove our helmets for some much-needed ventilation. The team leaders had their work cut out for them controlling the formations and making their commands heard through their helmets. The echo system – whereby each member of the team shouts a repeat of the command as they hear it – was imperative.

The heat was draining, and I was finding myself taking longer to process commands into actions. It was only a split second, but that's all it takes. Everyone was struggling to various degrees. With every command to "Box Left!" Or "Stack Right!" Somebody would always move momentarily to the wrong position before correcting themselves. It was me just as often as it was not. But if we ex-pats were struggling due to the heat; our local brothers were having a whole other set of problems.

It was becoming clear that a lot of the Manusians simply had no concept of what we were doing. Their constant state of bewilderment belied the fact that most of them had supposedly completed the IRT course with G4S. With our reactions already slowed by the heat, things were getting even slower than we could afford given the fact that we not only had to think for ourselves, but for our battle buddy as well. As we switched from one formation to another, guys were literally having to grab their buddy by the arm and drag him into position.

We would break it down, each ex-pat explaining to his buddy what his job was and what to do when the command came. The response was always the same. Whether it was through face-saving or simply lack of comprehension, our vacant-eyed buddies would simply nod.

"Yes, yes."

The fundamental lack of understanding became painfully clear as we rehearsed junction drills. In the hot mid-afternoon sun, marching in full-kit up and down Manus's unsealed jungle roads was not fun. The junction drill came when upon reaching a blind corner, the squad would fan out to cover the frontage of the road. The team-member of the extreme left or right of the line (depending which way the corner was) would report on what he could see around the corner to his team-leader.

To practice reports and reactions, the trainer would sometimes position role-players (whose intentions may or may not be clear) on the road. Other times there might be nothing. Whatever they saw would dictate their report.

"TWO PERSONS ON ROAD!"

"THREE HOSTILES ON ROAD! APPEAR TO BE ARMED!"

"NOTHING SEEN! ROAD APPEARS CLEAR!"

All this might seem obvious, but problems became apparent when we started giving the locals a chance to practice as corner-men. Weather it was lack of confidence or comprehension, they would invariably just repeat whatever the last corner man had reported on the previous drill, regardless of what was actually on the road. We had to start rearranging the team make-ups to ensure the locals were not put in positions that could cause embarrassment whilst also leaving the team situationally unaware.

Their lack of aggression was also a concern. We had been told up till know, both by previous trainees and veterans of the riots, that the most difficult thing would be keeping the locals on a leash. We all had the impression from those stories that the Papua New Guineans were all wild jungle warriors, but that wildness didn't seem to have translated from the mainland to these laid-back island folks.

Whether it was building clearances or room extractions, unarmed tactics or arrest training, or being shown the effectiveness of your shields and armour by having the trainers hurl bricks and bottles at you, we were constantly having to prod them forwards. They were timid, almost frightened at times. Aggression just wasn't natural for them. Given the role they were being trained for, this was worrying.

It was easy to become frustrated with the Papuans, even if deep down I knew it wasn't really their fault. Contractual obligations and inter-government agreements were throwing them into a role that was too complex for them. We all had completed far more intensive training in the military prior to this. The small-unit tactics and instinctive commands were already ingrained in us. Not to mention the decade-plus of schooling we had received growing up. We knew how to learn, and were simply adapting something we already knew into new conditions.

Most of the Papuans, however, had only basic education and had spent most of their lives as fishermen or subsistence farmers. That was pretty much the economy on Manus. Few of them had ever held a job as we would understand it before the MRPC arrived. As it was a more prestigious appointment, most had been chosen for ERT training based on tribal and family connections rather than aptitude. They didn't seem to really comprehend what was going on. Despite this, they were being given three days to be theoretically trained up to the same level as us. It was never going to happen, but we did our best.

* * *

Whilst we all shared concerns about our local counterparts, there was no such worry about the Aussies (and Kiwis) on team. Like everywhere on Manus, there was a lot of familiar faces.

Drew and Freddie were the "old men" of the team. Drew had been the feature of an article in the Army newspaper a few years earlier when he had joined up at forty years old in the same intake as his son. He was supremely fit, and back at our old unit had routinely run laps around guys half his age.

Freddie was our resident fixer. We called him "The Pirate". You know how in every war or prison movie there is that guy who can get his hands on anything and everything? That was Freddie. He built up great networks with the locals and always had something on the go.

Roy was fresh out of the army and father to a young son. He was doing his best to juggle his commitments to family life back home. Ken had spent a stint in Canada post-army working the ski resorts and still had one of those funny trans-pacific accents, so many young Aussie travellers seem to develop. It was even more pronounced when on the radio.

Travers and Evo were ex-soldiers and young fathers as well, and no doubt were trying to balance home life with the challenges of FIFO. Travers was a former paratrooper and amateur boxer who had a personal training business back home. Evo had been working on Nauru and had come across to Manus to help on that first day. He had done some training with the ERT on that island and was to be a big help in setting up our own capability.

Hadrian was one of the most experienced guys on the course. He had spent time with the Northern Territory Police riot squad after leaving the army, as well as qualifying for their Tactical Response Group. He had been on the ground with G4S during the riots, so his understanding of crowd behaviours that night was invaluable to the team. It was timely too, as we would get an insight into the realities of a fired up MRPC quicker than we imagined.

* * *

By the end of Day Two our bodies had started to get a handle on the heat. We headed to the MRPC in the afternoon to return our gear. We still had more stuff to get through, but the rest of the day would be theoretical and spent in the welcome air-conditioning of the Bibby.

Returning our equipment to the on-duty ERT every day had become a game in itself. The trick was to return the black gear bags and riot shields without the transferees in the compound seeing them. We didn't want to risk them getting worked up. The irony of causing a riot by being seen preparing for one would not have been appreciated by Immigration.

We were about to leave when we got word that we were needed in Foxtrot compound. It was nothing exciting, in fact quite the opposite. The head count in the compound was short. This was not an unusual occurrence, especially after IHMS runs. Transferees would swap their ID cards whilst mingling and return to each other's compounds. It was a game really, and they got great amusement watching the staff try and figure out what was going on and who was meant to be where. This time though it was taking longer than usual, and the call had been made to conduct a 100% face-to-photo check of the compound.

This was an extremely manpower-intensive task and the on-duty ERT had been called in to assist, as well as the trainees and trainers, fire-fighters and pretty much everyone who wasn't busy at the time. It soon became clear that it was going to be a frustrating and near-impossible task to complete. For some reason we were not allowed to simply muster every transferee into the open ground at the centre of the compound and count them from there. I guess it would be harassment or something for us to disturb their card games and afternoon naps. It seemed to be perfectly OK for them to screw us around though.

We had to make our way around the compound as they went about their business, finding and ticking them off one-by-one, trying to find out who was missing and who shouldn't be there. It was like herding cats. I started hearing yelling and jeering from the neighbouring Mike compound, but didn't think much of it. Sports were played in the open areas this time of day — it was probably just an enthusiastic crowd.

The noise grew louder and louder, and suddenly the atmosphere began to change. I started seeing the on-duty ERT guys running towards the rear gate of the compound. As I was not technically on-duty I didn't have a radio to hear what was going on, but as one of the boys ran past me I heard theirs crackling:

> "Code Black, Mike compound! Code Black, Mike compound!"

SSAs in need of immediate assistance. That's all we needed to hear. I made straight for the rear gate, passing through Green Zone between the two compounds and into Mike. My first thoughts when I saw it:

> "*Oh shit.*"

It seemed like the whole of Mike compound was crammed into the open ground between the two accommodation blocks that served as a multi-purpose sports field. Up above, the stairwells and walkways of the accommodations upper-levels were overflowing. In the middle of it all I could see a thin-line of green — the ERT had formed an extended line between the corners of two blocks. Behind them was a small but defiant group of Sudanese and Somalis. In front of them was a much larger and far more vocal mob of Iranians.

I weaved my way through the baying Persians and was warmly welcomed into the ERT line. I looked around, trying to figure out what was going on. I began scanning for threats, but there was just too much movement. The transferees crowding the walkways above us were concerning – every time I saw a movement up there in the corner of my eye I internally flinched, expecting a wall of projectiles to come raining down on us.

Amongst the crowd, I could see two of our most intimidating-looking ERT guys were leading the negotiations. Kane was a former power-lifter and body-builder who spoke good Arabic and Asher was a solid Muay-Thai kick-boxer who had been with the ERT on Nauru. Both were ex-infantry and no pushover in a stoush but even they looked like they could be overwhelmed by the increasingly agitated crowd. I could hear Asher trying to talk some sense into Wushu, who had of course presented himself as the mouth-piece of the Iranian side.

Our tactical situation was not good. Every man we had was holding the line and covering our negotiators. We had no rear-protection. There was nothing to stop the crowd simply running around behind the buildings, along the fence line and attacking us and the Africans from behind. We were outnumbered at least ten-to-one. Maybe our crowd-parting wedge techniques were about to get a work-out sooner than expected. If so, it didn't look good for us all getting out unscathed.

Suddenly, out of nowhere, a transferee dressed in nothing but a set of tiny red underpants ran out into the small opening between us and the Iranians and threw his hands in the air, screaming out something in Farsi. Judging by the howls of laughter that came from the crowd, I could only assume it was as hilarious as his appearance. People who just seconds before had been yelling and arguing turned their heads to look. It began to calm things down and slowly the crowd began to disperse.

What could have been a potential riot situation had been averted by a man in his undies.

The on-duty boys stayed in Mike maintaining a presence for the rest of the afternoon. The mood was calm. We finished unloading the gear and returned to the Bibby. I don't know who completed the head-count in Foxtrot, but I was glad it wasn't me. That evening everyone involved gathered in the Bibby lounge and I got an idea of what had happened to spark to whole situation.

It was school yard stuff. The Iranians and Africans had had a disagreement over which sport to play on the multi-purpose field. One group had wanted soccer and the other volleyball. It wasn't clear who had thrown the first punch, but the Africans had been quickly descended on by the Iranians. Bodhi had been first in and pulled a group of Iranians off a Somali who was getting well-and-truly pounded, only to have the mob turn on him. He was briefly cornered and trading blows when Kane and Asher got to him, literally hurling Iranians over their shoulders as they worked their way through the crowd.

It could have all ended badly, had it not been for one gallant soul. Asher summed it up best.

"That guy in the red jocks – what a fucking legend!"

* * *

We finished up the course the following afternoon with one final scenario. It tested pretty much everything we had covered up until that point – contact in open-ground, obstacles, barricades, building entry and room clearances, even a spur-of-the-moment hostage situation which had not originally been part of the scenario but just kind of happened. The ERT guys role-playing gave no quarter and got none back, and by the time it was all over everybody was thoroughly battered, bruised and exhausted. We couldn't have been in higher spirits.

Despite the complexity of the scenarios the trainers threw at us however, none of the training could replicate one critical factor – numbers. In all these exercises, our team always had the numerical superiority. As we had seen in Mike the day before, a real situation would see us as a very small group of fish in a very big pond. Training and teamwork would be our only equalisers.

I did one final shift in the compounds before flying out. I was looking forward to a full-length break, but also to coming back as a member of ERT. After the chaos of the early deployment and undermanned changeover, Wilson had finally established its rotation system for manning the MRPC year-round. Four identically organised teams had been stood up, with two to be on the island at any given time to cover each side of the clock. I was assigned to Team 3.

After two rotations on the floor listening to every request, grievance, whinge and insult the transferees could send my way, this new opportunity was something I was keen to make the most of. Things were going to be getting a lot more interesting for me on Manus Island.

CHAPTER 7

OFF THE STONES, ON THE TOOLS

I had a great three weeks off, mainly due to an improvement in the company I was keeping back home.

Zoe had caught my eye the moment I laid eyes on her, and they have never been off her since. We had met for the first-time months before I started working offshore and when I was in my downward spiral. I hadn't made a good impression and she made it clear that she wasn't interested in taking things any further.

I never got her out of my head however, and we were soon back in contact online. She seemed to notice a positive change in my attitude and I managed to secure a second date. She almost didn't recognise me when we met at a bar on the Brisbane River. Since we had last met I had embraced the Manus Island grooming standard of long hair and a beard, and looked something akin to a wild man emerging from the jungle. It seemed that whilst I had been gone however that hipsters had overtaken the Brisbane hospitality scene, so most other people just assumed I was an off-duty member of staff.

We spent nearly every moment of my break together, but all too soon my return flight to Port Moresby beckoned.

My first day with the ERT was in fact my first official day shift at the MRPC. Except for the initial inductions and the ERT course, I had never gone to work in the morning on Manus Island. I was soon to see just how much of a different world the centre was during daylight hours, but first up I was to start my workday the way ERT always does – at the gym.

Whilst the SSAs doing the hard yards in the compounds would

start their day dealing with queue-jumping Iranians in the breakfast line, ERT got to hit the weights. It was another reason I was grateful for my new position. No other team (except the fire-fighters) had PT scheduled into their shifts, and most had to get up early to beat the mad rush for the limited gym space. ERT had no such problems, in fact, our biggest problem was finding enough stuff to do in there for the hours we were allocated.

Not that a lot of guys had trouble with that. There were some serious athletes amongst the team. I wouldn't say it was intimidating, but I felt a similar phenomenon to what I did in the army. It's easy to feel like a slug when you are surrounded by so many supremely-fit people – it's only when you go back amongst the general population that you realise that you are doing all right.

Luckily for me, I have long been blessed with "retard-strength" – the ability to move heavy loads whilst apparently making it look easy. It was funny (and more than a little gratifying) to hear guys that had done special-forces selections in their former lives tell me they envied my strength – even if they did leave me for dead in the cardio department! This strength became my force multiplier on the team, earning me a place at the front of any barricade-breach and headman in any arrest team.

The Bibby did have a dedicated gym, but it was painfully inadequate for our needs. It was big in size but consisted of little more than a few treadmills and exercise bikes and some child-sized dumbbells. Clearly the builders had not fitted it out with a few hundred iron-hungry ex-soldiers in mind. Over time, the guys built it up into something passable, shipping in loads of barbells, plates and even a squat rack at their own expense.

The trusty Bibby master then attempted to reassert his authority by trying to take ownership of the equipment. At one point he even announced that we weren't allowed to take our own gear out of the

gym to work out on the wharf when the weather was agreeable. I
thought he should have spent more time worrying about the random
local crew members who would wander the upper-floors of our
accommodation unexplained and unaccompanied, and the resulting
cases of things going missing. But that's another story.

The ERT would split 50/50, with half training in the early morning
and the other half in the mid-morning, to take advantage of the quiet
time in the centre, we would have all hands back on deck for when
most transferees began to wake in the afternoons. It wasn't all just
vanity PT though – with the courses complete and signed off, 'H' had
come aboard as the permanent ERT trainer for Team 3. It was his
job to organise the all-important continuation training. This could be
anything from refreshing Level 1 and 2 tactics to medical, language or
legal instruction. He also had the unenviable task of trying to integrate
the Manusians into all this. There is no time like Island Time.

In addition to H, Drew, Freddie, Hadrian, Roy, Rich and Ken had
all come onto Team 3 with me. A lot of the other guys already on the
crew were familiar to me as role-players in our scenarios, and we all
got along great.

Whilst Ranger One was responsible for liaison with control, our
boss on the ground for day-to-day running was predictably known
by the call sign Ranger Two. On our rotation this was Jake, an ex
New Zealand Army NCO who had been with G4S during the riots.
Jake was one of those guys who was physically gifted at everything.
Whether it was sports, cardio, lifting, combat sports, he was good at it
all. He topped this off with a fierce motivation and was one of those
guys that could literally do anything he put his mind to. The only
downside to this was that you could feel like a real slug beside him,
and he wouldn't be afraid to let you know.

Also hailing from New Zealand and ex G4S, Joey had been an
aviation mechanic in the RNZAF before spending a few years as a

policeman in some of the roughest neighbourhoods in Auckland. He had moved to Brisbane with his young family and done a short working stint with the private-prison system before coming to Manus. Joey was calm and collected and a good man to have with you in a crisis. He knew how to talk to people as well, especially when they were worked-up and irrational, something we would deal with a lot.

Rounding out our Kiwi trifecta was Billy. Originally of Tongan descent, Billy had travelled the world with the New Zealand Navy before moving with his wife and young kids to Queensland. Power-to-weight ratio-wise, he was one of the strongest guys I had ever met. He was giving Jake a run for his money, which in turn made them both push harder.

Leading each of the three sections on our team were Horse, Gene and Justin. Gene and Justin were fresh out the army, but Horse had been out for a few years and had tried his hand at a few different business ventures, including running a coffee shop. I found it hard to imagine Horse in customer service, but he was a smart guy who I suspected was never fully mentally-stimulated by his surroundings. He was studying his MBA and had a perverse sense of humour, which drew us together immediately. One night to stave off fatigue, he and Gene engaged in a lively discussion on string theory and the multi-verse. Minds were blown.

Every group has its Crossfit crew, and we had Mason, Braith and Sully. All three had served in the same battalion and trained at the same "box". Whenever the three were together the talk was all-WOD. Mason had been a recon-patrol commander and took on the role of assistant-trainer for H, whilst Braith had a baby daughter back home who he doted on like any young father does. Sully only stayed on Manus for a short while, as he discovered soon after joining ERT that he had been accepted into the Queensland Fire and Rescue Service after two years on the waiting list. He was replaced by Rob, who following his army stint had worked as a bouncer in Surfers Paradise.

He sure had some stories to tell, and none that can be shared here.

There was Rich, who had been with me on that messy overnighter in Port Moresby and had his pockets fleeced whilst sleeping on the Bibby. Jock had been in air defence back in the army and had even passed the infamous SASR selection course, only to be rejected due to his youth. Proving just how small the world was, Jock and I discovered that we had gone to the same school. I had been two grades ahead, but we had a lot of mutual friends and had probably gone to a lot of the same parties over the years but had just never connected. Yet here we were on Manus together.

Rounding out the team was another couple of G4S crossovers, Abe and Alex. Abe had been a paratrooper in the Australian Army before spending a few years as a policeman in the UK. Alex had been in the artillery and had left the army after spending the last few years in the Federation Guard, leading ceremonial parties to commemorate Australia's war dead in Europe and Gallipoli.

* * *

When not training, ERT's home at the MRPC was referred to as F-Block. This was in reality a long, narrow corridor of connex offices, adjacent the old crazy bin "D-Block" which now housed the offices of various other stakeholders (mainly the cleaners, caterers and local labour-hire companies). While E-Block housed the escort team and the other government and non-government agencies such as Immigration (Australian and PNG), IOM and STST (Survivors of Torture and Serious Trauma, a psychological service there to provide support for those transferees deemed to have previously suffered such acts).

Despite the importance of all these groups, I never saw any of their staff and would struggle to recognise one if I did – I guess leaving their air-conditioned offices wasn't in the conditions of their employment contracts. People could say the same about us though. Over time, the various ERT teams succeeded in making F-Block rather comfortable. As well as the office and kit storage room, we converted one of the connexes into a home theatre, complete with couches and a wall-to-wall projector.

F-Block was neighboured on one side by the Oscar compound and the staff mess and control room on the other. This put us in range of control (both Wilson and Transfield) WiFi nodes. Quickly the other SSA's labelled the ERT "Eat, Rest, Train" or better yet "Eat, Rest, Text". It was mainly in good fun, but it really brought home the luxury we had compared to the compound teams, especially when it came to opportunities to communicate with home. Mobile phones were forbidden in the compounds, and in any case the WiFi signal didn't reach there anyway.

This isn't to say we spent all our time loafing around F-Block. Whilst half the team would remain there on QRF (Quick Reaction Force) to respond to any calls of assistance, the other half would be out roaming the compounds. Usually we would split into groups of three, but occasionally we would roll-heavy as a presence if there had been intelligence regarding a possible disturbance or just general atmosphere. For the most part, the days remained quiet. Our biggest concern would be finding the shadiest spot in the compound, or the best vantage point for the incoming ocean breeze.

We still tried to interact as much as possible with the transferees, to build up our networks and to help us get a feel for what was going on in the centre. But it wasn't like before. The transferees clearly noticed the way we moved from compound to compound and how we were spared the mundane static tasks such as mess duty and phone/internet groups. Some thought we were whiskies, but others were more suspicious. Whilst some openly questioned us about it, many were stand-offish. This was particularly true of the "big-players" in the compounds. We were watching them, and they were watching us.

Guys on the other teams had more success at this than us. Kane was good at building relationships, and managed to gain quite a rapport with two of the big players in Oscar. Most days on shift change we would find the three of them together in the shade, chatting like old friends. Blackbeard and D-Bol were two of the most physically intimidating men in the compound. Both were Lebanese, which was a change from the usual Iranian domination.

Blackbeard was nicknamed Blackbeard for his resemblance to the pirate character. He seemed quiet and polite, but I never trusted his demeanour. He was on several Interpol lists according to rumour, but for what we never really found out. We did learn however that he had a brother in one of the motorcycle gangs in Sydney.

D-Bol was Blackbeard's 2IC. He had been a power-lifter back in Lebanon and was nicknamed for his expressed fondness for the substance. He was the friendlier of the two, and also spoke better English. Like many transferees however, Blackbeard's grasp of English was a lot better when the situation suited him.

Another prominent character was Smiley. The former Iraqi policeman spoke excellent English and was one of the friendliest and most helpful detainees in Oscar. SSAs often found him a great help when trying to navigate the complex goings-on amongst the transferee community. Many of the guys on my own team sought him out when we passed through the compound and became quite friendly over time. I tried to keep my distance. I still chatted regularly with him, but I felt uncomfortable. I think it came down to the questions I had about him.

Smiley always spoke about his family back in Iraq. With the insurgency still fresh, the life of a policeman in that country was obviously a dangerous one. That danger extended to his wife and children. Why then, had Smiley been boarding a boat from Indonesia to Australia whilst his family were still back in Iraq, presumably facing great danger? I asked him this one day, hoping to maybe hear something that everybody else may have heard to make them like this guy so much. All I got was the same vague answer we always got from everyone.

"I just had to leave."

"But why did you leave *them* there?"

"I just had to."

"But *why?*"

"I had to."

* * *

There was nothing personal about any of this. We were there to do a job, one that by its nature brought us into contact with the less-likeable personalities in the MRPC. We may have disliked many of them for their actions, and distrusted them from what we knew of their previous lives. We always tried to remain professional. It became very clear one day though that some transferees were not so willing to maintain the work/personal divide (in all fairness though, there wasn't exactly a work/personal divide from their side of the equation).

Horse and I were making our way through Oscar when we were approached by an Iranian we had dubbed 'Monopoly Man' due to his distinctive moustache. Apparently, he had been some sort of fashion model back home, but here at the MRPC was a far cry from those photos we had seen. He was highly unstable and had been prescribed anti-psychotic medication which he was refusing to take. He was so prone to violent outbursts that he was banned from attending any medical appointments without an ERT escort. The fact that he was now approaching us with a massive smile on his face immediately made the hair on the back of my neck stick up.

"How are your daughters?" he asked Horse. "They are all blond like you. It's very nice."

I saw the briefest of flames in Horse's eyes. How did this little psychopath know about his family? Monopoly Man caught his reaction and his grin widened. Just as quickly though, Horse regained his composure and returned his smile.

"They are well, thank you."

We excused ourselves and continued our walk. Afterwards we headed straight to control to report this unnerving encounter to the intel boys. Corey was the on-duty officer that night. With his post-service hair growth and boyish features, he didn't exactly look like a former military intelligence operator. I suppose that worked to his advantage. It was Corey's job to know what was going on in the centre, and it was something he did well. He confirmed our suspicions, and told Horse that he was not the first to be confronted in such a manner.

"It's not just the transferees either – journalists and refugee advocates have been stalking guys online. I'd be careful about what information you share and what connections you make. Remove any mention of you working here, just to be safe."

Most guys had already done this and maintained a discreet online presence anyway when it came to work. But it didn't take the transferees long to hit pay-dirt. Within weeks, screenshots of SSA's personal online profiles were being shared on advocacy web-pages in a pathetic and hypocritical attempt to "name-and-shame". Advocates had a field day, with descriptions such as "sadist" "jackboot", "Nazi", "bigot" all being thrown around.

The double-standards of this invasion of privacy made me sick. None of these people criticising us knew us or had been here to see what we were dealing with. Their only sources were people like Wushu – some of the most untrustworthy people, I had ever encountered. They were all pushing an agenda that relied on exaggerating or outright fabricating our actions whilst remaining silent on their own violent and dishonest behaviour.

Stuff like this we could all handle. It was part-and-parcel of working in such a sensitive area. Where it became unforgivable was when they used it to threaten our families. Transferees would often make these threats. They had our personal information to flesh out their taunts, and hid behind the knowledge that we were bound by professionalism not to retaliate.

It was both sickening and gutless. We could mainly brush it off as mere empty threats from cowards, but there was always the niggling thought. What if it *wasn't* just bravado? What if they really *did* have those connections to bikie gangs and other violent people back in Australia? At the end of the day, we really didn't know that much about them. What so many of these advocates didn't seem to understand (or *want* to understand) is that whatever it was that some of these guys may have been running from might be chasing them for a damn good reason.

In the end, we just put our heads down and went back to work. We maintained our integrity and our agreement to confidentiality, and the media stayed silent about these vile and cowardly threats from so-called refugees.

* * *

Moving so freely around the centre gave me the chance to see how things ran in a whole new way. It also gave me an indication of what day-shift had to deal with in regards to the other stakeholders. I thought it had been bad dealing with them at night when there had only been a few but during the day the centre was crawling with them. The growing differences in opinion between the different organisations was continually showcased.

I was standing by the Delta gate one morning, chatting with the compound supervisor. Nick was a little nugget of a guy who was forever the butt of jokes about his height. He took it well though and gave as good as he got. He was a great supervisor – firm but fair. He was hated by many transferees for this, but respected by just as many. As we were talking, a case worker approached him as she was leaving the compound.

> "Excuse me, when are the cleaners due to come by?"
>
> "They came through once already after breakfast," Nick replied. "They are due to come back in a few hours after lunch. Why is that?"
>
> "Um, I just saw a couple of empty water bottles up against the back fence. Would you be able to call them in now?"

Nick and I exchanged glances. She was completely serious. It was hard to keep a straight face, but to his credit, Nick was diplomatic in his reply.

> "I'll let them know when I see them, but I don't think it will be a high-priority for them."
>
> "OK, well as long as you call them. I really think you should."

I should have bit my tongue, but I just couldn't help it. Contracted cleaners came through each compound three times a day to clean up after the transferees, yet here she was trying to absolve them of the simple responsibility of *not littering*. It wasn't like somebody had defecated on the mat in the prayer room.

"How about they just clean up after themselves?" I suggested. "It's not really that hard, is it?"

She looked at me with a scowl. Was what I had suggested really that offensive?

"They deserve some dignity."

"Isn't there dignity in not just throwing your rubbish on the ground and expecting somebody else to clean up after you?"

Moments after she left, probably on her way to write up a complaint about me, a young Iranian man emerged from the rec-room and opened a bottle of water. Looking straight at me, he took a few gulps and simply tossed the still half-full bottle onto the ground as he walked away. It was if he had timed it perfectly just to annoy me.

I had never been so glad not to be tied to the compounds.

* * *

Day shift introduced us to another new practice that Transfield had imported from Nauru – the excursion programme. These excursions could be anything from soccer games on the oval across the road to walking and running groups along the hilly jungle tracks surrounding the MRPC. The ones that attracted the most interest (and the biggest headaches) were the beach excursions.

Excursions were mostly the bag of the escorts team who worked alongside the Transfield activities staff, but it seemed that every time there was a visit to the beach behind the centre that ERT would get a call. Some transferees were determined to see how far they could push us. For once, however, the Iranians didn't seem to be the main culprits. On this occasion it was the Africans' time to shine.

During beach excursions any transferee going into the water was instructed not to go out beyond waist depth. This was a safety precaution. Few of the transferees could swim and given the fact that none of the SSAs or Transfield staff were certified lifeguards meant that nobody was keen to risk a drowning. Nonetheless, nearly every beach excursion would result in the same inevitable call over the radio.

"Any available Ranger call-sign to the beach front."

Those of us on QRF would make our way out to the small beach behind Delta compound. Transferees would be piled up along the fence-line, giggling and heckling at the farce that was unfolding. Those that had been on the beach excursion were huddled in the shade below one of the many palm trees dotting the cove. The Transfield and Wilson's staff were mainly concerned with what was still offshore – namely the trio of Somali transferees that had well and truly ignored the waist-deep rule. They were over fifty metres out, with only their heads poking out above the waterline.

They weren't exactly drowning – we knew that there was a sandbar there that allowed a person to sit quite comfortably with the water at chest-level. Now the tired old game would begin. SSAs would call out in vain for the transferees to come back ashore. Negotiations would begin. They even brought out a Somali interpreter with a megaphone to try and coax the men back in. Finally, they brought out the canoe.

Zane, our ERT Manager, had acquired a locally-made twin hull canoe which was stashed at a small inlet at the other end of the beach. Usually once he paddled his way out to the sandbar, the absconding transferees would simply grab on and follow him back to shore. This time however, things didn't really follow the script.

Almost as soon as Zane's canoe made its way around the cove, it began to take on water. By the time it was directly in front of us – and in full view of the entire centre – it had begun to sink. Soon it was completely beneath the waterline, and Zane was left standing on the sandbar. The Somalis he was supposed to be picking up made little effort to conceal their amusement, and neither did the rest of the MRPC that was watching on. Their laughter could probably be heard in Lorengau.

Some local fishermen soon came and brought the group back to shore. The remainder of the excursion was cancelled – once again a few idiots had ruined it for everybody else. The quiet Rohingyas and Tamils shot some resentful looks the Somali way – but towards us there was nothing but weak smiles and accepting nods. At least they seemed to understand. The Somalis, on the other hand, were already launching into the same tired argument.

> "Why? Why are we going back in? We were supposed to be here for two hours!"
>
> "You were asked not to go out beyond waist depth for safety. You disobeyed the safety rules."
>
> "No, we didn't!"
>
> "Yes, you did. We saw you. All these people here saw you. And when you did you ignored directions to come back in."
>
> "No, we didn't!"

I doubted that they truly believed that a different chain of events had occurred – they were just being argumentative for argument's sake. About this time, they would usually resort to a political tirade against the Australian government. Their noses really got out of joint when they were temporarily banned from excursions.

There was something about the Somalis – they were just as aggressive and dramatic, but in a different way to the Iranians. Something said that they had to be taken more seriously. Whilst most of the Iranians seemed to be middle-class blowhards, whose idea of intimidation was acting like characters from Jersey Shore, I had no doubt that the Somalis had lived violent lives. Whatever it was, I was glad that their numbers were in the minority. Had the Somalis had the numerical advantage of their Persian neighbours, things at the MRPC could have been very different.

* * *

The use of the Somali interpreter on the beach was the one and only time I ever saw this protected species used to assist Wilson. The interpreters were by far the most highly-paid workers at the MRPC, but despite the obvious need for their services they seemed to spend most of their time in their air-conditioned hut sucking up the WiFi. They emerged so rarely that SSAs started to refer to them as "unicorns".

The reason for this was not exactly the interpreters' own fault – they could only be used for official correspondence (such as medical appointments and interviews with DIPB or IOM) and had to be booked in advance. They weren't there to be utilised by Wilson or Transfield for day-to-day tasks. This wasn't as much of a hindrance as it first appeared – there was often enough language skills on both sides of the conversation between SSAs and transferees to get a point across. For anything that required something more substantial, Wilson had another card up its sleeve in the form of our Cultural Advisors.

The "Charlie-Alpha" team were all SSAs of Arabic ethnicity. They spoke the language and had an obvious understanding of cultural nuisances that those of us of predominately European descent didn't. They were all second-or-third generation Australians and like most SSAs came from military or police backgrounds.

Paul was a Lebanese-Australian and former infantryman. He had applied for a regular SSA gig just like the rest of us. It was only when the person interviewing him bothered to glance at his resume (and presumably his face) that they noticed that he spoke Arabic. On the rare occasions that he could be spared, H would arrange for Paul to give lessons in Arabic slang.

English was still the universal language in the MRPC – Tamils and Rohingyas, for example, would speak with the African or Middle Eastern transferees in English as it was the common tongue. It was strange to watch – kind of like how in the movies where everyone converses in accented English regardless of where they are from. Various Arabic dialects were the mother language of the Arabs and Africans, but as it turned out most of the Farsi-speaking Iranians knew it as well.

Balancing Paul on the Charlie Alpha team was Loretta. In a working environment dominated by young men, it would be easy to dismiss this "little old lady" as an office assistant or some other form of administrative position. Nothing could be further from the truth. Loretta was also of Lebanese descent and spoke Arabic fluently. She had a way of being able to engage with transferees in a way that we couldn't in such a testosterone fuelled environment. She never backed down or showed the slightest sign of intimidation whenever one of them became aggressive.

We never did learn much about her background before Manus Island. We knew she had worked a lot at the detention centres on Christmas Island and Curtin, and had spent a lot of time with government departments in Canberra. Her language and people skills led many to speculate that she had worked in the intelligence community – some even went as far as to believe that she was still working for them in some capacity.

Everybody on our team really took to Loretta. She was one of the few non-ERT members to have an open-invitation to ride on our bus (ERT was assigned its own sole-use mini-bus and land cruiser, for us to react quickly from the Bibby to the MRPC). The boys were fiercely protective of her as well, as one transferee quickly found out when he made the poor decision to spit in her face.

Whilst Loretta and Paul were the epitome of valuable assets, the same could not be said about Yemi. The only use for Yemi was to provide a laugh at the absurdity of his situation. If you did not laugh you would go mad trying to figure it out whilst cleaning up the mess.

All organisations make bad hires, and Wilson was certainly not immune. In the early days of the rushed recruitment process there were some people who simply shouldn't have been there. Most of them were sorted out quickly. Yemi was another story though. He had gotten the job as a cultural advisor on the basis that he spoke fluent Arabic, Farsi, Pashtun and Pidgin. He was the perfect combination and almost seemed too good to be true. That's because he was.

I suppose those conducting the interview took him in good faith. Why else would you tell them about the very skill that you are being hired for when there is no chance that you could fake it? But he did. It became apparent immediately that Yemi could in fact speak none of these languages. It would have been funny really if it hadn't been so serious.

Apart from being obviously incapable of doing the job he was hired for, Yemi made situations worse. He had no negotiation skills whatsoever. SSAs would often call for Charlie Alpha to mediate disputes with transferees, but if Yemi was the one to turn up you could guarantee the situation was about to get worse before it got better.

His way of communicating was to open his eyes wide, move his hands around a lot whilst speaking loudly and slowly in English in a blatantly patronising manner. This only served to antagonise the transferees further. It was a complete farce. Transferees would look at us as if to say, *"Who the hell is this guy?"* We couldn't help but agree.

The only thing Yemi did worse than his job was being a room-mate. Thankfully I was never unfortunate enough to be forced to share space with him on the Bibby. Those that did told horror stories

— he certainly didn't have the close-quarters living awareness us ex-military guys had. He would make phone calls from his bed in the early hours of the morning whilst everyone was trying to sleep, and was quite loud when performing his ablutions. To top it all off, he was a snorer.

It was amazing that it took them as long to fire him as it did. Even then, it was suggested by somebody in HR that he simply be busted from Cultural Advisor down to SSA! He had been hired solely based on his so-called language skills and had no security background to speak of. He had proven in the compounds to be completely unsuitable for the task. How could they even think about keeping him on? Thankfully wiser heads prevailed, and Yemi was eventually dismissed.

* * *

It would be easy for most people to assume that apart from the Cultural Advisors our workforce was predominantly an Anglo-centric affair. Whilst this was true for the majority, there were some notable exceptions. I often wished I could have introduced some of the guys I worked with to critics who labelled everything we did as racist. They might have been more than a little surprised to learn that some of the so-called jackboot thugs they accused of abusing refugees had actually been refugees themselves.

This was especially true of our "Spasians" (Spanish Asians) Normie and Manny. Normie had been a few of the boys' Platoon Sergeant back in the army, and was a great guy. His fiancée was a German scientist who was awaiting her permanent residency status to be approved. He flew back to Europe to see her on almost every break, and the team all celebrated on the day she touched down in Australia permanently.

Like Normie, Manny had also been born and raised in the

Philippines. He had grown up in poverty, and his family had waited for five years after applying for the chance to migrate to Australia. They had long given up on the possibility when one day they received the news that they had been approved. Manny was already a teenager when his family had arrived in Melbourne. He took to his new life with both hands, working several factory jobs before eventually becoming manager of a mobile phone store.

> "The day I was eligible to apply, five years after arriving, I walked into the army recruitment office. I wanted to give back to my new country."

I found Manny's story inspiring. Some of the transferees however, found his presence amongst us offensive. It was as if his citizenship was an affront to them. Nearly every time I was in a compound with him a transferee would take it upon himself to challenge him about the perceived double-standard.

> "Why does Australia accept you and not us? What makes you so good? How can you stand there and look at us the way you all do, when you are no better than us?"

Manny always rebutted them bluntly, yet politely, never letting himself to be dragged into a petty argument.

> "It's not about anybody being better than anybody else. It's about the process. As for Australia accepting me, I worked hard and became part of Australia. I even became a soldier because I wanted to defend her."

> "You had the chance! How does Australia know that I would not become a soldier to defend it?"

The transferee – an Iraqi – was pleased with his statement. But Manny hit back in flash. It was the first time I came close to seeing him lose his composure. I could hear the emotion in his voice.

"Your country is under attack right now, but you're not there defending it. You left your family and your country in danger and paid a people smuggler knowing that what you were doing was illegal. I don't think you would do anything for anybody other than yourself!"

Later in private, Manny expressed regret that he had let his emotions get the better of him.

> "I hate it when the Iraqis and Iranians say that I am the same as them. My family was in poverty back in the Philippines. We would have loved to have just gotten on a boat, but we didn't because we knew that that was not how things worked. I see their Facebook profiles – they weren't poor! It's all cars and drugs and nightclubs, fancy clothes and expensive watches!"

* * *

On the rare occasions I spoke to people back home about my job, I often encountered refugee advocates. I respected their beliefs, even if I did find it difficult at times to separate in my own mind the difference between a disagreement regarding the overarching government policy and the behaviour of the individual transferees I encountered.

I was having a drink one evening with some old school friends. The bar was in Brisbane's West End, pretty-much the epicentre of left-wing thought and not the place where a "border bouncer" for the Abbott Government would be welcomed with open-arms. One school-friend introduced me to some of her self-described "hippie friends" and although I wasn't the one who said it, the subject came up that I worked on Manus Island. One of them widened their eyes, as if she couldn't believe she was sharing the same oxygen as me.

"Oh my God. You're not cruel to them, are you?
"No. Why would I be?"

That seemed to be enough to relax her. My schoolfriend, who herself was opposed to offshore processing, just shrugged.

"*Somebody* has to work there for as long as it's there."

With that we ordered more beers and the subject changed to something far less serious. It's funny how well everyone can get on when there is more alcohol and less politics involved. I always just found it easier not to talk about it. Zoe could never understand why I was so cagey about it, or why I got annoyed when she blurted out to people where I worked.

"It's not that I'm ashamed or that I want to look mysterious or something. I just don't like sharing my personal details with people I've only just met, especially when there is a chance they might react negatively, because that will just make the night awkward for everybody. Nobody wants to be the guy who ruins the party."

When we did discuss the MRPC, I would endeavour to impart on people just how non-prisonlike the facility was. I don't believe there could be a prison anywhere in the world whose inhabitants had as much freedom as they had on Manus Island. We couldn't even legally stop a transferee from simply walking out of the centre if they so chose. We could only negotiate and convince them that it was better to stay.

Where would they go anyway? Inside the centre they had free food, bedding, medication and access to telephones and internet. Despite how much they complained, they certainly had it a lot better than those held up in the squalid UN refugee camps that thousands of others found themselves in around the world. They didn't even have to look that far. Outside the fence the locals of Manus Island had it far tougher.

Despite this lavish endowment of taxpayer money which they gladly accepted, they continued to complain. They continued to demand entry to Australia. They continued to demand "Freedom". They continued to cling to the notion that freedom means getting whatever you want when you want. They were free to leave the centre whenever they wanted. They simply couldn't enter Australia uninvited – just like every citizen of every country in the world.

In a practical sense, nothing showed how non-prison-like the MRPC was than the weekly farce we knew as "compound sweeps". These words conjured up images of tossing cells and other prison movie clichés whilst looking for contraband. The only way an SSA could obtain the legal authority to touch anything inside a transferee's accommodation to perform a proper search was in the company of the PNG Police in the execution of a warrant.

Search warrants were few and far between. They required a long period of intelligence-gathering to present grounds to the local constabulary for a warrant. And even then, it only happened if the local coppers felt like doing it. But whenever they did happen, we always hit pay-dirt. We didn't care about the contraband – the drugs, the pornography (illegal under PNG law) or the mobile phones. It was the makeshift weapons that worried us.

Whilst our safety was being placed at risk to satisfy some bureaucratic red-tape, a malevolent element within the transferee population was stockpiling for a showdown. As if to rub-in the fact of how powerless we were to prevent this, management had ordered us to undertake a predictable pattern of pointless exercises known as "sweeps".

Try to imagine a search without searching – that's what a sweep was. You were literally just walking through the accommodation blocks hoping to see something dodgy lying out in the open.

We tried our best to maximise our chances of getting lucky. ERT would trickle into the compounds – a pair here, a pair there – trying in vain not to make it obvious that something was up. The transferees – especially those who probably had something to hide – would pick up on us straight away and head straight to their rooms. We would move through the accommodation, legally unable to touch anything that didn't have a Transfield sticker attached to it. Transferees would ask us what we are doing. Our excuses got feebler each time.

"We are checking for rats."

"We are checking for expired safety stickers on electrical items."

"We are checking to see if the air conditioners are all working."

They saw straight through it, and eventually we stopped even trying. The whole exercise was pointless. We just wanted to get it over and done with, so we could sign it off. The transferees were aware of the restrictions placed on us. They would simply hang sheets around their bunks, rendering our visual sweeps redundant. They could have had a samurai sword and a box of hand grenades under their bed and we were powerless to even check. The Iranians took great pleasure in tormenting us about this fact. We would enter a room to find them sitting in a group, laughing at us.

"Ooooo, so close officer, just missed it! Hahahaha!"

We weren't laughing. Our visual checks told us quite enough. Every bunk bed had the safety railings missing from its steel frame. Every fan had at least one blade missing. Checks of the toilet and shower blocks would reveal missing pipes and fixtures. The bad element in the centre was arming itself for war and there was not a single thing we could do about it.

CHAPTER 8

JUST ENOUGH ROPE

Like everyone employed at the MRPC, we relished the chance to get out of the centre and see more of the island. Most of the government departments seemed to keep regular office hours and only worked nine-to-five, Monday to Friday, giving them plenty of time to explore. For us though it was a steady routine of twelve-hour blocks, with our time away from the centre being spent on or around the Bibby.

There was a brief window during the changeover between day and night shifts where you had twenty-four hours to yourself. Some guys used the opportunity to head into Lorengau, or to try out the surfing, fishing and diving around Manus Island's beautiful coastlines. Most guys though just tried to stay up as late as possible to get into their night routine.

As ERT we were lucky in the fact that not being tied to individual compounds gave us a little more freedom. When conducting our team fitness tests, for example, we took our bus to a pristine deserted beach around the headlands. We finished our run and other components and managed to fit in a quick dip in the ocean before heading back to the MRPC. Having enjoyed this brief respite, we were quite excited to learn on our return to F-Block that we were being warned out for an outside tasking in support of the Australian High Commissioner's upcoming visit to Lorengau.

The amount of political background work going on to keep the MRPC going was incredible. Australia gives over a half-billion dollars in aid annually to PNG. I'm sure the positioning of the centre was written into it somewhere. Despite all this one-way cash-flow however, it always seemed like PNG was the one calling the shots. It was no secret that a lot of the money Australia was spending on the MRPC was going directly into PNG government pockets. They gladly accepted this financial windfall but continually demanded further financial concessions.

Whilst government ministers were the ones benefiting most from the agreement, the same couldn't be said for the local people of Manus. The MRPC was certainly bringing in great opportunities in the way of local employment and business. The local people may not have shared their government's high-level corruption, but they certainly seemed to share their kleptomaniac tendencies.

I know that it's easy to judge them coming from a Western-developed background, and I realise that poverty breeds opportunism, but it was frustrating to watch it all unfold. The people of Manus Island were able to really put this increased Australian investment to good use and to develop the island province, yet they were squandering it with greed and short-sightedness. There seemed to be no sense of planning ahead for the day when the centre and all it brought with it would invariably end. It was more a case of take as much as you can, as quick as you can, and don't worry about which bridges you burn.

The reason for the High Commissioner's visit was to address the concerns of the residents and to consult with the provincial government on how Australian aid could best be utilised. The local constabulary were to oversee security during the visit, which was set to include an open meeting with local community members in Lorengau. Manus wasn't exactly a high-threat environment, but seeing as that the ERT was arguably the most capable asset on the island that answered to the Australian government, it was decided that we would provide a presence there too. We didn't have any legal authority to actually do anything in Lorengau should anything occur, but we were still keen to go along for the ride.

'H', Jake and Zane headed out to do a reconnaissance on the

meeting site and briefed us on the plan they had come up with. It was all to be a relaxed affair – plain clothes, a loose cordon, pretty much out of sight. The only thing that looked like it could throw a spanner in the works was the timing.

The whole job was due to occur on our changeover day. Team 1 (our opposites for the last two weeks of each rotation) had flown in the day before and would be taking over the daytime ERT capability for the centre. We would be losing our rest-day to cover this commitment in town, but the biggest problem then was who was going to cover the night shift? Nobody was keen to work a twenty-hour shift, and in any case, it was unlikely Wilson would be keen to cover the overtime.

In the end somebody decided that we would work a special 10a.m. – 10p.m. shift, thus allowing us to cover the High Commissioner visit as well as the busy evening period at the MRPC. This would leave the centre uncovered by ERT for the period of 10p.m. to 6a.m. the following morning when Team 1 came back on deck, but as the old saying went, if it hasn't happened by ten it probably won't happen at all.

In any case, we would still be on call. What could go wrong?

* * *

"Wake up bro! We're being reacted!"

Jake's distinct Kiwi drawl had roused me from a deep sleep. What was going on? What was the time? I didn't get a chance to ask. His silhouette had already vanished. Then instinct took over. I jumped down from my top bunk and began to get dressed. I fumbled around in the dark. Jake could have at least turned the light on when he woke me up!

The high commissioner's visit had gone off without a hitch. The team had simply parked our mini-bus and land cruiser behind the meeting hall and spent most of the afternoon waiting it out in air-conditioned comfort. Two guys had originally been tasked to wait inside the meeting hall's back-room, ready to provide assistance to the high commissioner in the unlikely event that the crowd became threatening.

In the end they hadn't been required. Apparently, the threat was deemed so low that the local police officers who were assigned to her as escorts spent most of their time out the back trying to bum smokes off the ERT boys and finding shady spots to sleep.

For Billy and myself – who had drawn the thrilling task of early warning – it meant a few hours at the end of the road connecting the meeting hall to the main drag of Lorengau. Should any vehicle turn off and head towards the hall, we would radio the main team and let them know. As it happened, we spent the whole afternoon sipping sugary PNG soft-drinks and sharing the shade of a palm-tree with the local unemployed. The only excitement came when I entered what I thought was an abandoned shack to relieve myself – only to discover that it was a family home. The family and I both laughed about it however, making my intrusion a little less awkward.

We had a few hours off to relax and hit the gym that afternoon before taking over from the day shift guys at the centre at 1800. When we had left at 2200 as planned things at the centre had been quiet. Now it was looking like our little rostering gamble had blown up in our faces.

I stumbled out the door, pulling my boots on as I went. I expected to see the hallway buzzing with activity. It was eerily empty. Jake was nowhere to be seen. The only thing that convinced me that it wasn't a dream was the sight of Mason stumbling out of a room a few doors up, looking just as confused about the situation as me.

"What the hell is going on?"

"I got no fucking idea!"

We bounded down the stairs – the elevators were out of order once again. We passed the second floor. We saw no-one. First floor. No-one. Surely if things were serious enough for us to be reacted then everybody should be up? Maybe everyone was forming up down in the lobby? Surely, we would find out what was going on when we got there.

The lobby was deserted. The only person there was the Entry One. This was the call-sign for the SSA's assigned 24/7 to the desk at the front entrance. It was a sought-after respite position, especially on night shift. Air-conditioning and WiFi with nobody to bother you. The SSA was sitting there quietly, looking completely unbothered. If things were kicking off down at the centre, he sure wasn't letting it get to him.

"What's going on mate?"

"Apparently there is some sort of disturbance in Oscar compound. Several personnel trapped inside the mess. Not sure about much more exactly."

The radio on the desk in front of him was silent, not crackling with activity as you would expect in this situation.

"Is this legit?" Mason asked. The SSA just shrugged. As we made our way out the door, he called out to us:

"The bus has already left! You'll have to get up there on foot!"

The first thing that came to mind when I heard that? This *must* be a drill. The vague situation reports? The conveniently missing vehicle just to throw a spanner in the works? The unexplainable lack of personnel responding? Surely somebody in charge was using this night of all nights to test our reactions. As we jogged down the gang plank onto the wharf, I could see several figures in the distance, running in the direction of the MRPC. We took off after them.

Tired, dehydrated and wearing boots, the run was harder than it should have been. I always thought that in the event of a real call-up the adrenalin would kick in and take over, but it wasn't. Maybe in my subconsciousness I wasn't convinced that this was the real thing, so my body wasn't giving up the goods. As we huffed and puffed towards the MRPC, I heard something that I had never heard there at this time of night.

Along the perimeter fence approaching Oscar from the Bibby are a pair of enormousness generators providing power for the MRPC. Usually they are so noisy that you simply cannot hear anything as you pass them. At that moment however, there was a sound that was overpowering even them. It was the sound of voices.

Angry voices. A *lot* of them.

Finally, the adrenalin took over. I picked up the pace. As I rounded the corner and the outer fence of Oscar came into view, I saw an SSA holding open the perimeter evacuation gate ushering us inside. We darted inside.

I immediately saw movement to my left, down the man-made corridor formed by the Oscar accommodation blocks arranged along the fence-line. Half a dozen SSAs holding back an equal number of screaming Arab transferees who seemed hell-bent on getting around the corner. Before I could even register what was going on, I heard a voice yelling out to me:

"GET UP HERE!"

I saw Horse standing up on a step at the side entrance to the Oscar mess. As I ran around the corner of the accommodation block, the extent of the situation filled my view from all sides. Through the floor-to-ceiling perspex windows of the Oscar mess, I could see chaos inside. Table and chairs lay broken and strewn everywhere. Transferees lay writhing on the floor, struggling to fight back against the SSAs. There were bloodied faces on both sides.

"HOLD THE LINE! HOLD THE LINE!"

Dozens of SSAs – it must have been the entire night shift – had formed an extended line in front of the mess, from the corner of the accommodation blocks to the entrance to the multi-purpose/prayer room. At the other end of the Oscar dozens of transferees were similarly formed up, leaving a kind of no-mans-land in the centre of the compound. It was like two medieval armies forming up for battle.

Scanning the faces on our side of the line, I could see just how all-hands-on-deck the situation was already. There were SSAs from every compound, Whiskeys and Charlie-Alphas. Control-room dwellers and guys from the investigations and intelligence cells. Even the fire-fighters were in the line. Everyone was there.

Everyone except the ERT.

Except for Horse, Mason, Jake and myself, I couldn't see anyone from my team. Hanno, Carlos and a couple of the guys from Team 1 were there. How had this happened? We were supposed to be the centre's go-to guys for when stuff like this happened. We spent every day training for it. But now that it was happening for real we weren't even on the front-line. We weren't even *all here*. There was barely a half-dozen of us on the scene out of two full teams and we were standing around confused and disorganised in the safe area behind the cordon.

None of us knew what was going on at that moment, but all this had started over an argument in the mess over what to watch on TV. At night after the evening meal, the Oscar mess was converted in a makeshift movie theatre. The argument between a group of Iranians and group of Pakistanis over which movie to play next had turned into a fist fight. SSAs had intervened only to have both sides turn on them. It became an all-in brawl.

Our big rostering gamble had been called in the worst possible way. With no ERT to respond, the call had gone out for the other compounds to be locked down and for every available SSA to make their way to Oscar. The call had then gone back to the Bibby, but all warnings about the problem of having us spread throughout separate rooms had now borne fruit. It had become a simply matter of *"grab who you can and get there ASAP!"*

The problem for the Pakistanis here was that in taking on the Iranians in the mess they were effectively taking on most of the compound. As the rest of Oscar became aware of the fighting, dozens of Iranians had emerged from their rooms and prepared to go to the aid of their countrymen. The Pakistanis too, had sent a handful of reinforcements – those men we had seen being restrained when we first entered the compound. Thankfully the SSAs had gotten there first.

From my vantage point behind the line however, I could already see a potential disaster in the making. The Iranians had nothing to stop them snaking around behind the accommodation blocks and rolling over the handful of SSAs and Pakistanis there. Hopefully the Iranians' lack of situational awareness continued, we ran the very real risk of being surrounded.

Whilst the Iranians formed up ahead of us, we could see Blackbeard, D-Bol and the other Lebanese sitting off to the side, watching the whole show unfold. No doubt they were waiting to see who would come out on top. I could see the little brown faces of the Tamils and Rohingyas peering out through the accommodation doors. They didn't want any part of this.

The Iranian numbers were growing, but they seemed oddly calm.

Monopoly Man and a few of the serial-agitators were out the front, attempting to whip them up into a frenzy. Despite their best efforts, an eerie silence was descending over the compound. The stand-off was ensuing.

"STOP HIM! STOP HIM!"

I spun around. One of the Pakistanis near the gate had lunged at an SSA, knocking him to the ground. He took off at full speed towards the mess. I was the only person in between. Without realising it, I was already mentally calculating the points that our paths would intersect. I rushed towards him. I tucked down my head, dropping my shoulder. My feet actually left the ground as I ploughed into him at full-force, smashing him into the perspex windows of the mess.

As the shock-wave was still reverberating across the perspex, I threw my arm under his shoulder and yanked it up into an underarm lock. The momentary shock of my tackle had quickly worn off however, and his face quickly shot out in the direction of mine. He gnashed his teeth at me whilst letting out an almost inhuman growl. I slammed his body as hard as I could into the window again. No way was I going to let him bite me. He could lose his teeth for all I cared.

Two other SSAs were with me in a flash, locking his arms behind his back and dragging him towards the gate. I was about to follow them when I heard a call:

"ALL ERT ONTO ROUTE CHARLIE!"

Why were we being called out of the compound? Obviously the other SSAs had Oscar under control, but all I could think of at that moment was how thirsty I was. I ran after the other guys, managing to grab a lukewarm bottle of water that had been lying unopened near the gate. As we raced out, I caught a snippet of radio traffic from the guard-hut – a large crowd was gathering at the front gate in Mike, and they were becoming agitated.

Route Charlie was eerily quiet. The usually bustling Oscar fence-line was unattended, whilst the transferees gathered in the neighbouring Delta appeared curious but calm. All the compounds had their gates shut – the closest thing to a lock-down at the MRPC. Skeleton crews had been left in the guard-boxes outside each compound to observe and report in any change in mood. I didn't need to listen to the radio to hear what the atmosphere in Mike was like – we could hear it from the other side of the centre.

I passed the water around to the other guys before gratefully gulping down my first H_2O since waking up. Carlos was grinning at me.

"Sweet tackle."

Here we were – five guys securing the main thoroughfare through the MRPC whilst disturbances kicked off at opposite ends. The noise coming from Oscar had obviously alerted transferees everywhere that something was up, but it was Hanno who said what we were all thinking.

"They're probably on the phone to each other right now organising this shit."

"If Mike gets into Fox again they can get onto Route Charlie – then it's going to be on."

Jonny was another ex-Adgie who had been on the line with G4S during the February riots. He knew all too well what the danger of our current situation was. On that night the transferees of Mike had breached the internal fence into Foxtrot and had then attempted to force their way onto Route Charlie. The G4S guards had only narrowly been able to fight them back. For all we knew, this was what was about to happen now. We had two full ERT crews on-island in order to counter just this kind of scenario – but right now that force was reduced to just the half-dozen of us standing cleanskin in the middle of the centre. We didn't even have radios.

I don't know how long we waited there for – it felt like ages. I was excited but apprehensive at the same time. Eventually though it seemed like the situation in Mike seemed to be calming itself and we called back into Oscar. There was unfinished business to attend to.

The threat of an Iranian charge on the mess-hall had now subsided, but now we had to get the bruised and battered Pakistanis out. The decision had been made that ERT would spirit them from the mess doorway to the Oscar gate and then into the neighbouring IHMS compound, where the on-call medical staff had by now arrived from the Bibby and were already treating the injured SSAs.

Given the way they were cowering behind the other SSAs when we went into the mess, I would have thought the Pakistanis would have been keen to get out of the compound as quickly as possible with the minimum amount of attention. But as always, they surprised us. With an ERT escort on each shoulder, we ran the Pakistanis the short distance from the mess to the gate. Now, with an ERT close-escort and an extended-line of SSAs separating them from their Iranians, they were suddenly full of bravado.

"FUCK YOU!" The first evacuee fired off at the onlooking Iranians as he was ushered out. The Iranians started shouting, and for a moment it looked as if the whole thing was going to kick off again. The following Pakistanis did the same thing.

"For fuck's sake!" I saw Horse shaking his head with frustration. "Do these guys WANT to get bashed?"

Luckily, we got them out quickly before anything else could happen, and the compound returned to its uneasy state of calm. Eventually the crowd dispersed, and the SSAs returned to their compounds. ERT maintained a presence in Oscar for another hour or so, before being recalled to the Bibby for the rest of our ill-planned night-off.

* * *

ERT copped a lot of stick for the Oscar episode. We heard it all the next night as we made our way around the centre. Usually the boys in the boxes would let us have it as soon as we approached the compound.

> "Wow, here you are! We didn't even have to wait forty minutes this time!"
>
> "If you guys need any help, just call the Whiskeys and the cleaning ladies!"
>
> "Don't mind me guys, I'm just writing a report on any usual occurrences – right now I can see ERT in the compounds!"

A lot of it was all in good fun – and a lot of it wasn't. Some of the guys got really riled up about it. I just tried to roll with it, even joining in the jokes at my own expense. We just had to take it. The last thing we needed was to be prima donnas who couldn't handle the banter. It still pissed us off because it wasn't really our fault. The decisions that led to the whole mess had occurred way above our pay grade.

At the same time though, the other SSAs had a right to feel unimpressed. ERT got a lot of leeway and resources for training, and when a situation that required our capabilities had occurred we were literally caught napping. Some people were even going so far now as to question whether we even trained at all during our absences from the centre. We had to ensure that it never happened again.

If there was to be any positives occur from the whole mess, it was that we were finally able to convince the Bibby management to concentrate ERT members in the same rooms. Despite attempts to keep track of where everyone was billeted when the time came it had proven near impossible to locate everybody in a short space of time. It may have cut into our already reduced rest time, but once we had all moved into our own dedicated ERT rooms then at least we had the peace of mind of knowing that one particular problem would not be repeated.

* * *

Nestled in between Mike and Foxtrot compounds, behind the telephone and internet rooms, was a secluded little spot known as the Secure Accommodation Area, or SAA. It was the closest thing the MRPC had to an "isolation" area, and was used to house any transferee that for whatever reason, was required to be kept separate from the rest of the centre's population.

Seeing as that most of the transferees who found themselves at the SAA were there because of mental health or behavioural issues, the Whiskey team was its main custodian. It was a far cry from the old "Crazy Box" though – there was a sofa lounge, coffee machine, a big-screen TV with a hard-drive full of pirated movies and even an X-Box (FIFA was the most popular game). Hardly a hellhole. It wasn't surprising that the Whiskey guys used it as their office when it was unoccupied, much the same way the ERT used F-Block.

We often passed by the SAA whilst moving between Foxtrot and Mike, mostly to check-in with the Whiskey boys and their lodgers but also to check what movies were on. On this night I entered to find Manly playing cards with a transferee. I made a coffee for each of us and plopped myself down on the sofa.

"Been copping much?" Manly asked, referring to the now centre-wide sport of ERT bagging.

"Yeah mate, even the transferees are getting in on it now. Wushu just walked past me in Mike and made a joke about how sleepy I looked."

Manly actually had more reason than anybody to have a dig – he had been first on the scene to the Oscar mass fight that night, and had taken quite a few blows whilst giving just as many in return. He laughed and motioned to the transferee sitting across from him.

"You remember him turning up late don't you?"

The transferee just laughed and went back to sorting his deck. It took me a moment to realise though that Manly was motioning at me with his eyes – darting over towards the transferee and raising his eyebrows. Then I realised – it was the Pakistani I had tackled in Oscar.

"You from Oscar, are you mate?" I asked the Pakistani.

"Yes, yes." He nodded, glancing up at me. Manly smiled. The transferee didn't recognise me either.

"Why are you in here, then?"

"Nothing. Nothing at all. You were just sleeping, weren't you mate?" Manly could barely conceal his smile. He had heard it all.

"Yes, I was asleep. I hear noises outside and came out to see what it was. As soon as I came outside of my room Wilson grab me and drag me away for no reason and bring me here. I don't even know why."

Nothing about attacking SSAs who were *protecting* his fellow Pakistanis. Nothing about trying to *bite* me. I wondered if he would still be trying to tell the same story if he realised who I was. Or maybe he genuinely believed what he was saying. Somehow, I doubted it.

As I left the SAA, I could imagine that night at that very moment another transferee was sitting at a computer, distributing these same bullshit-versions of events to gullible advocates back home in Australia, painting Manly and me and all the other SSAs as some sort of monstrous thugs and themselves as frightened, confused angels. For all their complaints about not having a voice, it seemed at times like theirs was the *only* voice being heard, and they were using it to lie.

Just another night on Manus Island.

CHAPTER 9

WATCHING THE WATCHERS

Regaining our credibility with the rest of the Wilson team would take time and a lot of good humour. In the meantime, we managed to pick up a little ongoing task during our first night shift that would allow us to focus on something other than the criticism.

The intelligence cell would often distribute dossiers to us outlining the believed goings-on in the centre amongst transferees-of-interest. Our interests were more than a little peaked when the intel boys asked us to keep a discreet watch on one transferee in Oscar compound – we'll call him Lurch.

> "Basically, what's going on is that we have gotten snippets from various sources pointing towards this particular transferee. It's a possibility that he is looking to orchestrate some form of disturbance here at the MRPC, possibly in cohort with some transferees in Foxtrot compound."

That was pretty much all the information we got. I wondered if it was because that was all they knew or if they were intentionally keeping things vague so that we wouldn't get too enthusiastic and see something that wasn't there. Either way, we now had the exciting job of keeping tabs on Lurch. We just had to figure out who he was.

With thirteen-hundred transferees in the MRPC, I don't think anybody could claim to know them all on sight. Many were just faces in the crowd. Even those SSAs who interacted with transferees the most were surprised daily when a new person they had never laid eyes on before crossed their path.

We had a copy of Lurch's ID photo, but that wasn't much help. None of us immediately recognised him, and in any case most transferees didn't look much like their pictures anyway. In the months since arriving in offshore processing, many had changed their hairstyles, lost or gained weight, or grown or shaved their beards.

Ken, Horse and I wandered into Oscar that night with the initial task of identifying our mark. At first, we didn't have much luck. We thought about simply asking some transferees and going and speaking to the guy, making up some excuse about why we had to see him. Not wanting to spook him in any way though, we decided against it.

I noticed Manly and one of the other Whiskeys following around a transferee we had nicknamed Sideshow Bob on account his sizable afro. Sideshow had been on high-watch on and off since the whole Whiskey role started, and tonight was one of those nights that he was "on". He had been visibly manifesting his depression for quite a while now. He would trudge slowly around the compound with a brooding and mournful expression on his face, allowing the smile and spring in his step to return only during phone and internet timings, or when he was with his girlfriend, a case worker who would hold his hand and stroke his hair.

> "It's so horrible what he is going through," she would say after her visits "He had to leave Iran because the police were harassing him and his family. Now our government is doing this to him. It's so horrible. No wonder he is depressed."

Manly spent a lot of time talking with Sideshow, and the story he was able to share with us didn't contradict the story he told to his girlfriend, but it was able to add a lot of extra detail that she wasn't privy to.

"He used to drive around his university in Tehran in, get this, *a pink Nissan Skyline*, selling party drugs to the other students. Apparently, that is grounds for arrest by the police in Iran. Imagine that!"

Sideshow obviously wasn't as talkative tonight though, as I could tell by the bored look on Manly's face as he followed the fuzzy-haired Iranian into his room. I had an idea and immediately followed him. The Whiskey boys had a much bigger network amongst the transferees than we ever would. If they didn't know who Lurch was, they could easily ask another transferee without it raising suspicion. Checking up on people was their job after all.

Entering the room, Sideshow appeared to have (immediately) fallen into a deep sleep on his bunk, leaving Manly with nothing to do but sit silently at arms-reach and contemplate the absurdity of his tedious task. He looked grateful for the distraction when I leaned in to whisper Lurch's name and ID number and asked if he could help us identify him. I took over the watch as Manly went to make his inquiries. He returned barely two minutes later with an answer.

"That's his bed, over by the door there. He's sitting on the steps outside. Dark blue shirt. You actually would have just walked past him to come in."

I walked back outside – making sure not to look at the transferees sitting on the step – and made my way over to the undercover area where Horse and Ken were trying to follow the goings-on of the Farsi-language soap opera playing on the TV. In the wake of the mess fight, a second TV area had been set up to accommodate the territorial Iranians. During daylight, the area served as a gym, Transfield having purchased tens-of-thousands of dollars' worth of Olympic-grade weight training equipment for the transferees. *We* still didn't have a dumbbell bigger than twenty kilos in our gym, however.

"That's our man over on the top step."

As we assumed, he looked different from his photo, but looking at him now we could tell that it was him. Thus ensued a tedious surveillance job that would continue for the next two weeks of night shifts. Surveillance work sucks, especially when you don't really know what you are looking for. We changed teams constantly and tried to vary our routine as much as possible, but it was hard to remain discreet. If he really was a criminal mastermind, he would be expecting all of this. It didn't take long for him to make us, I'm sure of that.

We built up a long and rather mundane notebook on Lurch's movements. We always knew where he was and who he was talking to. We maintained a presence at IHMS and at phones/internet, taking note when he spoke with known agitators and community leaders from Foxtrot. Our opposite numbers on day shift got in on the act as well. Dorn (now ERT supervisor for his team) took it one step further. Over time he built up a whiteboard where Lurch was connected to every other known player in Oscar compound in a spiders-web of multicoloured lines.

Lurch wasn't stupid, and neither was the circle of cohorts he had built around him. As time went on, we noticed that we weren't the only ones running a surveillance job. The transferees ran their own system of lookouts and diversions, all of it well coordinated. Soon we were spending as much time observing and studying this system as we were watching Lurch.

The charade was well and truly over, so we changed tack. As it turned out, Lurch's room (and therefore the steps where he spent much of his time sitting and chatting) was directly adjacent to the internal gate linking Oscar compound to F-Block. We had long ceased using the gate as an access in all but major emergencies (it was a blind funnel, and we didn't much fancy copping a face full of boiling water were transferees to set an ambush). But the cut-out space near the lock enabled us to view the building's entrance and Lurch's main hangout without being seen. Even after we moved vantage points however, they certainly still knew they were being watched.

Boring as the surveillance work was, it was cool to have a little secret job and gave us something to focus on. Other SSAs started to pick up on the fact that we were up to something and started giving us a little less grief, which was a bonus. For me personally, I was most excited about the prospect of our work leading to a search warrant. I was excited about possible consequences for Lurch and his cronies. I was sick of seeing these guys get away with everything.

Sadly, we never did get to see the fruits of our labour. Our rotation came to an end and we handed over to the incoming teams, hoping that they would continue our work and not let things fall by the wayside. It was only when we returned to the island following our three-week break that we learnt that our surveillance had indeed led to a search warrant being executed by the local police, and that something had indeed been found.

Brewing was not uncommon in the MRPC. Stills were found on a pretty regular basis, usually when they exploded or when a transferee presented to IHMS with alcohol poisoning. In this case what they found cooking however was a little bit more potentially dangerous. Fermenting chillies, rubbing alcohol, ground pepper and filter papers – all the ingredients for home-made capsicum spray.

Lurch hadn't been stupid enough to hide all this under his own bed. There was no way really to prove it was his or that he was linked in any way. Even if there was, it's likely nothing would have happened. The PNG police didn't seem to have the will nor the actual investigative skills to follow any of this up. The warrant had just given us what it always does – the chance to remove an immediate threat, confirm some suspicions and gather some short-term intel on what was occurring behind closed doors. The root problems remained, growing bigger and virtually unchecked. Until somebody somewhere higher-up decided that there had to be consequences for these sorts of actions, nothing would change.

* * *

We were surprised to learn after returning from leave what had sprung up in our absence. The Managed Accommodation Area, or MAA, was like the SAA's big brother. Rather than being a chill-out zone the MAA was a dedicated naughty-corner. No X-Box. No coffee machines. No big-screen TV.

It was a step in the right direction as far as I was concerned. There may not have been a lasting consequence for criminal behaviour if the PNG Police were unwilling (or unable) to step up and actually do their jobs and enforce their country's laws, but it was better than what had been happening so far, which was basically us having to walk away from a situation whilst troublemakers thumbed their noses at us and received accolades from their mates. From now on any transferee that needed to be removed from their compound for behavioural reasons would be sent to the MAA, whilst the old SAA would be reserved for welfare-related cases.

The MAA was located down at The Swamp – the village of demountable shipping containers that housed staff quarantined for illness (gastro was still making its way around the Bibby at this point). The fire-fighters were also based here, as well as a contingent of local guards and their expat supervisors who were there to keep their eye on the adjourning warehouses that held most of the MRPC and Bibby-bound cargo unloaded from the neighbouring docks.

The MAA itself was two adjoining shipping containers, each converted to hold three rooms that opened up onto a small undercover courtyard. ERT immediately put the space to use rehearsing building clearance and room extraction drills. Previously we had used an old converted fisheries warehouse near the Bibby wharf for such training, but it had been demolished to make way for all the new infrastructure that DIBP was putting in to eventually replace (and hopefully improve on) the Bibby. Things were definitely starting to take on an air of permanence.

Apparently, the demolition of our old training space had revealed it to be full of unexploded ordnance dating back to World War Two – some of it lodged in the roof space! At least it wasn't asbestos.

Training at the MAA held other benefits too – if there was to be another riot or major disturbance then there would more than likely be many agitators transferred there. It was an obvious possibility that those same people could use their numbers to take advantage of the confined space to create another incident. We needed to know how to move around inside it, to know where all the blind-spots and funnel points were.

As it turned out, the MAA wouldn't have to wait long before receiving her first visitors.

* * *

For many in the western world, the sudden rise of the Islamic State in the Levant came as something of a shock. When these once-obscure fanatics – apparently disowned by Al-Qaeda for being too extreme – first emerged as the third belligerent in what was now the triple-sided Syrian civil war it was hard not to view them as just another in a long line of Middle-Eastern terrorist organisations. But by the time they started to make moves on the borders of Iraq, it was clear the ISIL was now more akin to a terrorist *nation*.

Whilst the world watched on in horror at ISIL's brutal march through the 'Cradle of Civilisation,' those of us working at the MRPC were keeping an eye on the more personal elements of the conflict that were brewing much closer. As ex-soldiers, we all had a mate still in the service. A lot of guys were still in the reserves. As it became more and more clear that the United States, Australia and a whole swath of western nations would be dragged militarily into the conflict, we faced the very real prospect of attending ramp ceremonies in the future.

As we hunkered down in F-Block, watching the live stream of ISIL rampage on CNN and Al-Jazeera, there was a group of people just metres from us who had a whole lot more personal and complicated relationship with the situation – those transferees who hailed from the Republic of Iraq. And they were to go about demonstrating this in their own peculiar way.

Accommodated mainly in Oscar and Delta, the Iraqis were far from the largest ethnic group at the MRPC, but they were easily some of the most vocal. This time though, the Iraqis were the complete opposite. A silent protest ensued in the form of a sit-in in the shady area adjacent the Delta compound gate. What exactly they were protesting and what they wanted to achieve wasn't exactly clear. Were they simply showing solidarity for their countrymen? Were they protesting the Australian Government's processing of them here in PNG whilst their country was being ransacked by religious extremists?

A Transfield case worker told us the reason for the protest, even though the transferees involved were refusing to utter a word to anybody about it, so I assume it was just her own opinion being projected on their behalf.

> "They are protesting because they are being treated like criminals for trying to escape violence in their own country. Our government is sending soldiers and fighter planes there to fight against Islamic State, so they have *agreed* that Iraq is a dangerous place. These guys can't understand why they are not being accepted as asylum seekers."

It was the same simplistic line, and one that didn't wash with me for a variety of reasons. I didn't say anything to her, it wasn't worth the hassle. Most of the time expressing a differing opinion to a case worker during a grown-up conversation resulted in a written complaint. But we let rip when back amongst ourselves in F-Block.

> "What are they sitting here protesting for? They keep talking about their families back home – who they abandoned there in the first place – and yet whilst ISIL are raping and pillaging their way across the country, these guys are here demanding a free ride to Australia instead of defending their homes!"

> "If they were really worried about their families, they would be taking the free flights and cash being offered to them and going home to protect them! They keep telling us how they used to be soldiers and policemen but they are here because they deserted and ran away. What a bunch of selfish cowards!"

These opinions must have sounded harsh – even deplorable – to outsiders. If it offended anybody then I am sorry they felt that way, but we stood by it. We were all ex-soldiers and a lot of the guys had families. They couldn't imagine the thought of abandoning their children in the face of danger. We all knew that very soon friends of ours could be deployed back to Iraq to help in the fight against ISIL. They would be risking their lives whilst these people whose fight it truly was were not willing to do the same.

Despite our feelings, we kept things professional. ERT gave Delta a wide berth whilst the silent protest was under way. They weren't being disruptive, and command prudently thought it best to give them as little an audience as possible. Social media began publicising it immediately, suggesting in their usual honest and accurate way that the protesters were terrified that we could attack them at any moment.

We rehearsed our drills in static-protest removals in case they were required, but we thought it extremely unlikely. But whilst things in Delta were quiet and calm, Oscar was not going quite the same way. The Iraqi population there was becoming far more vocal and agitated, and right in the centre of it was everybody's favourite Iraqi policeman, Smiley.

Smiley's sudden transformation from the friendly and jovial go-to man into a snarling agitator was shocking for some, but we all should have known better. A lot of the boys were disappointed, but I felt vindicated. I knew that we should never have trusted him. It was obvious that the events in his home country were having an effect on him, despite the situation being of his own making. I had to wonder if his pleasant and helpful demeanour had just been an act all along, or if it was well and truly a matter of circumstance. Either way, Smiley's stoking of the Iraqi fire was setting him on a collision course with ERT.

Once again, it happened in Oscar on our transition day from days to nights. It seemed like this was becoming a pattern. Luckily however, the day-shift team was on-hand at full strength when the Iraqi unrest had turned violent. We came on shift at the MRPC that evening to learn that there were a half-dozen Iraqi transferees now accommodated down at the MAA.

Smiley was not amongst them. For all his venom and agitation in the week leading up, apparently when things had kicked off he was nowhere to be seen. Without the immediate justification to remove him, he was left amongst the compound to sow his discontent. The whole incident had really upped the tension in Oscar. Kane, who had once enjoyed such warm relations there, was now considered *persona non-grata* – some transferees even submitted a written demand that ERT members be forbidden to enter the compound.

For night shift, this new development meant two-hour long stints down at the MAA to back up the Whiskey teams. The Iraqis there seemed to be calm for the most part, but they were clearly unimpressed that the privileges and leeway they experienced in the compounds were not applicable in these new surroundings. no cigarettes, no coffee or tea, No TV, phones or internet, with meals delivered in hot-boxes and rarely enough for seconds.

It was the closest thing they had ever come to real punishment at the MRPC, even though it would only be temporary. It was never supposed to be a holiday camp, but it was hardly cruel and unusual. Despite this, it didn't take long for the rumour to start making its way around Oscar (and the usual social media sites) that the MAA was some sort of "torture room" where the occupants were being starved, beaten and even raped. Nobody else from the compound had been there or spoken to anybody who was there, but that hadn't stopped them in the past. Why should it now?

This misinformation (less confrontational than calling it outright lies) spread around the centre like wildfire and threatened to set off another protest, especially in Oscar where things were tense enough as it was. The next day, somebody somewhere decided that the best thing to do to counteract these rumours was to take some trusted community leaders down to visit the MAA and hopefully share with their fellow transferees a more accurate picture of what was going on there.

Community leaders were chosen from each ethnic group. In their eternal wisdom, somebody selected Smiley to represent the Iraqis. He came back from his visit to the MAA and duly reported that yes, the poor protesting Iraqis were being denied food and water, as well as being regularly bashed and sexually assaulted by SSA.

The once-friendly Iraqi policeman had shown his true colours. His lies now threatened to spark more violence, putting the safety of staff and fellow transferees at risk. In the short-term, the effect of seeing their mates removed from the compound and taken away to places unknown seemed to provide a deterrent to anybody else considering a violent protest. When the Iraqis returned from the MAA a few days later, the whole thing seemed to fizzle out. But the damage to relationships we had spent so long building was well and truly done.

Nobody in ERT ever spoke to Smiley again. I never actually *saw* him again. I learnt some time later that he had taken the option to return to Iraq via IOM, taking with him a five-figure sum courtesy of the Australian government. Perhaps he had decided to go home and protect his family and fight against ISIL. Maybe he had gone to fight *for* ISIL. Either way, his actions had made it harder for us to trust many of the transferees.

We heard a few months later through the transferee grapevine that Smiley had indeed returned to Iraq but had left again immediately. Last we heard he was in Vienna, Austria. His family was still in Iraq.

* * *

The introduction of the MAA – and the all-important authority to use it being granted by DIBP– gave us another option when it came to deal with the bad elements. Although we still favoured the softly-softly approach, at least it gave us recourse to physically remove the instigators from a situation and allow things to diffuse.

The deterrent effects had lessened somewhat as transferees began to realise that it wasn't exactly the hellish Gulag it was said to be – rather just colossally boring and with less dining options. The very least it signalled a more robust approach towards transferees who up until now had been able to cause trouble without any fear of consequences.

When we sat down in F-Block one evening for our pre-shift brief, Jake shared with us some very welcome developments in management's decision-making process. The gloves weren't exactly coming off, but we could wiggle our fingers.

> "Basically, command is sick and tired of transferees threatening staff – especially IHMS and Transfield. From now on there will be no warning, no negotiation. They threaten staff and they are pulled out of the compound, end of story."

We knew things wouldn't work this simply in practice, but it was a good sign. Our frustration at certain transferees' behaviour was growing daily. We were tired of having to back down in the face of what was some of the most pathetic forms of intimidation imaginable. This wasn't just a pride thing, even though I'd be lying if I said that wasn't a factor. The further they pushed without consequence, the greater the risk became that something would give, and by the time we were finally authorised to act it would be too late.

It defied belief that the transferees could forget that just a few short months ago they had bitten off more than they could chew at the hands of the local Manusian population. But that seemed to be exactly what they were doing. As it turned out, we had a task on that very evening related to the matter of transferee-Papuan relations, and the first test of our new-found powers.

The often fought-over multi-purpose area in Mike was to be the focus of a meeting between Transfield representatives and the Mike community leaders. Meetings like this were enough to warrant an ERT presence as Mike was still considered the tensest of the compounds, and it had been a meeting like this between transferees and Transfield that had set off the fatal February riots. It may seem like the future of refugee status determination and the use of a multi-purpose area would be apples and oranges, but more and more even the most trivial matters could set the transferees off.

Transfield was keen to improve the facilities available to the residents of the compound, and the open area between the accommodation buildings used for sports was an ideal spot for redevelopment. The question was what did the transferees want? Did they want grass put down for a soccer pitch? Sand for a volleyball court? Level concrete for basketball?

This was the question that was going to be posed to the community leaders. It was bound to be anything but simple. Yet, there was also another agenda that Transfield wished to test the waters with, which was bound to be more inflammatory.

The issue of reintegrating the local staff was still a thorny one. It was lagging due to protests from the transferees, although we suspected it was more just a vocal minority who had reason to fear the Papuans due to the way they had provoked them during the February riots. Either way, it was another frustrating example of transferees dictating the way the MRPC operated. Not that they shouldn't have been able to make their concerns heard and that they shouldn't have been taken on board, but at what point was the line drawn?

The locals were still employed, especially on the comically over-manned external tasks, but for the most part this employment meant dozens of them with nothing to do sleeping in the staff mess, demolishing the canteen supplies and just generally demonstrating the absurdity of the situation. I'm sure those in charge on the PNG side couldn't have cared less if they were still getting their money, but they still made noises about them not being included in the running of the centre. On the other hand, I'm sure the Australian government was equally frustrated with having to continually pay the local staff to effectively do nothing.

Transfield had thus come up with a novel way of broaching the subject of reintegration with the compound most opposed. They were going to propose that whatever works were agreed to for the

Mike sporting area, that they would be completed by PNG workers. If the transferees did not agree to this, then they would not get their improvements.

The meeting was to be held in the movie theatre upstairs above the Mike mess hall. Before the community leaders arrived Abe, Hadrian and Roy had taken their positions at the back of the room. If at any time things got heated, they were to make straight for the agitators and prevent them harming the Transfield staff.

Horse, Rich and myself were waiting in the hallway outside, out of sight but still in easy earshot. We were there to stop any uninvited guests from trying to crash the meeting, as well as to extract and evacuate the Transfield staff if things got ugly, and help the inside guys if they had to fight their way out. This might sound excessive for a community meeting, but the discovery of the "snatch-kit" and the threats to kidnap staff members were still fresh in our minds.

The meeting started well enough. The Transfield representative explained her proposal, then the floor was handed over to the community leaders. A small Afghani man stood up and began speaking, but our attention was taken by the appearance of Wushu at the end of the hallway. We had all noted his absence at the start of the meeting and hoped it would have stayed that way. It would have given me great pleasure to tell him to clear off, but unfortunately his name was on the list. He made his fashionably late entrance and immediately made his presence felt.

> "We do not want the Papua New Guinea people in Mike compound! These are the people who in February attacked us and beat us and shot us. They killed our friend who had done nothing wrong! We Iranians are educated people, but they are savages! We did not come here, we went to Australia! We do not wish to live amongst or associate with them! Why do you try and force us?"

To her great credit, the Transfield representative had no time for Wushu's histrionics, and even less for his rude and abrasive entrance.

> "Excuse me, but I was speaking to this gentleman here. Sit down and let him finish, and I will speak with you in a moment."
>
> "WHY ARE YOU SILENCING ME? I AM A REPRESENTATIVE OF THE IRANIAN PEOPLE! WE HAVE A RIGHT TO BE HEARD!"
>
> "Yes, but you are being rude and disrupting this meeting. I will speak with you after this man has finished."

Horse and I shared a grin. It was good to hear a Transfield member show this kind of backbone, and for Wushu to be put in his place. But when he lowered his voice, the whole mood changed.

> "Nobody comes into this compound without my say so – not even Wilson. If *you* let them in here, there *will* be trouble. And *you* will be the one held responsible for what happens here."

I locked eyes with Rich and Horse. I wasn't the only one that had registered this statement as a threat. Without a word, we all began to pull on our gloves. We stacked up on the doorway. The new proactive policy was about to be tested, and best of all it was Wushu who would be the test case.

Then something unexpected happened. The little Afghan who Wushu had hijacked the conversation from spoke up. The Hazari interpreter on hand immediately went to work, translating the little guy's response as quickly as he heard it.

"*You* will be responsible, not her. *You* ruin everything here in Mike compound. *You* are the reason we can never have anything nice here. *You* do not speak for the whole compound."

The mood in the room changed instantly for the better. The Afghans present began to clap. Our own serious faces broke into smiles. It was great to see the usually timid Afghans stand up to the Iranians like this. Their boldness seemed to humiliate Wushu – his usual big mouth remained closed. I knew at that moment we wouldn't be grabbing him tonight, and I didn't mind. Him losing face like this was a far more effective than a trip to the MAA, which he would have turned around into a propaganda victory anyway.

The meeting finished without further incident, but without any agreement of the improvements to the sports ground. We still reported Wushu's failed threat, but what was more interesting was the growing Afghan boldness. These guys had taken the fallout for the Iranians' actions during the February riots and were obviously growing weary of their Persian neighbours' actions.

We began spending more time engaging with them, reassuring them that we would be there to protect them if the Iranians tried to intimidate them. It was a genuine sentiment, but we were still severely hamstrung by rules that seemed to favour the troublemakers. I think the Afghanis sensed that, but they also appreciated our offer. One of their leaders though made it quite clear to us that their time of lying down and taking it was ending.

"Just look the other way for an hour and we will fix the problem," he said to us. He smiled and laughed, but we could tell he was serious.

Intel later heard from their sources that some Iranians had spoken of smashing the mirrors in the ablution blocks and using them as edged weapons for a showdown with the Afghans. The same sources also indicated that, as we believed, it was the Africans in Mike who were the deciding factor. Both the Afghans and Iranians were courting them, and the boys believed that whoever they eventually threw their support behind would emerge as the dominant group. It sounded right on the money to me.

As for Wushu, it was about this time that his position and influence really began to deteriorate in the compound. A lot of it had to do with a legal misadventure he had embroiled himself in. For months Wushu had been in contact with a self-proclaimed "Human Rights Lawyer" in Australia, who had offered to take their case for unlawful detention to the High Court.

Wushu had convinced his fellow transferees to put up tens of thousands of dollars (many of the Iranians in particular were not short of funds, kept safely in overseas accounts) for the lawyer to come meet with them and begin working on their case. Unfortunately for them, the lawyer was turned around by PNG officials at the airport in Moresby and he returned home to Australia, unable to help him with their case. Wushu was now understandably less popular amongst his cohort.

Whilst we were off-island on leave, Wushu finally made the mistake again of threatening Transfield staff and was removed from the compound by ERT. During his stay at the MAA, he was said to have handled himself with his usual humility and grace. Upon returning to Mike, he was told in no uncertain terms that he no longer spoke for the Iranian community, if indeed he ever had at all. He was certainly a lot less cocky and sure of himself when we did return, and never again tried to insert himself into every situation that occurred.

He still tried to show off to us his shadow-boxing skills however. Not everything changes overnight.

CHAPTER 10

THE RETURN OF THE WONTOKS

It wasn't just security and construction work that was affected by the non-integration of local staff. The great and thankless task of cleaning up the mess made by the transferees had employed an army of cleaning staff. Those cleaners now spent their days and nights sitting around the staff mess smoking cigarettes and pilfering the canteen. The one thing they were still able to clean was our own staff ablution blocks, which they did with great regularity. Five or six times a day, in fact.

We wouldn't normally complain about this, except for the fact that it meant the toilets were now closed for "cleaning" for most of the day. There was another toilet block, but in their great efficiency the cleaners would close them both at the same time. Sometimes, if the need was urgent, we would push past the sign and open the door only to find them sleeping inside. There was no time like island time.

In-lieu of the locals, Transfield had been forced to bring in contracted cleaning-staff from Australia. These guys were quite possibly the highest-paid custodial staff in the world. They were reportedly on about twice our daily rate, but it came with a catch. They worked a punishing roster of four weeks on, one week off and were accommodated down at The Swamp. On top of that of course was the fact that they had to clean up after the transferees, who had a habit it seemed of defecating everywhere *but* the toilet bowl. From that perspective, they were welcome to the extra dollars.

The big problem with this whole situation though, apart from the extra expense for the Australian taxpayer, was that these fly-in cleaners were some of the dodgiest individuals I had ever encountered.

All where Lebanese-Australians from Sydney's western suburbs, which wasn't a problem. They weren't proud Lebanese-Australians like Loretta and Paul though, and seemed to be spending most of their time in the compounds holding court with the transferees rather than cleaning. This was apparent in Oscar, where most of the Lebanese transferees were located Their behaviour was suspicious right from the start, and soon we were watching them as much as we watched the big players – which wasn't hard, seeing as that they spent most of their time together.

The cleaners looked at and spoke to us with the same disdain that the transferees did, and run-ins became common. When one compound supervisor suggested to one of them that he actually start doing his job and cleaning instead of socialising, the transferee the cleaner was speaking with actually took off his shoes and hurled them at the supervisor's head. Needless to say, he ended up at the MAA.

Intel was working hard to build a picture on what – if anything – was going on. The cleaners were spending a lot of time with Blackbeard, and given his known links to the bikie gangs in Sydney it wasn't completely beyond possibility that the association was more than serendipitous. When Blackbeard openly declared his support for Islamic State, the paranoia went into overdrive.

The problem took care of itself though when the day finally came that the local nationals were fully re-integrated into the running of the compounds. With their services no longer required, the cleaners simply flew home and were never seen again – at least not in the flesh. When one of their photographs appeared on the TV news as that of an Australian jihadi killed fighting for ISIL in the Middle East, my blood ran ice cold.

We could never be one hundred percent sure that it was him, and nothing was ever officially confirmed. If it was, then I wondered if coming to a place like Manus Island had helped radicalise him. Had he seen it as an example of the West oppressing his fellow Muslims? Had spending time with Blackbeard influenced him? How many more people within the compounds themselves harboured similar ideologies?

* * *

I honestly didn't think that reintegration was going to happen. It had been left too long, and the transferees that were opposed had been given too much ground in a negotiation that should have never been a negotiation in the first place. The longer that it could drag out the harder it would be, and I honestly believed that the powers that be would just leave the things as is to avoid the headache.

I was wrong on all accounts. Not only did re-integration occur, but it was a total non-event. The first I even knew about it was when I turned up to shift one evening and saw local guards walking around with SSAs in a compound. I turned to the outgoing compound supervisor.

"The locals are back in the compounds?"

"Yep. Happened this morning."

"Have any of the transferees kicked up a stink about it?"

"Nope, not a peep. As far as I can tell it's just business as usual."

There was no rioting, no protests. No mass suicides or self-harms. All the rhetoric and histrionics had fizzled out like so much of the piss and wind before it. Even big-mouthed Wushu remained silent, and most likely out-of-sight. Almost overnight, the pointless external posts where disbanded. Supervisor, who until now had been running the compounds with just a handful of overworked expat SSAs now found their available workforce greatly increased. As much as the reintegrated locals assisted in the numbers game, they brought their own unique set of problems as well.

It's unfair to impose our own standards upon the Manusians, who had grown up in a neglected corner of an already struggling-to-develop nation. Most lived by island time and had never held a real job before. But when you're trying to run operations at a major facility like the MRPC, that novelty can quickly wear off and understanding can run thin. We were there to mentor them, but in many cases, this morphed into micromanagement.

Shift changes were always at 7 o'clock, but ongoing teams would rarely have their full complement of locals before 9, if at all. They had a habit of wandering off for hours, especially at night. Out on the externals, the locals' habit of disappearing had been funny, but here in the centre it just caused headaches and a whole lot of extra work for the supervisors.

I found Nick supervising in Delta one afternoon, and I could tell that he was pissed off. He was opening the gate for the catering vehicles to make their delivery. Usually this was a local guard's job, in fact their only job. For twelve hours a day he was detailed to sit in the guard box with a key to unlock the vehicle gate whenever required. But tonight, Nick was doing it himself.

> "I only had one local turn up tonight, I was supposed to have six. My gate-guy told me he was going for a smoke, but that was two and a half hours ago! I got no idea where he is."

Right on queue, the local in question appeared. When Nick calmly asked him where he had been for the last few hours during his cigarette break, the Manusian just looked at him and answered matter-of-factly.

> "I had to get a bus into town to buy tobacco."

If you were ever missing any of your local staff however, the one place you could be guaranteed to find them was in the mess during meal timings. Lucky as we are in Australia, we ex-pats were forever complaining about the quality of the food served up to the staff. A lot of guys even chose to eat with the transferees in their messes, believing the food served there to be of a higher quality despite the transferees' assurances that it was not. This practice was soon banned however, as it either looked unprofessional or was embarrassing to the caterers, depending on who you believed.

The locals though had no such complaints, and could be found lining up outside the staff mess up to an hour before opening. It seemed that meal time was the only timing that island time recognised. They had no concept of staggering, often leaving their posts around the MRPC abandoned. The reality was that these island folks had never seen so much food. It was all free too, and it wasn't uncommon to see a local pile up their plate with all three courses at once. Rice and curry mixed with cake and ice-cream, all washed down with sugary soft-drinks.

It was the issue of portion sizes in the staff mess that really began to strain relations between locals and expats. Whilst the locals would have their plates piled until they overflowed, the local servers would often ration what they handed over to us, often serving up just a tiny portion of undercooked meat to go with the overcooked vegetables. To a bunch of guys over 6 ft and pushing 100kg, who worked long hours and then trained afterwards, it was galling to receive a portion half the size to that given to a 5 ft Manusian with a rapidly expanding waistline.

This blatant double-standard held a secondary reasoning – the less they served to us, the more they would have to take home after the shift. More than once the caterers apparently ran out of food leaving the expat workforce to miss meals, only to find those same servers trying to smuggle unopened trays of meat out of the centre.

Standards of food preparation and hygiene were a lot lower than ours with food poisoning a common thing. It never affected the locals though, who had stronger stomachs than ours.

Whilst food poisoning may not have been an issue for the Manusians, there were certainly some health time bombs ticking away. Raised on a natural and healthy diet of meats, fruit and fish had led to them becoming quickly addicted to many trappings of the modern Western diet, namely sugar. It wasn't unusual to see them shovel a dozen scoops into a coffee, or even to sprinkle sugar onto meats and salads. Attempts to educate them on these nutritional pitfalls were met with either blank faces or laughter.

Apart from what was sure to be an explosion in diabetes over the next few years, I often wondered what long-term impact the MRPC would have on Manus Island society. We heard stories of villages becoming virtual 'Lord Of The Flies' territory, with children pretty much abandoned for days on end whilst their parents dropped everything to work at the centre.

With so many of the locals passing through the gates, the community was being flooded with cash. Many people who had never had a job as we would understand it were now flush with wages. Alcohol and betelnut use was sky-rocketing, adding to Manus's already considerable social problems. Shopkeepers were inflating their prices to take advantage of this, which disadvantaged those not employed at the MRPC and this led to even more problems.

Due to PNG's *wontok* system, those running the local labour companies were only giving the work to those connected to their own family, which was creating resentment and violence.

* * *

The reintegration of the locals led to a greater emphasis on our Manusian offsiders in ERT. Despite all the talk of us being one team, the reality was we didn't really have much to do with each other. The stayed down one end of F-Block and we stayed down the other. The only time we interacted was during training, and even then, it was only if we could find them. Like everyone else in the centre, our offsiders had a habit of disappearing.

We didn't consider them to be anywhere near competent or reliable, despite the hard work H and the other trainers put in trying to get them up to scratch. Part of the problem was the assortment of different local labour-hire companies that provided the workforce. We didn't know who we would get until the day, or what standard they were at. Half the time they hadn't even done the ERT certification course, and despite the hours the trainers put in with them their assimilation and retention on what they were taught was far below the standards we would have accepted for ourselves. Nevertheless, they were with us now, and we had to make it work.

I have no doubt that they had disparaging feelings towards us as well. They probably saw us as arrogant and dismissive and were no doubt frustrated about being left out of things. Although we would never become close with our Manusian team-mates, things generally remained cordial. There were instances though when things looked like they could really boil over, including one incident that centred on another of Manus Island's local inhabitants – the local dogs.

Manus was crawling with stray dogs, and in fact I don't think I ever saw a canine apart from the Mobile Squad's Alsatian that was domesticated. Perhaps due to Australia and PNGs shared prehistoric past as Gondwanaland, a lot of them looked like dingos. The longer the PNG Police dogs were there too, we started see a lot more pups getting around with a distinctively German appearance.

Australian's are a dog loving people, and our team was no exception. The strays must have sensed this, and over time we adopted quite a few of them. The locals had a different outlook though, regarding the dog's as little more than vermin waiting to be kicked. One affectionate local mutt had had a litter of pups in the undergrowth near the Bibby wharf, which the locals promptly exterminated by spraying with mosquito de-fogger.

These cultural differences really came to a head one morning whilst we were conducting joint training up near the old theatre. If we thought dogs and Manusians didn't mix, then things were really going to get messy when you threw in a Rhino.

Rhino had arrived on the island later then all of us, but that wasn't the only reason that he was an outsider. Unlike the rest of the team, he didn't come from a military background. That didn't mean he was inexperienced however – he had worked many years in corrections as well as various onshore detention centres, including Christmas Island where he had been a member of that centre's riot squad. A tower of a man who was also a competitive power-lifter, he had arranged the purchase and delivery of a squat rack for the chronically inadequate Bibby gym. But even this wasn't enough to bring him fully into the fold.

I never had a problem with Rhino, but he rubbed a lot of guys on the team up the wrong way. He was opinionated and perhaps rightly believed that his experience should have been considered. This wasn't Christmas Island though, and we had our own way of doing things, so his headstrong approach didn't exactly endear him to a lot of his new team-mates. A lot of guys wanted him out, and his own forthrightness was about to give them the perfect ammunition.

One of the numerous local strays had decided to follow us during our drills, and when we sat down for a break came over for a scratch and a pat. He made his rounds around the boys, and was certainly getting what he came for – that was until he brushed past one of the local boys, who delivered a swift kick to the dog's ribcage. It yelped and scampered away into the undergrowth. The local lads all burst into laughter – to them kicking a dog was nothing. Rhino didn't see it the same way though, and he let them know it in no uncertain terms.

"YOU KICK A DOG LIKE THAT AGAIN MATE AND I'LL FUCKING KICK YOU!"

The laughter immediately stopped. The Manusian who had kicked the dog shrunk away, his eyes wide with shock. The dynamic changed immediately. 'H' sensed the sudden onset of tension and announced an end to the break.

"Everybody back out on the road – junction drills!"

Everybody knew that nothing good would come of this exchange, but as we sweated it out in the already scorching morning heat, I don't think any of us could have expected what was to come next.

* * *

Hugging and crying. That is what this had come to. A few hours ago, I thought that this could have ended in physical violence, but in many ways, this was much, much worse.

Rhino's explosion at the dog-kicking Manusian had sparked a full-blown scandal, termed alternatively as either a "HR incident" or a "cultural misunderstanding". Given how important cultural sensitivities were to the contract and how expendable we all were at the end of the day, at best we thought Rhino was looking at losing his job or possibly being shipped back to Port Moresby. At worst we thought he might possibly have the offended local coming after him with a machete, high on jungle juice and backed by all his brothers and cousins out to regain face and avenge his honour.

When it was announced that the whole team would be attending cultural sensitivity training with the locals, we were all pissed off. We were supposed to be a riot squad. We were supposed to be able to take everything that was thrown at us. But now we were sitting down for a touchy-feely all because somebody had been yelled at for kicking a dog.

The presentation went for nearly an hour, and the Manusian speakers who seemed to have been pulled in from every corner of the centre droned off onto every tangent imaginable. When Rhino rose to his feet at the pre-appointed time and offered his apologies to his offended offsider, we were glad that it was almost over. But not before things were about to get a whole lot more awkward.

It started with a handshake, followed by a brotherly tap on the shoulder. Rhino clearly wasn't expecting the embrace, or the sobbing that accompanied it. At the behest of our cultural educators, our two groups — now further apart than ever despite the intent of this whole charade — filed down F-Block, shaking hands like a pair of opposing football teams following full-time. The Papuans were all crying now, and hugging each ex-pat as they shuffled through. It was embarrassing. I couldn't take it — I ducked out the back before any of the emotional hands could find me. Alex did the same.

"So much for jungle warriors! Can you imagine any of these guys backing us up in a fight now? I sure as hell can't!"

CHAPTER 11

THE LAW OF THE LAND

For all our moaning about both our management and the PNG authorities' lack of response to the transferees' often criminal behaviour, there was occasionally an instance where something happened. That usually only happened when the alleged offence was sexual in nature, and the alleged victim was a white Australian female. It sounds messed up, but that's just the way it was.

I arrived at work one morning to learn that I was to accompany the Investigations cell on a drive to the provincial court house in Lorengau.

The reason for this visit was a transferee we called Little Rez. Little Rez had the distinction of being one of the few transferees charged by PNG Police after a female case worker had alleged he sexually assaulted her during a meeting. He had been bailed back into the custody of the MRPC and was due to appear in court today. I was going along on the unlikely chance he tried something whilst we were there.

Little Rez didn't exactly look like a sex offender, if there is something a sex offender is supposed to look like. I sat in the back of the land cruiser with him on the long bumpy drive into town, whilst the investigator and interpreter sat in the front. He remained quiet the whole way. When we stopped briefly at the Lorengau police station, he became visibly anxious. He had spent a couple of nights here after he had first been arrested. It obviously hadn't been a pleasant experience.

We arrived at the court house and waited out front for the judge to arrive. We were the first case of the day but already it was clear that things weren't going to go smoothly. The judge was late and nobody knew where he was. The lawyers called repeatedly before finally getting hold of him. The waiting room had filled with an assortment of Manus Island's undesirables and our motley crew of white boys and Iranians was attracting some interesting looks.

The judge finally arrived, and was looking worse for wear. His teeth and gums were stained bright red from betelnut. He struggled to stay awake whilst addressing the lawyer. When speaking with Little Rez through his interpreter, he seemed surprised when he realised that it was not in fact the interpreter that he was presiding over and that there was another person in the room. He adjourned the hearing till a later date and staggered from the chambers.

I learnt months later that Little Rez had returned home to Iran. Apparently, the PNG authorities had agreed that they would drop the charges if he did so. Perhaps he was guilty and saw going home as the better option, or maybe he wasn't but realised that taking his chances with the Manus Island legal system was not in his best interests.

* * *

The transferees' understanding of PNG law was as varied as ours. There were more than a few lawyers amongst them (every second one of them it seemed on some days) and it was strange to see the way some of them tried to twist it to their advantage, no matter how long the bow was. The PNG Criminal Code is basically lifted from Queensland's, but with a few differences here and there.

One common thread they used was homosexuality, which is illegal in Papua New Guinea. Homosexual activity was rife in the compounds, both consensual and otherwise. It made things difficult for Transfield and IHMS, who wanted to provide the transferees with condoms and lubricant. It was their duty-of-care to look out for their health in this way, but as it could be deemed as encouraging a criminal activity it was disallowed.

The transferees found novel ways to "smooth the ride" – shampoo was one very popular method. It was interesting to say the least for an SSA when two bald transferees approached the box hand-in-hand, requesting a bottle of Head and Shoulders whilst smiling sheepishly.

In their warped understanding of the system, many transferees began to formally declare their homosexuality when attending interviews with DIBP. A case worker explained the logic to me.

> "They believe that because being gay is illegal in PNG, that by saying they are they will be refused refugee status here and that DIBP will have no choice but to send them to Australia. They say that if they are in danger of being persecuted in PNG for the same thing they were persecuted for in their home countries then Australia will have no choice but to accept them as refugees."

> "Do you think they are legitimate?"

> "I don't know. Some would be, others wouldn't. I guess at this point in time they are so desperate that they believe anything is worth a shot."

> "But if they came from a place of such persecution and were genuinely afraid of it here too, you would think that they would be more worried that by declaring it the PNG Police are just going to bust down their doors and take them away, right?"

I recounted the conversation to the boys back at F-Block. Horse made an interesting observation.

> "I wonder if they would stop threatening to kill themselves all the time if they knew that attempting suicide was illegal in PNG and punishable by one's year's imprisonment?"

"I think if the local coppers seriously followed any of this up, then Chai would be serving more jail time than any one here."

That last observation had come from Gene, and it was something we all agreed on. When it came to homosexuality and attempted suicide, nobody's story was as messed up as Chai's.

* * *

In a place where nothing was at it seems, Chai's case was one that at first glance seemed to be as genuine as it was tragic. Mixed Chinese-Burmese, and with a very good understanding of English, little Chai was at first one of the friendliest characters in the then still-peaceful Delta. Aside from the odd smile and wave as we walked past, we in the ERT had very little to do with him.

The Whiskey teams knew him well though, and in talking to them we learnt that his smile and politeness hid a dark secret. This first came to our attention when one day Chai apparently tried to scale the Delta fence to get at some transferees that were provoking him from the adjourning Oscar compound.

"What was that all about?" I asked the compound supervisor when we showed up to see what all the commotion was about. Henry was yet another ex-soldier. He was recently married and in between studying a sports science degree in his weeks off was training for a charity climb up Mt Kilimanjaro.

"Apparently the boys over in Oscar were calling him gay."

The authorities in Malaysia (where Chai had transited through and where homosexuality was still illegal) had agreed with this assessment and had arrested him several times for homosexuality-related offences. Chai was very slight and effeminate. His usual outfit consisted of a tight pink singlet and jeans shorts, so nobody had ever been surprised the many times in the past when transferees inferred this.

It was rich coming from these other transferees though, who – surprise-surprise – were Iranian. They as a group were responsible for some of the most prevalent predatory sexual behaviour amongst the all-male centre, yet still saw fit to bully and intimidate those they saw as gay. Speaking to Manly and some of the other Whiskey lads later however, we learnt that it wasn't the Iranians that were responsible for Chai's reputation.

> "It's really fucked up when you read the file. Back when Transfield took over, one of the Somalis offered Chai cigarettes in exchange for sex. Apparently, what wasn't made clear in the offer though was that all the Somali's mates were invited as well. About six Somali guys went through him in one session. He had to spend a few weeks down in the SAA recuperating. Now he is back in there with them."

It looked like the Iranians only considered you gay if you were the receiver and if you took it from a lesser race like the Somalis. Now Chai was having to live back amongst his attackers as well as take the ridicule of the transferee community. He was quickly becoming one of the few transferees I was feeling genuine sympathy for – not for their stories from before the boats, but for what was happening to them right here in the MRPC. What was worse was that it was happening at the hands of others that called themselves refugees who were savagely preying on those more vulnerable.

"Did anything ever get done about it?"

> "I don't know. I don't think he named the guys who did it. They offered for him to move compounds, but he refused because all his friends are in Delta. Not that they

could protect him because there is no way the Burmese will stand up to the Somalis. And even if he did, what would it matter? We all know that nothing happens to these guys when they do anything."

"This is so messed up. Little Rez gets taken down to the police station and flogged then taken to court when he touched up that Transfield woman. Yet these guys can commit a *fucking gang-rape,* and nothing happens?"

"I know, man. I've said it before and I'll say it again. This place is fucked."

* * *

"Code Green in Green Zone, Code Green in Green Zone!"

As we started making our way towards the Green Zone – an area between Mike and Foxtrot so named for its row of green demountable buildings used as telephone booths – we didn't really think much of it. Code Green meant that a transferee was attempting to abscond from the MRPC, and seeing as we didn't have any legal authority to stop them, it wasn't like there was a mad rush. After all, the most we could do was strongly suggest they do not leave, and remind them that once outside the centre they were illegals and under the jurisdiction of the PNG Police.

All that changed in a split second however, when a frantic call came over the radio.

"Code Black Green Zone! Code Black Green Zone! Chai's in the tree, he has a noose!"

We broke into a jog as we made our way through Foxtrot, where already a sizable crowd of transferees were gathering along the fence line. We could see Chai halfway up one of the palm trees that sat in the Green Zone. He had a bed-sheet tied around one of the branches, with the other end fastened around his neck. He was at least seven metres above the ground.

Just as Chai was about to leap, two brown flashes went shimmying up the tree. The two Papuan guards seemed to glide up the trunk with almost supernatural ease, and before I could even blink they had a firm grip on each of his limbs. They had him back down on the ground just as quick. We quickly turned our attention to dispersing the curious crowd, many of whom seemed to be more amused and entertained than concerned for their fellow transferee. Chai was bundled away to IHMS.

It had really been a sight to see. The Manusians had been awesome – who knows how it would have ended up had they not been there and done what they did. I had no doubt that if Chai had made the jump he would be either dead or at least badly injured. But what was more shocking to me was that it seemed like something I had never seen before at the MRPC – a legitimate suicide attempt.

The media like to throw around the number of recorded self-harm incidents that occur in offshore centres like Manus or Nauru. But what those numbers and statistics didn't show was how pathetic and staged most of these attempts are.

The scratches from a plastic fork on the outer forearm written up as a slashing incident. The barely tied bedsheets around the neck, the feet still on the floor, the conveniently placed gaggle of hysterical onlookers surrounding them at just the moment an SSA walks around the corner, as if by divine timing.

There were no quiet, solitary hangings in the dead of the night. No tragic cases of cold, unresponsive corpses being found in the morning. After all, you can't benefit from something if you go through with it without giving somebody the chance to intervene.

In their own warped view, the transferees seemed to think that doing this helped their case, that somehow the government would react the same way as those hysterical members of the public and reverse their policy. I have no doubt that advocates back in Australia were encouraging this sort of behaviour, all whilst expressing their shock and outrage.

Chai was different though. It seemed as if he had finally reached his breaking point. I was finally seeing what I thought could be a genuine refugee, only in this case it was his fellow refugees that he was seeking the ultimate refuge from.

* * *

Chai was at a high-risk watch for the next few days, but with time that was downgraded to a low-watch with visits from the Whiskeys every half-hour. It all seemed to be going well, until one-day Manly and another Whiskey – a big, friendly New Zealander by the name of George – were called to Delta with reports that Chai was hiding under his bed and would not come out. Understandably concerned for his welfare, George lay down on the floor next to the bed to try and talk to him.

At that moment, Chai shot out from under the bed and wrapped his arms around George's neck in a choke-hold. Shocked by this unexpected turn of events, Manly had to pry Chai off him and then struggle to restrain him. The little Burmese, who would have barely weighed in at fifty kilograms soaking wet, seemed to have acquired superhuman strength. Chai screamed like a banshee the whole time.

He was now back on high-watch, but his attack on George had changed the game. He was going to the MAA, and ERT would be going along as well. A schedule was devised whereby two Whiskeys and two ERT would be with Chai in the MAA always. By now Welfare and ERT both had Manusians shadowing us as well, so that number was punched up to eight when they were included. There would be frequent visits throughout the night by psychologists and medical staff.

All this might seem excessive for just one little troubled Burmese asylum seeker, but we were to soon discover that the numbers were needed in order to rotate us in and out from engagement in order to maintain sanity and composure. Those next few nights dealing with Chai in the MAA were mentally draining.

Chai shrieked and screamed all night, alternating between demanding we kill him to accusing us of being his attackers.

> "YOU KILL ME, IT OK! I SIGN PAPER, YOU KILL ME! IT OK!"
>
> "YOU FOR GOVERNMENT – YOU KILL ME!"

At one-point Alex entered the room to take his turn on watch. Chai looked up at him, his eyes widening. He pointed up at him and began to scream.

> "RAPE! RAPE! RRRRRAAAAAAPPPPEEEEEEEE!"

In between screaming, Chai would leap up and launch himself across the room, attempting to put himself head-first into the wall. We would restraint him, try and calm him, then once he stopped struggling let him go and await the next inevitable repetition.

We weren't allowed to use any restraints on him – the situation was far too sensitive for that. Nor were we able to use the force we would have used on the larger and more aggressive Iranians. It gets surprisingly tiring going at fifty percent against somebody that appears to be going through a psychotic episode. But nobody wanted to risk the fallout of four burly ex-soldiers injuring a fragile Burmese asylum-seeker – no matter how unhinged and aggressive he was.

We had to take his shirt away after he tried to strangle himself with it. We had to accompany him to the shower, but after he tried to wrap the shower hose around his neck that had to be canned as well. We had to accompany him to the toilet, where I dread to think about what he might have done. He seemed to need to go to the toilet every five minutes. It was as if he was trying to exhaust us, and it was working.

This went on all night. Every few hours, he would seem to tire himself out and fall asleep. But this would last just a few minutes, and then he would awaken and start screaming and the whole thing would begin again.

One of us had to be at arms-length engaging with him at all time. At first, we let the Whiskeys take the lead on this, but soon we too were rotating through to give them a break. We started to wear thin as well, so the decision was made to give the locals being trained up in the Welfare role a trial. It was a bad idea.

Much like we had experienced in the early days of the ERT, it was clear that the Manusians didn't really comprehend what they were supposed to be doing in their new role. The first *wontok* to take the lead on "Chai Watch" simply strolled into the room and stood over him. He stared down at Chai, his gaze unmoving and unblinking. Chai flipped out.

"YOU KILL ME! YOU'RE GOING TO KILL MEEEEE!"

The Papuan didn't blink. But he spoke.

"I could. I could kill you if I wanted to."

Chai went quiet for a moment, then went ballistic. We decided after that to not use the locals as the lead until they fully understood what Welfare was supposed to be doing. But all our nerves were running thin.

* * *

Chai continued like this throughout the following day and was still at it when we returned to take over for night shift. It was incredible that he hadn't crashed by now. Hands were being forced, and in the early evening a doctor arrived from IHMS to administer a sedative. It had to be administered intramuscular however, and it had to be jabbed in the buttocks. Rob had the unenviable task of restraining Chai and pulling down his shorts – given all his screaming about rape, God knows what he must have thought was about to happen.

The sedative did nothing. Chai kept going all night again. But in the early hours, as our patience began to fray, Alex and I took a chance and did a little experiment. The result was both disappointing and unsurprising.

For what seemed like the hundredth time, Chai leapt off the bed and ran head first for the adjourning wall. But instead of going to grab him as we had every time in the past, we let him go. Chai made it to the wall, but this time it was different. Realising that we were not restraining him, he stopped short of crashing and banging his skull against the wall as he had tried to in the past. He just stopped. He sat down on the bed. He began to scream and accuse us again, but this time it seemed more half-hearted.

If this had all been a game, then now it was up. Alex and I shared a look that said it all. Had Chai been playing us this whole time as well? In that moment the sympathy I had once held for him evaporated. I saw him as no better than those piss-taking Iranians that had made such a mockery of the Whiskey Watch, manipulating a system that was designed for their safety and well-being to suit their own purposes. It was a shit feeling.

This situation with Chai repeated itself every month or so, and nearly every team in the rotation had a turn at it. Over time Chai's character would truly emerge, and more and more what remaining sympathy I had once harboured evaporated. We even heard over subsequent months that he had become widely despised amongst the other transferees in Delta – not for his sexuality, but for his new-found status as an unlikely bully. He developed a habit of accusing everybody who didn't let him have his own way – staff and transferees alike – of raping him.

None of this prevented him establishing consensual sexual relationships however, which led to even more trouble. Chai's promiscuity resulted in his multiple boyfriends becoming jealous and clashing over who held prime spot in the line to the revolving door that was his bedroom. I don't know what the other guys had expected when they signed up, but breaking up fights between love-scorned Iranian men over a small Burmese man in hot-pants was most likely not it.

CHAPTER 12

THE FULL MOON PARTY

Ask any policeman, paramedic or emergency room worker and they will tell you that the lunar effect is indeed a real thing. I don't know what it is – maybe the moon's gravitational pull does something to people's brain chemistry the same way it affects the tides. Whatever it is, werewolves are the last thing we need to worry about on a full moon – we mortals cause enough trouble to worry about. Manus Island was no different.

We arrived for our shift that evening and were awed by what we saw in the sky. The moon was hanging low, it appeared so huge you could make out every crater. It bathed the centre in a light that left no shadow to hide in. Marty – the day-shift Ranger Two – gave us a warning of foreboding as he left. Marty was a transplanted Brit, having served in the British Army Parachute Regiment in his youth before moving on to a career with the City Of London Police (not to be confused with the London Metropolitan Police, we were told. We made sure we always did).

> "Back in the UK, the police commissioner in Brighton always rosters on extra officers during full moon. It sends people loopy. Enjoy your evening!"

To say there was already a weird and uneasy vibe settling over the centre would be an understatement. What day-shift passed onto us in the pre-shift briefing was not encouraging. Apparently, the crazy had already started before the sun went down.

"Whiskey's have a guy down in the SAA right now. They've nicknamed him the Scat-Man if you can read into that what you will. I'll leave that up to your imagination."

I could see everyone feeling around their pockets, double-checking that they had their gloves. I was doing the same. We also learnt that there had been an outbreak in one of the accommodation blocks in Foxtrot during the day. Transferees there had been going down on an hourly basis. What were they presenting with though? Scabies? Ringworm? Some other sort of tropical ailment?

"Seizures. Everyone in the block has been having seizures. About one an hour, like clockwork. They get cleared by IHMS and then go back where the rotation starts again. Most are up to their second or third by now."

The stories from the guys who witnessed it were full of praise for the performance. Anybody who has seen a real seizure can tell you how disturbing and upsetting they can be. It is such an unnatural and violent movement of the body, and difficult if not impossible to accurately choreograph. The transferees afflicted were giving it their best shot however, with all the over-the-top dramatics we had come to know and love.

With that in mind, we immediately set off for Foxtrot, keen to visit Ground Zero and see if anything in the air would also cause us to convulse. The odds were on our side. But we had not even reached the block in question when an almighty din rose up from the neighbouring Mike compound. Our radios burst to life:

"Code Black Mike compound! Code Black Mike compound!"

We moved at top speed through the Green Zone into Mike, joining every other available SSA who was pouring in as well. A melee had broken out in the covered area where transferees lined up for the mess. Dinner service was well underway, but now more and more transferees were running outside to join the ruckus. It was clear from one look that the tension between the Afghans and Iranians had finally spilled over. It was clear by the second look that the Iranians were getting well and truly worked over.

Everywhere I looked, the big-dogs of the Iranian community in Mike were separated and under attack. These same men that spent their days lifting weights and shadow-boxing whilst boasting to us of their fighting prowess and their military exploits were struggling to shape up with Afghans half their size. The little Hazaris were in some cases leaping into the air to deliver blows to the faces of their former Persian intimidators.

ERT went to work. We darted amongst the melee, grabbing anyone involved and frog-marching (or in many of the Hazaris' cases, carrying) them out into the dead ground between Foxtrot and Mike. Some of the Iranians resisted, but most were too dazed from their Afghan rough up. Anybody who struggled was placed in restraints. The MAA was activated, and the ERT mini-bus was soon on the way to pick-up the offenders. There would be a brief stop-off at IHMS — more than a few of the Iranians were nursing black and bloodied faces.

Throughout it all, the Somalis and Sudanese had been off to the side, watching and enjoying the show. I wondered if they had indeed sided with the Afghans over the compound's internal power struggle. I didn't see Wushu – when push had come to shove it appeared that the big-talking shadow boxer had decided against making an appearance.

We learnt later that the catalyst for the evening's brawl had been as simple as an Iranian taking issue with an Afghan looking at him whilst in line for dinner. By the looks of how things panned out he perhaps should have kept his grievance to himself.

* * *

A small ERT element accompanied the Mike transferees on the bus to the MAA, whilst the rest of us reorganised. The mood in the compound was still tense. The dust had barely settled when we heard crashing and noise from back in Foxtrot.

"Code Black Foxtrot! Code Black Foxtrot!"

Half the team raced for the gate, the rest of us remained in Mike in case whatever was happening next door kicked off another round there. The boys in Foxtrot soon got the fight there under control, although information was sketchy as to who was involved and what it was about. That was when I heard Ken on the radio, with an air of understated urgency in his voice.

"Any available call sign, make your way to the Green Zone."
Green Zone? What the hell?

I left on my own, depleting further our limited footprint in Mike. I later learnt that during the action in Mike, the SSAs supervising the phone groups in the Green Zone had left it in the hands of the newly reintegrated local guards, one of whom had managed to get Ken's attention as he was moving towards the fight in Foxtrot. I found Ken and the locals standing a short distance from a transferee, who was visibly distressed. I noticed that Ken had his gloves on. Then I noticed something gleaming in the transferee's hand.

At first, I thought it was a USB thumb-drive, a common enough sight in the Green Zone. I then noticed that it was in fact the steel buckle of a wrist-watch. A hysterical transferee with a sharp-edged object. A watch buckle might not seem like much, but with enough force and motion anything sharp and metal can open you up. We were about to see how.

Whiskeys arrived and tried to speak with him, but it was no use. With a blood-curdling scream he began to slash at his throat and face. It took a few goes but quickly the faint red lines that had appeared began to grow and flow.

Ken and I were on him in a flash. My hand locked over his wrist, my thumb pushing hard into the nerve. I slammed his arm against the wall, hearing the watch buckle clatter to the ground. The transferee continued to scream manically as we restrained his arms behind his back. The heightened emotional state had brought on superhuman strength, and it was taking everything Ken and I had to keep his arms locked in. We managed to control his lower body enough to sit him down on the ground, taking the explosive strength in his legs out of the equation.

At that moment I looked over and saw a group of wide-eyed transferees watching from through the Foxtrot fence. Given how prone the occupants of the MRPC were to misinterpret everything they saw, seeing two ERT holding down a screaming transferee with a bleeding face was probably not what we wanted right now.

"Get those guys away from the fence!" I yelled to the Manusians, who had been standing by and watching as Ken and I had wrestled the surprising strong old man to the ground. They took off, hopefully to do what I asked. The transferee was still screaming and thrashing, his eyes shooting daggers at each of us in alternation as he whipped his head back and forth.

Soon though, his screams and snarls became wails, and soon those wails became whimpers. Tears began to flow. Ken and I disengaged. Charlie Alphas and the man's friends were brought in to try and speak to him and find out what had set him off. The brief spike of adrenalin I had gotten began to wear off and I started to feel tired. I looked at my watch. We were barely two hours into the shift. It was going to be a long night.

* * *

The mood in Mike and Foxtrot eventually settled, but ERT soon found ourselves farmed out on a few different tasks. One was looking after the boys at the MAA. It was a pretty easy affair. The Afghans and Iranians were segregated in adjoining wings, and the Iranians spent most of the night sulking and nursing their wounds. The Afghans on the other hand were smiling and laughing the whole time, clearly still on a high from their victory. They seemed to be treating their trip to the MAA as an adventure. You couldn't help but feel happy for them.

Other guys didn't have such an easy night – they were assigned to help out the Whiskey teams down in the SAA looking after Scat-Man. When I walked in there for the first time I immediately saw why he had gotten his moniker – and I nearly retched. Scat-Man had decided to urinate and defecate on everything in sight. He had taken to not wearing clothes and adorning his very hairy body in such excrement.

> "Why the hell is he doing this?" I asked Manly, who had been there all night. "Does he think this will get him into Australia?"

Manly just shrugged. He had seen it all.

In between bronzing-up Scat-Man enjoyed activities such as trying to shove his penis into electrical sockets and masturbating in the corner, after which he threw his ejaculate in our general direction. He then crapped in a cup and offered it to each of us, which we politely declined. He made out like he was going to eat it himself, but it seemed in the end that he wasn't quite *that* crazy, so he just tipped it out and added it to his collection.

The worst part was that command didn't want to expose the cleaning staff to all this, so the sickening task of cleaning it all up fell to the SSAs. In a show of leadership, I will always admire, the man who came down and cleaned up the first lot himself. We couldn't really argue after that.

Normally behaviour like Scat-Man's would be enough to end you up before a judge, but we all knew better than that by now. Manly summed it up perfectly.

"In a few days of this he will get bored of this and it will be like nothing ever happened."

He was right. After nearly a week of wallowing in his own filth and sharing his bodily fluids with anybody who was unfortunate to stray close enough, Scat-Man literally stood up and put his clothes back on.

"I'm done now. I'm ready to go back to my compound."

The next time I saw him he was playing soccer with his friends. True to Manly's words, it was like nothing had ever happened.

* * *

We were getting more and more calls down to IHMS. Aggression from transferees towards medical staff had been on the rise ever since the locals had begun to take on more prominent roles there. We were warned out for a job, and told to prepare for transport to the MAA. A transferee had threatened one of the local nurses, which was unacceptable. I wasn't surprised to hear that it was Captain Jack. He would be going to the MAA as much for his own safety as anything else, as the local guards were apparently keen to rip his head off.

Captain Jack had been taken to IHMS for dehydration. He had been refusing to drink any water for days because of a toothache, but he was refusing treatment from the local dentist. He had long become tolerant to the pain killers, which he was now demanding in greater quantities. Given his narcotic history, this wasn't surprising. The nurses had attempted to give him an IV drip to get his fluids back up, which was when he snapped.

"YOU ARE FUCKING IDIOTS, YOU KNOW NOTHING!"

He was screaming at Loretta as we entered the room. She had been on the receiving end of this tirade for the last few minutes, but his vitriol seemed to be directed more at the local nurses than her.

"I KNOW WHERE NEEDLES GO – I WAS A HEROIN ADDICT! I PUT NEEDLES HERE, HERE, HERE!"

He pointed to spots between his fingers and toes and even on his neck. Loretta had been trying to calm him only until we arrived. Once we had taken our positions in the room she excused herself, leaving Captain Jack alone with Gene, Rob and myself. He knew what was up straight away.

"Okay Captain Jack, due to what's occurred here..."

Captain Jack launched himself off the bed and drove his fists into the fluorescent light that was flickering above. The room fell into darkness with the sound of the light smashing, and I could feel the glass showering down over my head. Rob and Gene were onto him in a second, but in the darkness, it descended into a mess of tangled limbs.

I saw the outline of Captain Jack's kicking legs and dived for them, wrapping them up as the other guys got a lock of his upper-body. We unceremoniously lugged him out into the light of the IHMS main treatment area. Captain Jack thrashed and screeched as we struggled to get the flexi-cuffs on. Finally, Rob pushed his knee down between Captain Jack's shoulder blades, effectively pinning him to the ground and allowing us to properly apply the restraints and check his circulation.

After a few moments he had calmed enough that we were able to get him to his feet and into the vehicle for his trip to the MAA, where he proceeded to be a royal pain for the rest of the night. He still refused water, instead demanding pain-killers. We brought an Australian doctor down to explain to him that he couldn't have any more as he was already taking more than the recommended dosage, but still he demanded them. I suspected he'd been told this before.

We had to remove the flexi-cuffs every ten minutes to check his circulation. We would have happily left them off, but every time they were removed Captain Jack threatened to kill himself and everyone else in the room, so back on they went. At around this time I started to feel a catching and graining sensation in my eyes. I went back to IHMS where they flushed out my eyes. Dozens of tiny shards of glass came out.

After a few days in the MAA, Captain Jack was brought back to Delta compound. Once again, there would be no lasting consequence. Quite the opposite in fact – he went straight to his case manager and lodged a complaint. It was hard for anybody to keep a straight face when Jake gathered us to tell us the result.

"He says he has been traumatised by what happened in IHMS, and that now he gets panic attacks whenever he sees Rob."

"Are you serious?"

"Yep, and it gets better – Transfield actually want you guys to have a sit-down meeting with him. They want you to apologise to him."

"For what? Doing my job?" Rob was incredulous.

"Yep. And until you do, you're banned from going into Delta compound."

What planet where these case workers living on? It blew our minds that they were even entertaining this. But it wasn't exactly unprecedented – Jake himself had been banned from entering Mike compound for the first few months of Wilson tenure due to transferee complaints following the riots. It seemed a few of the Iranians had taken issue with him taking them down whilst they swung metal poles at his head. The case workers had agreed.

It was serious from an employment prospect. Several ex-G4S employees had been let go because management had seen it as easier to give in to the transferees' complaints and just get rid of the SSA in question, even if there was no real evidence or basis to the accusation.

"Will Captain Jack apologise to me for smashing a light over my eyes?" I asked.

At the end of the day, Transfield was our boss, and what they said went. They didn't care that they were undermining us and asking us to apologise for doing the very job we had been hired to do. Captain Jack was brought to Echo Block where Rob sat down and explained to him why he had to do what he did, and apologised through gritted teeth for any distress he might have caused him.

Captain Jack put on a good show for the case workers, looking forlorn and nodding along before meekly shaking Rob's hand. On the way out, he flashed us a grin – he had gotten the last laugh. He had played the system and succeeded in humiliating the guy who had bettered him physically. At the end of the day, Rob got to keep his job and Captain Jack got to keep his victim-image. Captain Jack would live to manipulate another day.

CHAPTER 13

DOCTORS WITHOUT WATCHES

Transferee discontent with the medical service provided by IHMS remained a constant at the MRPC, and in a way, I could relate to their frustration. Even under ex-pat supervision, the local medical staff there worked to a standard far below what would be considered acceptable to the public in Australia, and probably Iran as well.

Waiting times blew out as island time took hold, and it was not uncommon for the medical staff to see just two or three patients in a four-hour period. The actual qualifications of the doctors and nurses were questionable as well. This applied to their treatment of staff and stakeholders as well as transferees. At one stage one of the local doctors was diagnosing every person who saw him as having gastro, despite not even one of them reporting any of the common symptoms. It was as if he had just heard an ex-pat doctor say it in another consultation and was just parroting it.

Alex suffered a lot at the hands of this questionable arrangement. He attended sick parade one morning for flu treatment, where the local nurse examined his throat. She announced that she was quite confident that there was no inflammation on his tonsils.

> "That's good to hear, because I don't actually have any. I had them removed when I was twelve."

On another occasion he suffered a serious outbreak of dermatitis on his neck, brought on by the tropical conditions. The local doctor administered the right medication but overdosed him by approximately four times the required dose, which really knocked Alex around. Had it been another kind of medication it may well have killed him. Rich went in to get sleeping pills and was given anti-depressants.

The other side of the equation when it came to the local medicos' lack of comprehension was the ease with which the Iranian transferees were able to exploit them. Not so much with drugs – not that they didn't try – but with other treatments. Often, it was the transferees dictating what treatment they received from the doctors, not vice-versa. The local medical staff, being every bit as docile as their counterparts in security, would adhere to them without question. Any that didn't would inevitably result in a written complaint to Transfield from the transferee in question.

The result was that an incredibly high number of transferees where walking around on crutches, and by that I really mean walking. It was a common occurrence to see a transferee return to his compound from an appointment with IHMS carrying a pair of crutches under his arm to be stashed in his room. They would only be brought out again for return visits to the doctor, whereby the patient would magically seem to have more and more trouble with moving the closer he got to the doctor, which would border on outright comical by the time he got there.

Given that a lot of the ex-G4S guys had reported crutches being used as weapons during the February riots and that most of those sourcing them now were known agitators, we knew that it was only a matter of time before this lack of oversight led to us copping one in the face. But as it turned out, the greatest victim of this game would turn out to be one of the Iranians.

Hamid was a young Iranian from Foxtrot, and not one that had really come up on my radar before. When he presented IHMS one night with a small cut on the top of his foot, nobody thought anything of it. It wasn't a major injury by any stretch of the imagination. The nurses treated it with a literal band-aid solution, and that should have been the end of it. But that wasn't what Hamid wanted. The young Iranian demanded a cast and a wheelchair, all for a small cut on the top of his foot that wasn't even bleeding by the time he reached IHMS.

This wasn't exactly unprecedented – in addition to the crutches, there was already a few Iranians with questionable ailments being pushed around the centre in wheelchairs by their dutiful Manusian valet's. The local nurse forwarded his request to her ex-pat supervisor, who rightly had no intention of entertaining it.

Hamid returned the next day, and it was clear that his injury had taken quiet a turn overnight. The band-aid had been ripped off and the wound re-opened. The nurses cleaned and re-dressed it, advising him to be more careful but reiterating that he would not be receiving the cast and wheelchair he wanted. Hamid made the usual noise but eventually left, dramatically ripping off his band-aid as he did so.

This process repeated itself for most of our rotation, and it seemed like Hamid was determined to get his wheelchair, even if it meant making sure his foot was well and truly incapable of being walked on. We would see him tramping around Foxtrot compound, ripping his growing scab off to open the wound and rub dirt into the bleeding crater.

"He's convinced that if he makes it bad enough that he will get into Australia," Manly told us one night after a conversation with the determined Iranian. The foot was becoming infected due to his efforts, and Hamid was developing a genuine limp. It looked as if soon he would get the wheelchair he wanted. The medicos would probably give him a cast as well, if only to stop him constantly opening and contaminating his wound.

When we finished our rotation, and flew home on leave, I didn't have any inkling that Hamid's efforts were going to have such dramatic and unintended consequences. When I first heard that a transferee from Manus Island had been brought to a hospital in Brisbane and was basically on death's door, I was shocked to learn that it was Hamid.

It turned out that the infection in his wounds had led to cellulities, which had then developed into septicaemia. Soon the blood infection had rendered him essentially brain-dead. The hospital that he was being treated in was just a few kilometres from my own house, and I drove past it every day. It was strange to think that somewhere in that building a person that I had just a few weeks ago viewed as a belligerent pest towards the medical staff was now at death's door.

Hamid's family made the decision to turn off his life support, and he soon passed away. Almost immediately the media storm started, and my hubris turned to frustration and anger. As expected, critics accused the government and MRPC staff of everything from gross negligence to manslaughter. Just like Reza Barati before him, Hamid was now being painted as a martyr – an innocent victim of a cruel and unjust system which they said existed for the sole purpose of perpetuation mental torture. As far as I was concerned, they were blaming the wrong people.

It should never have happened. Hamid's death was avoidable and completely unnecessary, but that did not absolve the part he played in his own demise. To blame IHMS was both unfair and ignorant, but I don't think the advocates really cared. The doctors there had done everything right, but what can they do when a patient is determined to aggravate his injury?

CHAPTER 14

HOME AWAY FROM HOME

Year's end was fast approaching, and it was amazing to look back at how things had changed. Physically the MRPC was all but unrecognisable from the February riots. Gone was the haphazard and piecemeal organisation that had greeted us on arrival. The centre had been slowly rebuilt piece by piece around us without anybody even noticing. It was only when you thought back that you noticed the changes. The reintegration of local staff, once thought impossible, was fully realised. The flimsy chicken-wire fences that had ringed the compound had been replaced by purpose-built security fences.

Outside the centre, the long-promised and delayed Transfield construction footprint had now taken a tangible shape. The thick jungle that had once covered the ground between the Bibby and the MRPC had been cleared and replaced with what was essentially a housing development of multi-story pre-fabricated accommodation blocks.

But the most important pieces of construction and symbol of change for offshore processing on Manus Island had occurred not near the MRPC but half an hour drive away in East Lorengau. This was the long-spoken-of open-camp where those at the centre determined to be genuine refugees were to be housed whilst they began the process of integrating into PNG society.

It was easy to forget the fact that the point of having the centre on PNG soil was not just deterring illegal immigration to Australia by sea, but to accommodate the deal with the PNG government for those transferees deemed "double-positive" – that is, declared as genuine refugees by the PNG Government and accepted for resettlement. It had taken a while for the PNG Immigration Department to get this programme off the ground, but now the process was becoming a reality.

The first status-determinations began being made in December. Those deemed double-positive would be offered the chance to move to the Lorengau camp and start the process of integration. From that point on they would cease to be transferees and become refugees. What was to become of those found "double-negative" however was less clear. Would they be deported? Would they be left in the MRPC indefinitely? Nobody knew.

There was also a third group to consider – those that had been found positive but refused to leave the centre and join the process. Even before knowing their outcomes, many transferees stated that they would refuse to move into Lorengau. They were being offered what they claimed they always wanted – recognition as refugees and a new start in life. But what they weren't getting was what they paid the people smuggler for – i.e. Australia. I guess they were confusing "Freedom" with just *getting their own way*.

> "We Iranian's are educated and cultured people," Wushu said, indignantly. "We cannot be expected to live amongst these people, they are little better than animals. The Australian government has the obligation to settle us in Australia."

There were probably a lot of people in Australia that agreed with him – the second point, at least. Wushu wasn't talking about the Burmese or Bengalis though, only the superior Iranians. I was more cynical. Most of the Burmese, Bengalis and Afghans I spoke to seemed excited at the prospect of a new life outside amongst the community. They were a little apprehensive, as was to be expected, but it was better than what they had come from. I was more inclined to think that the Iranians wanted Australia for its greater prospects of nightlife, drugs and welfare-money, not to mention their general air of entitlement.

We heard reports that some transferees were intimidating those that were considering accepting the move. We also heard that others that had previously accepted had changed their mind after learning that they would not be waited on hand-and-foot at the new centre. They would be provided a living allowance by the Australian Government and have comfortable facilities provided, but they would be expected to buy and cook their own food and generally take responsibility for their own lives. The days of sleeping till noon were over. This reality dampened their enthusiasm.

As for Wushu, he was fast becoming an asylum-seeker within his own compound. At his own request he was moved from Mike to Oscar. With the Afghans running things in Mike ever since the "Battle of The Full Moon" he must have sensed that his time there was up, and it was best to get of dodge. Management was quite happy to accommodate the move to sever any trace of remaining influence he may have still had.

Whether or not Wushu was able to regain any sort of status in his new compound remained to be seen, but he did provide us with some entertainment. I was sitting in the box at the front gate of Oscar one evening when he approached to speak with Nick, the compound supervisor. To our amusement, the shadow-boxer with the most perfect and fluent English skills of anybody in the Iranian community now addressed us in broken, faltering speech.

"Excuse me, officer, can I how you say, telephone? I...
Appointment. Yes, appointment!"

He gestured with his hand and made a telephone motion by his head. I couldn't handle myself and burst out laughing. Nick just looked at him with disbelief.

"Wushu, are you kidding me? We all know who you are, and we all know how well you speak English. Do you think that just because you are in another compound now we don't recognise you?"

Even after his fall, Wushu was still trying to manipulate. Some things would never change.

* * *

The knowledge that we would be spending Christmas on Manus Island wasn't relished, but it was accepted. We were all used to spending Christmas away from home. At least we would be home for New Years. One thing that sweetened the deal was an early Christmas present from Transfield – moving into our new accommodation.

We weren't sorry to leave the Bibby, and she reciprocated the feeling by giving us one final parting gift. The air-conditioning died. For those of us on the top floor, where the hot air rose to, sleep became all but impossible. It was like being locked in a hot-box with four of your best mates, all in a room that was designed for single occupancy. The Bibby was to be towed to Singapore in a week for a long-overdue refit, so none of the crew was doing any overtime to fix it. They all slept on the much cooler first floor anyway, so they didn't care.

Unable to sleep up top, most people took to sleeping in the lobby, which made the common-areas of the Bibby resemble a makeshift homeless shelter. I would awaken throughout the night to see the suspicious silhouettes of local staff creeping amongst the sleeping masses, no doubt looking for unguarded belongings to liberate.

A farewell party was held in the Bibby's honour, which most of the people who had lived on the Bibby were unable to attend due to work. It was however well-attended by the local villagers who made good use of the free catering and alcohol. As ERT, we had some flexibility to leave the MRPC to check things out. We saw a lot of familiar clothing adorning the local party-goers, looking a lot like the clothing in fact that had disappeared from the laundry over the last few months.

The move into our permanent accommodation, with its single-occupancy rooms and working air-conditioning, could not have come at a better time. Even if the long-promised fully-equipped gym didn't exist yet, facilities were a big step up. There were teething problems – a combination of cheap local labour and a construction subcontractor going bankrupt mid-build meant that a lot of corners were cut.

Unsealed floors and leaking showers led to corridors becoming inland seas. Horse had it worst – his door was at the point where all the water pooled. He had to dam his doorway with towels, bracing himself for the bow-wave that would ensue every time somebody walked past. Another guy came home from shift to discover that the air-conditioning unit above his bed had fallen off the mount and landed right where his head would have been.

They got around to fixing all this eventually, which was especially fun if you were on night shift and trying to sleep during the day. The sound of the local labourers crashing around and yelling right outside our door was soothing, as were the gifts of urine-covered toilet seats and unflushed surprises they left in our ablutions.

* * *

As Christmas neared, and the process of resettlement began to take shape, the mood at the centre began to change. What was most startling was the shift in incidents between the compounds. Mike, once the problem child of the MRPC, had been calm and trouble-free since the Afghan takeover. Oscar, always a hotbed, was beginning to occupy more and more of our time. Much to our surprise, so was Delta. If somebody had told me a year ago that Delta would become a trouble-spot, I would have laughed. But this was fast becoming a reality.

A discontented number amongst Delta, mainly led by the Somalis, was beginning to show considerable aggression whilst dealing with Wilson and Transfield staff alike. Whilst we were on leave, we learnt that the on-island ERT had entered the compound in force to prevent the disruptive elements' attempts to restrict entry into the compound. The most vocal of the Somali clan were two brothers, Heckle and Jeckle. They were quickly becoming identifiable as the key players within Delta's growing tensions.

Most of the discontent seemed to be based on the resettlement issue, and the intel boys began to receive a growing number of tip-offs that large, coordinated action was being planned in the lead up to Christmas. We stepped up our training and increased our presence in Delta, as much hoping to force the troublemakers' hand as to deter them.

Banners began to cover the fence-line around Delta, most demanding FREEDOM, the rest denouncing Tony Abbott. The Somalis then put another up across the front gate denying entry to Transfield case workers, who they now deemed "useless" and "liars".

Charlie-Alphas were sent in to try and negotiate for calm with Heckle and Jeckle before things got out of hand. When the mood of the Somalis became aggressive and threats were made, ERT got the call. We arrived to find the negotiation team in a precarious situation – basically hemmed in against a wall with no clear exit route. The mood in the compound was growing darker and the crowd was getting agitated.

We fanned out, trying to disperse the crowd of onlookers so that we only had to focus on the hard core. We weren't going to go hands-on unless a transferee physically attacked one of us or the negotiators, but something was already making the hair on the back of my neck stick up. Whilst we were forming a cordon around the Charlie-Alpha's, the Somali's were forming their own cordon around Heckle and Jeckle. They were marking us up.

As their leaders became more and more agitated, my adrenalin began to rise. But just as I was sure things were about to kick off, somebody at control made the call to de-escalate. The Charlie-Alphas ceased negotiations, and walked out of the compound. Once they were out, we followed on, with our tails wedged firmly between our legs. The Somalis erupted in a chorus of hoots and jeers, a major victory handed to them on a platter.

The adrenalin that had been coursing through my system was replaced by anger. These guys had done the supposedly unacceptable – threatening staff – and we had backed down right in their face. We may have prevented a large-scale altercation, but this was a bad precedent. Even worse was that on our retreat back to F-Block, having left behind the howling mockery from Delta, we now had to pass Oscar, who had also been enjoying the show. The usual peanut gallery had gathered along the fence, ready to throw in their two cents.

"Haha, ERT! Run away! Run away, ERT!"

Monopoly Man was loving the ruckus. He chased us along the fence-line, feeding on our humiliation.

"You see now, huh? *We* are Rangers too!"

Hearing the psychotic Iranian refer to our radio call-sign reminded me how personal this tension was becoming. The frustration boiled over for one of the boys, and as we passed through the gate into F-Block he bit back in no uncertain terms to the baiting coming from Oscar. Unfortunately for him, a group of Transfield case workers had chosen the area just inside the gate to have a meeting. They promptly reported him.

With no reference or understanding of what had happened in Delta, the do-gooders had taken it upon themselves to champion the cause of the very people that had banned them from the compound under threat of violence. Our guy *should* have kept his cool and not taken the bait, but it just went to show how wilfully ignorant so many of the case workers seemed to be to the amount of crap we had to take in the compounds, not to mention the rapidly darkening atmosphere that was beginning to build over the entire centre.

* * *

Intel continued to advise that something was brewing and that it was going to happen soon. But then in mid-December, something happened back home which attracted everybody's attention and changed everybody's focus. On that day a lone Iranian asylum-seeker, with a questionable background and an even more questionable mental state, took innocent men and women hostage in the Lindt Cafe in Sydney's Martin Place.

Like much of the Australian public, we spent hours in F-Block, watching live streams of the news coverage and wondering how much wider this attack could become. Thankfully it was isolated, the work of a lone nut rather than a coordinated campaign. We breathed a sigh of relief on news of his violent demise, but despaired that two of his hostages had suffered the same fate.

The effect of the siege on our immediate situation at the MRPC was dramatic. Our intel sources passed on that any protest action had been postponed – apparently the ringleaders had decided that public sympathy for Iranian asylum-seekers in Australia was not at an all-time high at this very moment. The new date for action was forecast as early in the new year, possibly close to the anniversary of the February riots.

We flew out for home a few days after Christmas, wondering in the back of our minds if it would all kick off again in the new year or if it would all blow over like so many of their threats often did. I just hoped it didn't happen whilst we were off-island. As much as I was looking forward to getting home and spending my first New Year's Eve with Zoe, I along with the rest of the team felt we had put too much time and effort into building the ERT capability to want to miss the action.

As it turned out, we didn't have to worry.

We got the first e-mail a week or so out from our return, asking if anybody was able to redeploy early due to the current security situation. The guys on-island had been keeping us up to date with developments, and by this time the media were on to it as well. The transferees' own social media pages were also giving a running commentary, and as you can imagine all three accounts were differing wildly.

They all agreed though that the PNG resettlement programme was the source of the tension. Delta was still on edge, and Oscar was still being its usual thorn in everybody's side. But it was over in Mike and Foxtrot that the biggest developments had occurred – full-blown hunger striking, or FFR (Food and Fluid Refusal) as it was officially known. Depending on the source, there were either several dozen or several hundred transferees involved.

Reports were also coming out some transferees had swallowed razor blades, but what shocked me most was the resurgence of something that had become synonymous with offshore processing in the past but had never been seen until now at the MRPC – lip sewing.

As we were boarding the plane in Brisbane, I still believed in the back on my mind that things would all blow over. The transferees would protest and hunger-strike for a few days, then get bored and give up when they realised it involved going hungry. Delta and Oscar would continue their bluster and bravado but fizzle out short of stepping up. Even the unpredictable Somalis would realise that violence wasn't going to help their situation. Whatever happened, I knew we would be in for a busy swing.

On arrival at the MRPC, the tension hung in the air low and thick. A knife would not have sufficed. We were briefed on the situation by Marty (who was staying on as acting Ranger One, filling in for Zane who was on leave). From what he said, it looked like this was the calm before the storm.

> "We have about sixty people on FFR in Mike and Foxtrot right now, and that number is growing every day. It's across all the ethnic groups, but it's not clear at this point if it's all volunteer or if there is an element of intimidation. The community leaders are claiming that they are discouraging it, but if that's true then they certainly seem to have lost influence. At this stage though it has remained peaceful, so engagement and negotiation will remain key."

A quick walk past the front gate of Foxtrot gave a good indication of the scale. A large marquee had been erected over the open area to provide shelter from the sun. Banners hung from it on each corner, denouncing Tony Abbott, the PNG Government and even Transfield case workers, whilst surprisingly leaving Wilson out of the firing line. In the shade beneath, transferees lay on mattresses dragged from their rooms. Most remained quiet, whilst others seemed to be making a point of writhing and moaning.

> "You've probably heard about the razor swallowing, and I can tell you that that is legit. In these cases though it seems that there has certainly been some form of coercion involved. It should also be noted that these aren't cut-throats they are swallowing – they are disposable safety razors. There may be a slight chance of damage on the way down, but the blades themselves will be disintegrated by stomach acid and the only thing that will pass out is the plastic. They may be aware of this, or they may not."

"As for the lip-sewing, I can confirm that has happened. It's not the kind of jobs you may have seen pictures of in years gone past, however. It's not the full lips, usually just a single strand in the corner, and often through one side. It's still self-mutilation though, and speaks towards the sort of determination we might be seeing here now."

"In Delta and Oscar, they have continued to threaten violent action, and Delta have demanded that all PNG staff be removed from their compound and refused any further communication with representatives of the PNG Government. They also presented a written request to management to be allowed to fight ERT."

We laughed, but then Marty showed us the document. It seemed the off-going team had been hanging a lot tougher with the troublemakers in the compound, which had served to heighten the tension. Whilst the mainly Somali cohort in question had been requesting a showdown, they also had complained that they were being provoked. That suited me just fine – maybe with those clowns down at the MAA all this would all blow over. Every day they remained in their compound they were adding sparks to the fire.

Our command however was keen not to add any more fuel of our own, and chose the softly-softly approach. ERT was instructed not to enter Delta/Oscar, so we were unable to get a feel for the situation in there. Instead we were tasked to help the overworked SSAs in Mike/ Foxtrot, taking on the role of stretcher bearers for the FFRs. This gave us a front row view as to how utterly farcical the whole situation was.

Transferees were now going down at a rate of one every fifteen minutes, and they were doing it with all their usual grace and drama. Like clockwork, they would approach the guard-box at the front gate, always accompanied by an entourage. On reaching the gate, they would dramatically collapse to the ground, eliciting the usual throes of histrionics from their friends.

We would take their pulse – which was always strong – and check their responses. They never responded to verbal, of course, but always winced a little when you pinched their earlobe or rubbed their sternum with your knuckles. We would then place them on the stretcher in the back of a vehicle, and watch them move about to get more comfortable despite being unconscious. They would be taken to IHMS, placed on an IV drip, re-fed and rehydrated then brought back to their compound, where the whole cycle would begin again. A steady parade of vehicle movements ensured, and by lunchtime the front gate of Foxtrot was resembling a taxi-rank.

We would sweep through the rows of accommodation blocks, looking for any transferee that might have collapsed on their own or in their rooms. We never found any. It seemed that they only succumbed to hunger whilst in full view of staff with an appreciative audience and quick transport to IHMS.

What we did find however were FFRs munching down on chips, muesli-bars and two-minute noodles, before heading back down to the marquee to take their next shift on hunger strike.

They didn't even try to hide it. The only official records kept of transferees eating at the MRPC was the meal registers in the mess, and they knew it. If you missed three meals on paper, you officially had not eaten that day. The whole thing was a joke.

By the end of that first day, I must have stretchered twenty people out of Foxtrot, some of them repeat customers on their second or third go-around. If they were trying to convince us that they were legitimately trying to starve themselves to death, they were failing. But if they were trying to tie up all our resources and elicit maximum media attention, they were succeeding big time.

That night the internet was full of claims on refugee-advocate sites that hundreds of transferees on Manus were at death's door, and no doubt folks sitting in front of their computer screens back in Australia believed every word of it. I tried to put it out of my mind, and drifted off into what was going to be my last decent sleep for the next few days.

CHAPTER 15

LOCKDOWN IN DELTA

The atmosphere in the centre the next morning was tense. We knew something was up when we found the intel boys waiting for us in F-Block. I was expecting to hear that something had happened in Oscar or Delta overnight. It turned out that it was something far more immediate.

> "Guys, we are receiving word from a number of sources last night that the disruptive element are looking to step things up a notch. For some time now, we've been hearing that the goal has been a death – not us, but one of them. Media attention is more focused on the MRPC now than it has been in some time. It's looking likely that this is the time frame they are intending to make that happen."

It was a sobering thought. Those early days of the snatch-kit and threats of hostage-taking seemed like a lifetime ago now. But they had wised up enough to know that the death of a transferee would get them far more sympathetic publicity than the death of an Australian, especially when they knew they could count on the media to ignore any part the victims played in their own demise. It was chilling to think that we were dealing with people who may well be contemplating this course of action. Coming at us was one thing – they saw us as oppressors, rightly or wrongly. But to consider doing this to one of their own? That was cold-blooded, pre-meditated murder.

We mulled over the situation as we waited on QRF in F-Block. The guys on the team that had been through the February riots – Alex,

Hadrian, Abe and Jake – admitted to a foreboding feeling. Things felt a lot like they had before the last time.

> "How do you think they'd do it?" I wondered. "Stage a murder to make it look like a suicide?"
>
> "I reckon they'd try and make it look like *we* killed them. They are still clinging to the belief that if enough bad shit happens here then the government policy will fold, and they'll get flown to Australia."

We spent the rest of the morning locked down in F-Block. We had no idea that whilst we were sitting there talking, transferees in Foxtrot where putting into practice the very scenarios we were hypothesising.

* * *

> "Everybody outside now, we have a job on."

Jake pulled his head out the door as quick as he had put it in. Antsy from sitting around with no updates all morning, we all jumped to our feet. As we piled out into the corridor it was clear that something big was up – all the command elements were there, as well as the intel guys. Marty waited until we were all out then began to brief us:

> "Guys, we have a situation developing down in Foxtrot. About fifteen minutes ago transferees in the marquee began wrapping one of the FFR's head to toe in plastic wrap. We're not sure where they got it from – Transfield most likely left it in the compound after art classes but we're not sure. At this stage though he is basically mummified and has a sizable group of transferees refusing to let anybody near him. This person is in serious medical danger as he will be unable to regulate his body temperature effectively.

Couple that with dehydration and he could be looking at real trouble."

"They are actually trying to kill one of their mates to prove a point?" Gene asked in disbelief.

"Is this guy just going along with it?" I asked.

One of the intel guys stepped forward to give us some background to the situation.

"Apparently this guy has been told by other transferees that his family that are already in Australia have had their bridging visas revoked and are being deported. This is complete bullshit of course, but it would go some way to explaining his motivation. Whether those who told him are the same ones that are orchestrating things is unclear, but the obstruction from other transferees is indicating that this is premeditated."

"This is being deemed a medical emergency. This man's life is in danger. We are going in there to pull him out. There is to be no negotiation. We're going to get in there, and get out. We won't be drawn into anything. We'll worry about the mess later."

The plan was simple. ERT would stream rapidly through the Foxtrot gate and head straight for the marquee. There we would immediately split into two teams. The primary team would go straight for the patient and pull him out. The cover team would push ahead of the primary, providing a cordon against intervention by other transferees. We would collapse back as soon as the primary team had their man.

We were relying on speed and surprise, and aimed to be back out the gate with the patient on the way to IHMS inside thirty seconds. As we formed up behind the staff mess in the blazing mid-morning sun, nervous butterflies began to dance around my stomach. This really had the potential to kick off a major clash. Even if Foxtrot didn't go off, Delta probably would, such was the level of tension in that compound right now.

Part of me hoped that somebody in Foxtrot would have a go. I hated the mockery they were making of everything with their hunger-strike. I hated the way they were trying to emotionally blackmail the Australian people without going hungry. And I hated the way they were trying to kill one of their own and make us look like the bad guys.

We waited for the call to go. We waited. We waited. We waited some more. Then after several agonisingly slow minutes, we were told to stand down. It turned out that somebody up top had decided to negotiate after all. We were no longer needed. We trudged back to F-Block, both frustrated and relieved – then I felt tired. We had pumped ourselves up for a fight and now the adrenalin-dump was kicking in.

Turns out that whilst we were premature, we wouldn't have to wait long.

* * *

"HIGH ORDER! HIGH ORDER!"

This was it. After all the training, all the drills, all the rehearsals – the black suits were finally coming on for real. Despite the tension in the air and the noise in the distance, things in our little corridor in F-Block seemed strangely calm. There was no more yelling, just the familiar hissing and cracking of zippers opening and Velcro stretching.

I don't know why I felt so calm. I had felt more nervous waiting to go into Foxtrot – and that had been cleanskin and without the din in the background. Maybe I had just broken the seal for the day, or maybe my subconscious just thought it was a false alarm and that we were about to be stood down. But once my ear tuned in to the situation reports coming over the radios, I knew for sure that wasn't going to happen.

In the hours since our aborted rush into Foxtrot, we had been pretty much quarantined into our holding pen in F-Block. Everyone seemed flat. Lunch had passed with very little appetite from anybody. But things began to liven up when word came that the protest leaders in Delta had arisen from their morning slumber and were starting to make their voices heard again. Keen to one-up their mates in Foxtrot, they announced that in addition to refusing entry to their compound of any Transfield or PNG Immigration employees that they wanted all local security staff out as well.

Not wanting to risk a confrontation at this moment, command had conceded and ordered the local guards out. In a practical sense this wasn't really an issue – the local guards in Delta were mainly employed on escort tasks to IHMS and other appointments. Given what was currently going down, all non-essential appointments had been cancelled anyway and that manpower could be better used ferrying FFRs out of Mike/Foxtrot.

But ceding to this demand set a bad precedent. Command was understandably trying to avoid a major confrontation, but giving in to threats was just emboldening them. The more threats there were, the more likely that one of those threats could become reality.

Negotiations began with the protest leaders, and soon it became clear that the withdrawal of locals had been a temporary measure. They wanted to cool down a heated moment, and try and talk some sense into the transferees. They needed to realise that threatening lives was not the way to get their point across, and that it was unacceptable no matter how desperate they felt their situation was. The locals were coming back in one way or another. There was no question about it. This was *their* country.

Marty briefed us on the situation, and outlined the part we would play.

"Right now, the transferees are being told that at 1500 HRS the local guards will be returning to Delta. They will be accompanied by our local ERT boys, as well as cultural advisors and Whiskeys. It's going to be a softly-softly re-entry, with a lot of talking. Given how Heckle and Jeckle are with sensible conversation, we're not expecting a positive outcome. We'll be here on stand-by, and DIBP have authorised high-order if the threats turn real. This is the make-or-break point, lads. Make sure your kit is squared to go."

We were already in low-order when 1500 rolled around. We each sat on our kit bags, the remainder of our gear within arm's reach. Further up the corridor, our shields were stacked for easy access. The mood was tense, but spirits were high. I still believed in the back of my mind that when faced with an ultimatum, Delta would back down.

When 1500 hit and the locals went in, things got tense straight away. Then they got noisy. From the updates over the radio net we knew that large groups of transferees were beginning to circle the guard box just inside the Delta gate. I could hear Ron, the old cavalry warrant officer who was the compound supervisor, being drowned out over the net as the transferees began to chant:

"FREE-DOM! FREE-DOM! FREE-DOM! FREE-DOM!"

The noise began to grow louder, echoing throughout F-Block. My heart began to speed up. Maybe this was going to happen after all:

"HIGH ORDER!"

With our helmets on, the bedlam outside was muffled to background noise. But I could hear my own thoughts racing. What would happen when we went in there? Would the sight of us kitted-up cause them to turn tail and run? Would it embolden them, making them think that now was finally the time to fight?

"Stand by guys, stand by."

The waiting felt like forever, but it had only been seconds.

"Whatever happens out their guys, we do what we have to do. We go in there together and we come out together. Stick with your mates!"

What was going on out there? I reached up and pulled my helmet away from my ear, trying to hear the radios.

"Delta call-signs pull back to the gate! ALL DELTA CALL SIGNS PULL OUT NOW!"
"RANGER CALL SIGNS GO GO GO!"

We were moving before I even realised, but the mad rush to start slowed to a congested shuffle as twenty men in body-armour with shields attempted to move at speed down the corridor. The end of F-Block suddenly seemed a lot further away than usual. As we emerged into the hot afternoon sun and peeled right down Route Charlie, the din that had been noisy from inside was now positively deafening.

Transferees were piled against the fence-line, not just in Delta but in Oscar as well. Up ahead, we could see locals and SSAs piling out the Delta gate under a flurry of blows and projectiles – rocks, chairs and wooden planks.

"GET THERE! GET THERE! GO! GO! GO!"

Now it was Delta that suddenly felt a long way away. I could see Ron and the SSAs frantically pulling the compound gates shut behind them. It looked as if a wall of human rage was right behind them. Transferees were grabbing the gates as well – but rather than trying to pull them back open, it seemed as if they were also fighting to get them shut. It was a lock-out, not an escape.

This was going to be a siege.

"CORDON! CORDON! CORDON!"

We stacked in shoulder-to-shoulder across the breadth of the gate. With a metal barrier now protecting them from the rampaging transferees, the Delta SSAs had us at their back. But this show of force didn't deter the transferees at all – if anything, they became even wilder.

"FREE-DOM! FREE-DOM! FREE-DOM! FREE-DOM!"

I saw Heckle and Jeckle, leading from the front. They stared daggers straight at me. Behind them I saw Captain Jack, flailing around like a madman, whipping up everyone around him into a frenzy. Then I noticed the battle the Delta SSAs had on their hands.

"Get the locks! GET THE FUCKING LOCKS!"

The SSAs weren't trying to *lock* the gates. In the scuffle, the emergency locks that usually faced outwards had been flipped around and were now facing *in* to the compound. A fight for control of the deadbolt that would allow the gate to be locked from within was under way. I saw Sam, one of our big-strapping Kiwi lads, jam an empty water bottle into the slot to prevent the bolt getting through. He was promptly met with a barrage of dirt and gravel hurled through the fence straight into his eyes.

The gravel was flying thick and fast. I could see it bouncing off my visor, but the clean-skinned SSAs stuck against the gate in front of us were copping the full brunt.

"GET BEHIND US! GET BEHIND THE SHIELDS!"

They couldn't hear us. Between the noise and the tunnel-vision, the boys were fighting to keep control of that gate. Then the rain came from above.

"ROOF UP! ROOF UP!"

A barrage of rocks was pouring down from over the fence. They bounced harmlessly off our helmets, but the Delta boys were completely exposed. Our shield roof immediately went up, linking together in an overhead barrier which we slammed into the gate above their heads as hard as we could. This action seemed to intensify the barrage. Soon the rocks were being joined by every kind of projectile available. Water bottles, wooden blocks, plastic chairs – pretty much anything they could get their hands on.

"There is no way they've just picked up these rocks right now," I heard Jock yelling over the noise. "They must have been stockpiling this shit for weeks!

"Of course they have!" Ken yelled back. "Haven't you noticed all the waste-bins have been disappearing?"

We saw a transferee appear in front of us, filming us on a smart phone.

"Hey, that dude's got an iPhone 6!" Ken yelled. "How did he get one of those? I'm still on the damn waiting list!"

It seemed like every second transferee in the compound was now filming us. Behind them (and conveniently out of camera shot) others were prowling the length of the fence, brandishing makeshift weapons. Bed-poles, fan-blades, even wooden sleepers that must have been ripped up from the old ablution block.

"ARRRGGGHHHH! FUCK!"

I saw one of the Delta SSAs, Tommy, fall back from the gate, holding his wrist. He had been fighting to get control of the lock when a transferee had swung one of the wooden sleepers at the gap. I could see blood streaming from his hand – the sleeper had still had a nail in it, which had gone straight into Tommy's palm.

"Did you fucking film THAT?" I heard someone yell at the transferees with the phones. Seeing Tommy get hit spurred a wave of aggression through the cordon.

"HIT THE GATE! HIT THE GATE!"

We surged forward, crushing Ron and Sam between our shields and the gate. The transferees were similarly pushing back against it from within. We managed to get the clean-skins out, then we surged again, this time in unison.

"HEAVE! HEAVE!"

It was like a rugby scrum, but we were getting nowhere. The transferees had managed to get the bolt across and secure the locks. The rocks were still coming, not just from above now but from behind, as Oscar had also decided to join in.

"ALPHA SECTION SECURE THE REAR!"

Abandoning the futile fight for the gate, we peeled around and found ourselves facing off with the Oscar compound. Much like Delta, these guys must have been stockpiling for some time, such was the volume of rocks that were coming over the top. With further to travel, most were spudding in short, but more than enough were finding their mark against our shields.

Monopoly Man was leaping about manically, punching the fence with his bare fists. I could see the whites in his eyes – he looked positively insane.

"REMEMBER ME! REMEMBER THIS FACE! I WILL KILL YOU! I WILL CUT YOUR FUCKING HEAD OFF!"

He picked up one of the few plastic chairs that had not already been hurled over the fence and launched it over his head. Unfortunately, it didn't make it over the top, bouncing off the lip and crashing back down on the head of the transferee next to him. Monopoly Man didn't even flinch, he just kept thrashing against the fence, screaming with rage.

"FUCK AUSTRALIA! FUCK PNG!"

"Ooooo, that isn't good." Ken mused. "Not with *those* guys watching."

Down at the end of Route Charlie, a small crowd of SSAs and command staff had gathered to watch the commotion. Whilst we were oblivious to the radio traffic, the situation had now been declared critical and a Code Grey (Major Disturbance) had been called. All non-essential personnel were being evacuated and the MRPC was now effectively in lock-down.

Jock's observation was directed at the two PNG Police sergeants who were standing amongst the command group. As if right on cue, one of the transferees proceeded to drop his pants and flash his cock right at the PNG coppers.

"FUCK YOU! FUCK YOU PNG!"

The PNG cops' eyes widened and one of them proceeded to make a cut-throat gesture at the transferee.

"Anyone else think that guy just signed his own death warrant?" Ken asked, sounding as if he was only half-joking.

Charlie section peeled off towards the side access gate, desperate to create some sort of distraction. Usually kept locked except when the caterer's vehicles were in, transferees were already barricading the gate courtesy of a trailer that had inexplicably been left unattended in the compound. The feint failed, drawing only a cavalcade of projectiles down upon the section. Back at the main gate, transferees were barricading the entranceway with everything they could find, even skull-dragging the guard-box off its pallet.

When Charlie Section re-joined the line, a strange sort of casual air descended over us. With no prospect of getting into the compound and the projectiles becoming fewer, we all started to relax. Visors went up, and guys were leaning on their shields. I looked over at Drew, who had taken position next to me.

"This didn't really go the way we thought it would did it?"
I laughed.
"Not at all." Drew shook his head, grinning.

A stand-off ensued. We watched as the transferees in Delta continued to fortify. We heard via radio that Oscar was now doing the same. After what seemed like forever, the call came for us to withdraw to F-Block. There was nothing more we could do here. As we walked back down Route Charlie, we were followed by the inevitable jeers and cat-calls from the compounds. It had been our first big run of the ERT and we had come off second best. It was a shitty feeling.

Cheech, a googly-eyed Pakistani who had always seemed to have a few screws loose, was sitting in the Delta guard-box, his feet up on the railing. He called out to us as we passed.

"I'm the compound supervisor now! If you want to come in, you can fill out a request form!"

We couldn't help but laugh. SSAs patted us on the backs and clapped us through as we re-entered F-Block. We passed the slip gate the connected our corridor to Oscar. It was now completely inaccessible, the locks clogged with dirt and exercise equipment from the outdoor gym jamming against it like a mad game of Tetris.

As we de-kitted and took stock, pouring some much-needed water down our throats, Alex flashed us all a knowing grin.

"This is it now guys. Say goodbye to sleeping."

CHAPTER 16

UNCERTAIN DAYS

The night-shift crew arrived early that evening, having been awoken from their afternoon sleep when the Code Grey had been declared. We spent an hour filling them in on the situation, and began to compile a target list. We trawled through the transferees' ID photos, attempting to identify everybody who had been involved. We soon had over thirty faces – and those were just the ones we recognised. Finding whoever had hit Tommy was our main priority, but our search proved elusive.

We handed over to the night-shift crew and headed back to our accommodation, fully expecting to be called back before the night was through. The small staff village was a hive of unfocused activity – with all non-security personnel now out of the MRPC, a lot of people seemed to be wandering around unsure of what to do with themselves.

Having been evacuated from their facilities at the centre, IHMS had now taken up residence in the only air-conditioned space that was large enough to handle their patient load – the staff mess. We would be eating our meals outside next to the dumpster for the foreseeable future, swatting off flies and watching the never-ending parade of hunger-strikers coming and going. At one stage there were too many patients to even fit inside, and they needed to form a waiting area on the front deck. Feeling uncomfortable in the muggy evening air, a few of the supposedly unconscious FFRs jumped up off their stretchers and went to wait in the vehicles where the air-conditioner was working.

We retired to our beds, wondering how long we would be able to attempt to sleep. Online, the media was already running stories about the disturbance. I got to watch a video of myself standing outside Delta that ran on the evening news. The Australian government wasn't giving much away, and the PNG government was denying that anything was happening at all. The refugee advocacy networks were running with the story that the violence had begun when security personnel attacked a peaceful protest and began beating hunger-strikers.

* * *

We were woken just after midnight, but it turned out to be a false alarm. We still got dressed and waited by the radio, until we were confident that we could stand down. Most of us slept in our clothes. We rose early to get down to the centre and relieve night-shift a few hours early as payback for their early arrival the day before. It had been an interesting night.

> "We got Oscar back last night boys!" Normie beamed as
> we entered F-Block. "And we got Monopoly Man!"

Whilst Delta had held up their blockade overnight, Oscar had started to crumble when it started to dawn on them that dinner was not being served. Oscar had the advantage over Delta in that the mess took its catering deliveries via a back gate that was separate from the main compound, so food could still be brought in. The Oscar ringleaders, however, had declared that the whole compound was now on hunger strike, and any attempt to break the embargo would result in violence and mass-suicides.

Via CCTV, we knew that the mostly-Iranian ringleaders had promptly looted the Transfield-run canteen, netting themselves a hearty supply of chocolate, chips and two-minute noodles to sustain themselves during the siege. The unfortunate Tamils and Burmese, who had taken no part in the disturbance and wanted no part of the whole ordeal, were not so lucky.

The ringleader though, had forgotten that a siege was a 24/7 job. By the early hours of the morning, most of them had gone to bed. The Tamils and Burmese had seized this moment to remove the barricades and allow food to be brought in. The Iranians awoke to find food in transferees' mouths and SSAs roaming the compound.

The ringleaders took as much food as they could from the early-morning resupply before announcing that whilst they would now allow the SSAs to remain within the compound, the hunger strike was still in effect. No more food was to be delivered, or else violence and suicide would follow. No doubt the suicides would conveniently be Tamils and Burmese.

As for Monopoly Man, he had simply chosen a poor location to have a cigarette. Sitting under the shade-cloth right next to the newly-reopened Oscar gate, he had been sitting there puffing away with not a care in the world when one of the night-shift ERT had simply marched in and picked him up by the scruff of his neck. Neither he nor any of his mates made a peep in protest as he was taken out of Oscar and down to the MAA. Turns out somebody had remembered his face after all.

Marty filled us in on the rest of the previous night's developments at our morning brief.

"As you're probably aware guys, this is now a critical incident and it's gone all the way to the top in Canberra. Wilson has gone into high gear as well and reinforcements from the off-island teams are being called in as we speak, both from Manus and Nauru. Command is obviously still hoping for a peaceful resolution, but it will come to the point where that is no longer an option. As for when and what that other option will be, right now your guess is as good as mine."

In the early hours of the day, whilst most of the transferees were still in bed, we took advantage of the quiet time to do a lap of the Delta perimeter. Bed-sheets had been draped along the ends of each corridor, making it impossible to see what was going on inside. The barricades had been reinforced though, and the locks had been vandalised beyond use by breaking off plastic cutlery inside the housing.

Social media was already giving us a fascinating glimpse of life inside. Transferees – mostly Somali and Iranian – posed in photographs with bedsheets wrapped haphazardly around their necks, declaring that they were willing to die. I'm sure it was designed to elicit both concern and sympathy from the public at home. If it was supposed to intimidate us, it wasn't working. We all wanted nothing more than to get in there and sort this out once and for all.

* * *

Any forced entry into Delta was going to take time. We needed to figure out how to get in, and we needed reinforcements. Even with both day and night teams on deck we could only muster around forty ERT. This was not including the locals, whose quality and reliability was still an unknown factor despite nearly a year of mentoring. Either way, there were more than two hundred transferees in Delta. Even if we assumed that more than half of them were not wanting to be involved, it was still a rabbit warren were our numbers could easily get swallowed up.

Delta would be the negotiators' bag for now. FFR was still in full swing in Mike/Foxtrot, but for now was remaining non-violent. ERT's focus would remain on pacifying Oscar, by removing as many of the agitators as possible. Rather than going door-to-door and risking another repeat of Delta, however, we were going to go the soft option. We were going to lay bait.

Whilst IHMS had been moved up to the staff mess, it had been decided that a few key staff would return to provide a limited medication service. Nobody from Delta was coming for obvious reasons, and most of the residents in Mike/Foxtrot were moving through IHMS like a revolving door anyway, so it was only really Oscar that was coming to get their meds. We didn't expect most of the ringleaders to turn up, but if any of them did, ERT would be waiting for them with an all-expenses paid trip to the MAA.

It turned out there weren't many takers at all for meds that morning – those that did turn up told stories of intimidation from the Iranians and feared repercussions when they returned. Some asked to be moved to another compound, as they feared more violence. We made sure each of them got the chance to scoff down an energy bar and some bread, which was the only food we had on hand.

It really pissed us off. These guys – mainly Burmese and Tamils – were the real victims of all this, but we were being forced to let the Iranians call the shots. We were about to give up hope of nabbing any agitators in our little sting when in walked our favourite afro-headed Iranian, Sideshow Bob.

Sideshow had become quite active amongst the Iranian discontent as of late, and had been seen by everyone whipping up a fervour during the barricade the day before. As soon as he saw us, he knew the game was up. He grabbed his medication and followed us to the waiting vehicle for the short drive to the MAA. I was about to hop in with them when Horse stopped me.

"I need you to stay here with Joey, mate. Oscar has got a guy who is going IOM who needs to be processed before going to the SAA. They want you guys to do it in IHMS."

This wasn't that uncommon an occurrence in normal circumstances, as transferees who elected to repatriate were often targets for harassment from hard-liners. But I could barely contain my shock when I saw Wushu walk into IHMS, grinning from ear to ear.

> "Crazy what is going on in compounds, yes? People act crazy, it very bad."
>
> "Yeah, I know," Joey said, deadpan. "But you didn't know any of this was going to happen, did you Wushu?"
>
> "No, no. I don't get involved in any of that."

We helped the property officers process his belongings, which included seven platinum watches, mountains of designer clothing and bundles of US currency. The whole time he spoke about how everything was going on was the PNG and Australian governments' fault and that all the protests had so far been peaceful.

> "Of course, they are," I agreed, trying to keep a straight face. "The way Delta and Oscar behaved yesterday was extremely peaceful. And I'm sure nobody in Oscar has any weapons in their rooms right now, do they?"
>
> "No, of course not. We are peaceful people."

The self-control needed to have this conversation was enormous. It was the same game we had played with Wushu for nearly eleven months, and he was playing it out until the very end. He knew that he had pushed his luck as far as it could go, and now was the time to get out.

> "Why are you going home now, Wushu? I thought you said it was too dangerous for you back there?"
>
> "I sorted it out."

"Of course, you did" Joey said, eyeing off the cash. "Money talks, doesn't it?"

As we watched Wushu head off towards the SAA, it felt like a chapter in MRPC history was over. Wushu was one of the most dishonest, conniving and manipulative human beings I have ever met. I had absolutely no doubt that he had helped sow the seeds of the trouble that he was now fleeing, that we were going to have to clean up.

> "He knows that if this goes bad and the PNG Police come in, he's a dead man," Joey pointed out. "They've had a target on him since the last riots. He's bailing while he still can."

Wushu did leave us one final gift, however. Within hours, the transferees' social media page was reporting that poor Wushu had been taken by force to the MAA, where he was of course being beaten, raped, starved and denied medical attention. The internet was bombarded by naïve do-gooders condemning this inhumanity and demanding his immediate release.

We knew that Wushu was a moderator of that very page, and that he had two personal smart-phones with internet access with him down at the SAA, where he had his feet up playing X-Box whilst the rest of the MRPC festered. He could have set the record straight at any time, but he let the lie continue. According to the SSAs there with him, he even laughed when reading his supporters' responses. He would be content to kick back and let others bear the fallout from this mess he had helped orchestrate.

* * *

Negotiations had continued throughout the morning with the Oscar leaders about the service of lunch. Well-fed on chocolate and chips, the Iranians refused. The hungry Tamils and Burmese watched on silently from their rooms, too afraid to get involved. Not keen to let anybody go genuinely hungry through lack of action, command made the decision to test the Iranians' bluff.

Even without the current level of tension, Oscar usually remained quiet throughout daylight hours. The lack of shade made the air-conditioned accommodation blocks the location of choice. This coupled with the ability of caterers to enter the Oscar mess without having to go through the compound gave us an opportunity to break the hunger strike right under the enforcers' noses, much the same way as the night before.

If last night was any indicator, those ringleaders would probably emerge, eat, then get indignant and start making threats. Then the whole farce could continue for a few more hours before we repeated it again. It was the only way that worked out with benefit to everybody – the Burmese and Tamils got to eat, the Iranians got to save face, and we got to avoid a major confrontation and possible casualties. It was a band-aid solution, but better than nothing.

ERT maintained a discreet presence in the compound, observing for any signs of trouble and trying to get a fix on any early-warning systems the ringleaders might have in place. I was given a (literally) cooler task within the air-conditioning of the mess. I hovered over the catering staff – if there was any sign of trouble or a call to evacuate I was to pull them straight out. I articulated this to the catering staff, making it clear how important it was for everyone's safety that they followed my instructions.

> "The moment I say to move, I need you to stop what you are doing and head straight out the back door. Leave your things, leave everything. Just move. Okay?"

The caterers all nodded in agreement. As they began to unload the food into the bain-marie, a small but curious and no-doubt hungry crowd began to gather outside. But before long the radio traffic made it clear that this was not the only attention being drawn to the mess.

> "Be aware we have some POIs outside the accommodation blocks, they are moving in the direction of the mess."

I could hear a commotion forming outside. It grew louder, and more animated. Then it came.

> "Pull out of the mess now!"

Things were still calm, which was good.

> "Okay guys, we have to go now. Leave what you were doing, let's go!"

The catering staff immediately began to dawdle. This was *not* good. One of them continued to unload the food.

> "Guys, let's go. *Now!*"
> "Um, yeah okay. Just let us grab this..."
> "No, *now*..."

A rock smashed against the mess door, causing the perspex to reverberate loudly.

> "I SAID MOVE NOW!"

That seemed to light a fire under them. The yelling was getting more intense as we filed out the back door, and I heard another rock or two bouncing off the windows. I moved them out the rear gate and out onto Route Pugwash. It was clear now that Oscar was heating up.

"All Ranger call-signs back to F-Block now!"

I broke into a run, heading straight for the MRPC's front gate. The rest of the guys who had been in Oscar would have to go the long way along Pugwash via IHMS – Route Charlie had been closed to foot traffic since the day before, as anybody moving to it was likely to get rocked. By the time I arrived at F-Block, High Order had been called. The QRF was already half-kitted up as I scrambled to get to my bag.

The whole team was soon fully kitted up, and then we waited. We waited. We waited some more. And then finally, the call came.

Stand down.

We de-kitted. The sweat I had built up from running back and then waiting in high-order had already saturated my gear. I knew that soon the fatigue would hit. Adrenalin might be a good thing when you get to use it, but every false-start like this was draining. The frustration was building amongst the team. We just wanted to get it done.

The latest word was the negotiations had been set a deadline of 1500HRS on Monday. We were barely halfway through Saturday.

* * *

The rest of the afternoon was tense but passed without incident. That evening, the first of our reinforcements arrived. The e-mail had gone out company-wide, and plenty of folks were answering the call. Even more were due to arrive in the coming days. Some of the guys had only been home from the island a couple of days and were back for more. Others had come straight from Nauru.

We arrived the next morning with a full night's sleep under our belts and started it like every other with a brief from Marty. Marty was doing a great job in the Ranger One position and was just as keen to get stuck in and resolve this stand-off as the rest of us. He had just come from a meeting with command, and by the looks of it things had been quite interesting.

> "Zero-hour hasn't changed gents, but we got word from a representative of the PNG Government that there *will* be consequences for what is happening here. Any transferee that has broken the law by being involved in this disturbance will be charged and prosecuted by the PNG authorities. Those found guilty will be sent to prison, most likely in Port Moresby."

Nods were shared around the group. This was a good development, and a long time coming. Ever since we had been here we had to stand by and watch as these same transferees who were responsible for this whole mess had walked around with virtual impunity. They could attack staff, they could damage property, they could even rape each other, and nothing was ever done about it. They took no responsibility for their actions, they just played the victim. Now the PNG government was finally stepping up to actually charge people with the crimes that were being committed on their soil.

It was looking less likely by the hour that the Delta situation would be resolved peacefully. Negotiations were going nowhere. Protest leaders were continuing to threaten mass violence if the PNG resettlement plan went ahead. The possibility of mass self-harm was still very real. Although we thought it unlikely, there was the very real possibility that there was already dead bodies in Delta.

It wouldn't be the transferees' usual style to keep something like that quiet, but they had already surprised us this week. If it became clear that people were (or had already been) hurt, then we would be forced to mount a quick attack. This would be messy, not to mention difficult in the fact that we still weren't sure how we were going to get in.

We had a number of options available – bolt cutters, angle grinders, even some jaws-of-life – but we already knew it was near impossible to get near one of the gates undetected. Somebody even suggested using one of the fork-lifts to ram a hole in the fence and have us all pour in through it. It sounded cool and crazy enough to work, but I couldn't see it happening.

We tested the various breaching methods on the F-Block internal gate, which was exactly the same as the ones in Delta. The angle-grinder was found to be noisy but surprisingly slow in cutting through the bolt. The manual cutters on the other hand made pretty short work of it.

The situation was starting to get more and more traction in the media, which definitely wasn't helping. Refugee advocates were encouraging those on FFR – not to eat, but to maintain the struggle. More stories of razor swallowing began to surface, as well as reports of transferees drinking shampoo and laundry detergent. The advocates defended all these actions however, claiming that the Australian public was simply not sophisticated enough to understand their situation. I wonder if they would have had the same opinion if they had been there to see how much of a farce the whole thing was, and how some of these people were truly behaving.

The transferees in Delta were really milking the media attention as well, happy to give the impression that they were the victims of the blockade, rather than the perpetrators. Ridiculous videos began to surface on the internet showing the transferees scavenging drinking water out of a leaking down-pipe – just metres from a pallet loaded with water-bottles that was conveniently out of frame.

Another showed them vainly reaching under the fence for a similar pallet of water that was just out of reach. They cried throughout the video that the pallet had been placed there deliberately to break their spirits. The truth was that the fork-lift driver that had been delivering them dropped the load short when he started getting pelted with rocks.

CHAPTER 17

DELTA RESOLUTION

We rose early on Monday, and were at the centre before sunrise. We relieved the night-shift early, allowing them to get back to their beds. They wouldn't be getting any extra sleep though – we had a busy afternoon planned. Reinforcements had continued to trickle in throughout the previous afternoon, and a few more were even due in this morning. They'd be in for a hell of a welcoming party.

Zero-hour couldn't come soon enough. All the tension and false-alarms were wearing everyone down.

* * *

Mike compound was quiet, just as we had expected. There was none of the malice that lay thick in the air throughout Oscar and Delta. It was the middle of the day and the sun was at its hottest. None of the FFRs ever went down between noon and mid-afternoon – the wait for a bed-space in the air-conditioned mess was too uncomfortable then, so it was better to stay in the shade of the Mike covered area until the collapsing resumed their schedule. This lull in activity had become routine over the last few days – it was almost like a bizarre gentlemen's agreement, as it allowed the SSAs detailed to evacuate, FFRs a chance to grab a breather and some lunch.

When intel had warned us about some sort of disturbance brewing in Mike, we had been suspicious. The warning was incredibly vague. Zero-hour was getting closer, and Oscar and Delta were beginning to stir – this wasn't the time to be down the other end of the MRPC on a wild goose chase. Nevertheless Horse, Ken, Jock and I set off for Mike to investigate.

The SSAs in Mike were just as puzzled as we were. They didn't have any indications of anything going down, and their fingers were more on the pulse than anyone. We were waiting in the shade by the Mike guard-box, trying to figure out what might be going on when the radio net erupted to life.

"CODE BLACK OSCAR! CODE BLACK OSCAR!"

Fuck! Just like we feared. We were on the other side of the centre and Oscar was kicking off. We broke into a run and it happened – my left calf cramped up and began to spasm. Great timing. I pushed on in agony, following the others out the Mike road access gate and onto Route Pugwash. As I limped after them, the radio handset I usually wore strapped over my shoulder came loose and was swinging in the air beside me. The net was still going crazy, but I could only hear every second or third word.

What I heard though, made my heart both skip and stop at the same time.

"(Inaudible) SNATCH SSA! (Inaudible)."
"Oh shit."

Our greatest fear since the first day stepping foot on Manus was unfolding. If an SSA had been snatched in Oscar, then the game had just changed irreversibly. I prayed that I had heard it wrong. At that moment, the professional frustration I had felt for so long gave way to rage.

Peaceful protest? *Peaceful fucking protest?*

Terminology be damned. These ringleaders were my *enemy* now. If one of my friends was in trouble, if one of them was being hurt, then

God help the transferees. We pussy-footed around so much, yet they still played the victim. Now the stakes were rising dramatically. Those gloves were coming off.

Up ahead, I could see the QRF flooding out the centre's front gate and sprinting towards IHMS. It was just a few hundred metres away, but right now it felt like miles. Horse, Ken and Jock picked up the pace. I tried, but my calf was screaming. I felt myself falling further and further back. They were already out of my sight as I limped past Oscar compound and turned down the driveway into the abandoned IHMS. As I turned the corner towards Oscar's internal compound gate, Horse was already turned around and tearing back past me.

"BACK TO F-BLOCK! HIGH ORDER!"

I immediately pivoted, sending another spasm through my cramping lower leg and pushed my way back through IHMS and out on to Route Pugwash. The entire team had already lapped me by the time I made it through the front gate and into F-Block. I don't think I drew a breath as I pulled my body-armour on. Fully kitted-up, we commenced our now familiar standby. But there was no quiet impatience this time. Everyone wanted to know what was going on, especially me.

"What the fuck just happened in there?"
"Some guys just tried to snatch Ricky!"
"Is he OK?"
"Hell yeah – he dropped the guy!"

I didn't know Ricky that well, but the relief I felt was immense. My anger subsided considerably, but my nerves didn't. I still wanted to get into Oscar and tear the place apart, and to find the guys that had done this. As it turned out, the intended victim had beaten us to it.

Ricky hadn't just punched the guy who tried to grab him – he chased him. His head had taken over however, and he quickly realised that chasing his failed abductor deeper into the compound was a bad idea. He headed back to the front gate and waited for back-up. The transferees' would-be snatch squad however didn't think to get too far out of sight, and when the QRF had arrived moments later Ricky had led them right to the guy. They pulled him right out and the gate was slammed shut. Oscar was now back in lock-down, but this time from the outside.

> "Who was it?" I asked, my mind already flipping through
> the likely suspects "Was it one of the Iranians?"
> "Nah man. It was one of the Tamils!"

That threw me big time. We had never had any problems with them. How could one of the small, timid Tamils be behind this? Ricky wasn't exactly a soft target. Maybe the Iranians had put them up to it, perhaps under threat of violence?

Other questions now started to come to mind – had this been somehow related to Mike? Had the ringleaders somehow planted the information that had led half or QRF to be down the other end of the MRPC when this had happened?

We would have plenty of time to run this through our minds. We waited for the call to storm the gates of Oscar, but once again the call never came. We stood down and de-kitted, enjoying some much-needed ventilation. Zero-hour was fast approaching, and for the first time we received a full run-down from Marty on the plan for breaking the blockade. It even had a name – Operation Delta Resolution.

In a few hours it would all be over. The only question now was what kind of place the MRPC would be when it was.

* * *

At the end of the corridor closest to Route Charlie, the fire-fighters were stockpiling fire-extinguishers. I had never seen so many in one place before, it must have been every cylinder on Manus Island. It would have made it quite difficult to actually get out of the corridor to Route Charlie – had that been the way we were going to go.

From our little garden at the end of F-Block, the firefighters were going to work on our own fence with the angle grinder, cutting a large man-sized hole for us to slip through. Our shields and kit-bags had been handed through, then piled onto the buses which transported them to IHMS. We followed through in small groups, piling into vehicles that joined the parade of now resumed evacuations taking the FFRs from Mike/Foxtrot up to the staff mess. Anybody watching from Oscar wouldn't think anything of it, we hoped. But we would be taking the turn-off into the IHMS driveway. From there we began kitting up. Every one of us remained silent, lost in his own thoughts.

It took a lot of shuttles to get us all there. We had nearly seventy ERT on island now. Both us and the night-shift crew stood at twenty men a-piece, when our locals were considered. The off-island and Nauru boys that had answered the call gave us the equivalent of a third crew. We didn't have enough shields and equipment for all of them, except for helmets. But we had dug up a large consignment of stab-vests that had been delivered months ago but never unpacked. Whilst our two shield wielding teams would present the hard front, the over-timers would provide a highly-agile snatch and arrest force.

Looking around at the huge force we had assembled, I was hit by a groundswell of confidence. Today was going to be different. We were going to win this time. None of us were going to go down. We'd all go in together and we would come out the same way.

I had absolutely no doubts that we were doing the right thing. No matter what facts and actions the media chose to ignore, the people we were going in there to confront had shown their true colours time and time again. This could end the easy way or the hard way, and that choice had always been completely up to them. The barricades were still there. Now we were going in and there was no way we were coming out until the job was done.

There were still uncertainties in the back of my mind as to what we would find inside. Would we be finding rooms full of bodies? Would the ringleaders have an actual defence planned? Would they fight, or would they run? I had no doubt we would win the day, but what would happen beyond that was more uncertain. Politics had a way of making the simplest things complicated.

Up at Delta compound, the diversion was beginning. There was a pedestrian gate on the side of the compound adjacent to Echo block. It had been here that negotiators had been speaking with the protest leaders over the last three days, mainly because the adjoining Echo roof provided safety from rock throwing. The locks had been sabotaged just like the other gates, it was too small and its surroundings too constricted to make an effective entry point, but that also made it the perfect location for our feint.

We knew that whilst the angle grinders were loud, they were ineffective at quickly cutting the bolts. But the transferees didn't know this. As the fire-fighters went to work on the Echo-side gate, the noise began to attract a large and vocal crowd. Several of the ringleaders appeared, whipping the crowd into a frenzy. But here at the Echo-side gate, the closely surrounding buildings left them all completely blind to the large open sporting fields at the other end of the compound.

We could hear the commotion from our forming-up point. The anticipation was nearly unbearable. I strained to hear the radio. But then I heard the words we had all been waiting for.

"Ranger One, Ranger One – Go! Go! Go!"

The echo made its way down the column.

"GO! GO! GO!"

Everyone lurched forward, pouring around the corner into Route Charlie like a stampede of armoured wild animals. SSAs had lined the sides of the driveway, clapping us through like a football team taking to the field. The atmosphere was electric.

"Get in there boys! It's all you!"

As I made my way around the corner, I could see that the first guys in the column had already hit the gate. H had been leading the charge, bearing not a shield but a pair of bolt-cutters. He hit the gate and sliced through the bolt like it was butter. The wave of ERT behind him had then steam-rolled through, pushing the blockading trailer out of the way without barely a pause.

We were in.

The gap was only wide enough for one man at a time to get through, which was slowing us down. The first man through had gone straight down the fence-line, coming to a halt in line with the ablution blocks.

"CORDON! CORDON! CORDON!"

Every man that followed covered off from the man in front, and within seconds we had dozens of men inside, forming a wall of shields on the boundary between the sporting fields and the built-up area of the compound. I found myself in the centre of the line, staring down one of the compound's main corridors. Transferees were beginning to appear, their eyes wide with shock.

"ADVANCE! ADVANCE!"

We rushed forward, quickly reaching the first row of accommodation blocks.

"HOLD, HOLD, HOLD!"

Transferees were now spewing down the thoroughfare directly towards us. Many had their hands in the air and eyes wide with terror. Others were brandishing bed-poles, fan-blades and other makeshift weapons, their faces contorted with hate. The rocks began to fly, hurled right at our shields from point-blank range. The impacts reverberated through the perspex, creating a deafening racket that echoed down the corridor. As we weathered this front-on barrage, the throwers adjusted their elevation, and the rocks began to rain down onto on heads.

"ROOF UP! ROOF UP!"

Shields were thrust up overhead, creating a mobile perspex box around us. Moving as one, we charged forward, trampling the rock-throwers that had dared to get too close. As we broke into the open ground, the guys who had been moving up behind us immediately peeled off to cover our flanks. Behind us, the arrest teams were scooping up the resistors and back-loading them to the teams of cleanskin SSAs that were now flowing into the compound.

I looked to my left and right, and saw that the same process had been completed the length of the corridor. Teams had broken through the bottlenecks and now formed an island of shields in each intersection.

"FRIENDLIES LEFT! FRIENDLIES RIGHT!"

We pushed forward again, repeating the process at the next

corridor. More and more transferees were streaming towards us, their hands above their heads. Mainly Tamil and Burmese, some were hit by the rocks being thrown from behind them, others were falling to their knees to show that they didn't want to fight. We had to get them out of here.

"COME TO ME! COME TO ME! SAFETY THIS WAY!"

I motioned to them as best I could from behind my shield. It must have seemed scary and confusing – giant men in riot gear telling you to come at them for safety. But most of them understood and ran towards us, their heads tucked down to avoid the projectiles that were still flying thick and fast. We slipped them under our shields and they were ushered into the arms of waiting SSAs.

"GET HIM! HE'S AN AGITATOR! ARREST TEAM FRONT!"

Captain Jack had appeared in front of us, with a lump of rock in his hand. As he went to throw it, our shield wall opened up and a three-man snatch team bolted forward and wrapped him up. The Iranian could barely let out a yelp as he was pulled back behind our line and the shield wall re-closed. The transferees that had been on either side of him dropped their rocks and ran.

"FORWARD! FORWARD!"

We punched through again, and it happened before anybody could even register. As we cleared the narrow walkway between the accommodation containers, Joey had darted out to secure his side of the flank. As he did, a plank of wood slammed straight into his side. The Iranian wielding it immediately dropped the weapon and hightailed down the corridor. Joey had dropped his shield with the impact, and was immediately tackled by a towering Somali.

Joey and his assailant had barely hit the ground before Ken and Billy were on them, prying the Somali off and slamming him face-first into the pavement. Joey was already up and about, picking up his shield. He was looking about wildly for the transferee that had hit him, but the Iranian was nowhere to be seen.

"HOSTILE FRONT! HOSTILE FRONT!"

Cheech – the googly-eyed Pakistani stoner that had declared himself compound supervisor – appeared in front of me, brandishing a metal pole.

"PUT IT DOWN! PUT IT DOWN! GET ON THE GROUND!"

I could see him hesitating. He wanted to hit me, but he knew what would happen.

"PUT THE FUCKING POLE DOWN!"

Cheech leapt at me, swinging the pole down towards the top of my shield. I thrust it up to meet him, the impact of the collision sending it flying from his grip. I scooped upwards, catching his knees with the bottom of my shield. He hit the ground hard, and the arrest team were on top of him before he even knew what had happened.

"FORWARD, FORWARD!"

We had made it to the last corridor. Behind it lay the ablution box and then the fence-line adjacent Echo Block. They would have nowhere to fall back to now, it was either make a stand or surrender.

I had seen a few of the ringleaders taken down. Most of the non-combatants had already passed through our line and been evacuated to safety. Anybody left now would have to seriously consider their options. It should have been a no-brainer.

As we punched through to the final corridor, I saw that the teams that had cleared along the fence-line on Route Charlie had already swung their axis around and had pushed down across our front. Those transferees that remained were now backed into a small clearing in the lower corner of the compound. With the ERT bearing down on them, most were following directions to get down on the ground. But then one Somali decided to jump to his feet and start ripping off his shirt.

"FUCK YOU! FUCK YOU!"

It seemed like everyone in the cordon went for him at once. Some transferees then decided to fight, others were just caught up in the melee. Soon the clearing was like a tangled mass of limbs as

transferees were taken to the ground and restrained. It was a free-for-all. As I applied my last set of flexi-cuffs to a struggling Somali, I could already hear yelling and crashing reverberating down the corridors. It wasn't over yet – the room clearances had begun.

Quickly but methodically, teams were making their way down the corridors. Ripping open the bedroom doors with enough force to take them clear off the hinges, any occupants inside were left in no uncertain mind about what was going on.

"GET OUT! GET OUT!"

Most of the rooms were empty, and were promptly turned upside down to confirm the fact. Some transferees were in their beds, seemingly oblivious as to what was going on outside. Others were hiding under them, terrified. This moment, unfortunately, was not a time for kind reassurance. Anybody who didn't follow commands to vacate immediately was dragged out, and those who resisted were restrained.

One Iranian refused to leave his top bunk and was pulled down by his shirt. Once on the ground, he thrust his face towards Gene's leg, gnashing his teeth as if to bite him. Marty, who had pulled him off the bed, grabbed the back of the biter's hair in mid-motion, snapping his head back just as his teeth were about to make contact. Further up the corridor, another SSA had already had a brush with some fangs.

The biter had been Chai, and his victim none other than George. The Whiskeys and other SSAs had moved into the compound after the ERT to help with the evacuation of the non-combatants. But Chai had one of his trademark psychotic breaks whilst being moved to safety, and had latched his teeth firmly on George's calf, biting through his pants and right into his skin. George, reacting the way anybody would, had promptly knocked Chai for six. He then scooped up the little Rohingya and carried him to safety.

With other teams clearing their way through the accommodation blocks, Ken and I started our way down the ablutions. I opened my first door to find a terrified Tamil literally with his pants down. His white-knuckled hands gripped the toilet seat as he looked at me and screamed. Ken opened the door next to me and found another guy in the shower, oblivious to the chaos outside.

"Um, get out of here when you can, guys."

I was on a high – we had broken the barricade of Delta and completely dominated that compound. We had gotten the innocents out safely, and we had shown the resistors in no uncertain terms that they no longer called the shots. I was ready to walk out that gate and march right into Oscar and repeat the process – and judging by the exodus of ERT out of Delta, that was exactly what was going on.

"REORG, ROUTE, CHARLIE! REORG, ROUTE, CHARLIE!"

Outside the compound, things were a hive of activity. The usually empty Bravo compound was full of Delta evacuees. Those transferees that had fought back when we breached the compound were being loaded onto buses that were running a shuttle service to the MAA. Most of the ERT were already in Oscar, whilst the rest of us remained out on Route Charlie in case the evacuees decided to change their minds and kick off.

A local guard walked up the line, handing out much-appreciated bottles of water. I didn't realise how thirsty I was until then. I ripped off the lid and poured it down my throat. Beside me, Ken was already pouring his down the back of his neck.

"Fuck!"

The water was boiling hot. It must have been left on a pallet out in the sun, baking for days. We yelled at the water-boy, who seemed oblivious to the problem. He returned a few moments with a fresh batch, but as he handed me a new bottle I eyed him suspiciously.

"Are these ones hot too, mate?"

"Yes."

"Well fuck off with it then!"

The vacant look on his face really pissed me off. We were baking in the hot afternoon sun. Fully kitted up and sweating heavily from our fight through Delta, we were in danger of heat exhaustion. Hot water was not helping in the slightest. But if that snafu hadn't happened, then Joey would not have gone into Bravo looking for a cold batch. And he wouldn't have seen the Iranian who hit him with the wooden beam sitting amongst the evacuees.

It turned out that Joey's assailant wasn't the only one. We moved throughout the evacuees in Bravo and found a number of transferees who had been involved in the violence. They had come forward, thrown rocks or swung poles, then run around the corner and approached another team with their hands up. They had come close to slipping the net, and no doubt there were more that had. But these guys were not going to be so lucky.

"Grab your shields guys, we're moving into Oscar!"

Oscar was eerily quiet as we moved through the gate. The rest of the ERT had formed a cordon across the open ground in front of the mess, but out in front of them the compound was empty. Not a soul was moving around outside. When we had first breached Delta they had been piled along the fence, chanting and hollering and whipping themselves into a frenzy. At some point though the mood had changed. After so long of us not responding to their provocations, they had seen the gloves finally come off. I would have loved to have been a fly on the wall in their rooms right now.

We took our place in the line and I could see that one of the boys, Nards, was really struggling. He was facing the wrong way and seemed a little spun out and confused. He had gone hard in Delta and now the heat was hitting him. He was pulled out of the line and moved into the shade, getting his helmet and chest plate off to allow some ventilation. The boys couldn't help having some fun with him though. Nards was confused and asked why he was sitting down and what had happened to make him feel so out of it. They told him that Chai had roundhouse kicked him when we first breached Delta. Nards believed it for a while – until he came to his senses.

An air of confident relaxation descended over the line. Visors went up and blokes leaned on their shields, enjoying our first hits of cold water since the breach. As we did so, the arrest teams walked from door to door around the Oscar accommodation blocks, calling out the names of the agitators we had identified from the previous days. All came along peacefully and were fully compliant. They were led to a waiting bus on Route Pugwash, from which they were taken to the MAA.

It was funny to see so many of the compound's tough-guys behaving so meekly. In a place where perception was everything, they had lost face in a big way. I saw Blackbeard let out an anguished cry as the bus pulled away.

"Oscar! Oscar!"

I don't know whether it was a cry of distress or a call to arms, but either way it got no result. We collapsed the line and retreated to the air-conditioning of the Oscar mess. There, we stripped off our riot gear and revelled in our success. This was our day, and we had won it. None of the feared transferee corpses had eventuated, and as far as we could tell nobody had been seriously injured on either side. The PNG Police had not become involved, which was a good thing. It was about as perfect a resolution as we could hope for. Best of all, those responsible were finally going to face consequences for their actions. It had been a good day, but things were only just beginning.

* * *

The MAA was absolutely bursting at the seams when we arrived. It had only ever been designed to hold maybe a dozen at the absolute maximum, and that would have been considered crowded. Right now, there was at least thirty. But instead of the usual dramatics and complaining you would expect with that many Iranians and Somalis in one place, there was dead silence. It was as if everyone knew that their actions were finally catching up with them. .

There were about half a dozen ERT at the MAA, and by contrast our spirits could not have been higher. We had been sent to back up the Whiskeys, but the transferees were so defeated that we weren't really needed. At one point some senior PNG Police officers arrived to do a walk through, and you could have heard a pin drop.

Gloves was there – he had been with his rotation's Whiskey team for a few months now, and was one of the many SSAs who had flown in early to lend a hand. As we sat and sucked down water, the fatigue began to set in. My eyes hurt, and my head pounded. All the adrenalin built up in the last few days was being dumped from my system, and I just felt wrecked.

The Iranian who had hit Joey spent the entire time staring at him, and Joey showed the patience of a saint to keep his cool. No doubt in the Iranian's mind, Joey had simply pulled him out of the crowd of Bravo for no reason at all. As if to confirm what I was thinking, the man's friend piped up, calling out to us in English.

"ERT, why do you bring us here? We did nothing wrong. We were being peaceful when you attack us! Why do you bring us to this place?"

Joey considered his words before responding, his voice remaining calm the whole time.

"I think it's time you stopped lying, mate. It's not going to help you where you are going."

As if on queue, a convoy of buses driven by the PNG Police arrived outside the MAA. The transferees were cuffed and herded onto the transports which would take them somewhere far harsher than the MRPC would ever be. Up until this point many probably thought that it would be a day or two at the MAA and then back to business-as-usual, but now the reality of the situation was settling in. More than a few broke down into fits of sobbing and wailing as the buses pulled away into the darkness.

* * *

Compared to Lorengau prison, the MAA was luxury. Like the MAA, things were pretty basic. There was little more than a narrow concrete corridor with a corrugated iron roof. A tiny dirt patch served as the exercise yard. It would have been crowded with ten men inside, let alone thirty. Unlike the MAA however, the custodians here were not likely to put up with their nonsense the way we did. They were in PNG custody now, and their whole world was about to change.

The first sign that things may not have been as simple as first thought came when the head warden came outside to greet us, a look of confusion on his face. A heated discussion ensued between the warden and the senior policeman. Whatever the confusion, the transferees were soon off the bus and herded into their new surroundings.

Many of them had spent time in prisons in their home countries (Heckle had even spoken of doing jail time in Libya) and we could tell by the looks on their faces that they recognised a harsh place when they saw it. MRPC was a holiday resort compared to this joint, and they knew it.

Some of the younger Iranians – those sheltered by a more middle-glass existence than their African and Kurdish cohorts – were still acting cocky. Maybe they thought getting their way here would be as easy as it was at the centre, where a complaint form or a pack of smokes slipped to a local guard was enough to tip the situation in their favour. When the head warden lined them up and began explaining the rules and expectations he had in place for them at his facility, one of the young Iranians rolled his eyes.

The warden stepped forward and punched the young Iranian square in the face, dropping him in a heap. The free phones and cigarettes, internet and X-Box games were a thing of the past. As we left them in the charge of their new custodians and drove back to the MRPC, I certainly didn't envy them. But I didn't feel any sympathy either. Everything that would happen to them now was the result of their own choices. It was something many people could do well to understand.

* * *

It was nearly midnight by the time we got to bed, but we weren't getting much sleep. The PNG Police had obtained a warrant to search Delta compound, and we would be supporting them. We were due to meet up with them at 0430 to begin the search right on daybreak at 0500. Unfortunately, the PNG Police were running on island time. They didn't turn up until 0630, and then headed to our staff mess for a free breakfast. We didn't make it to the compound until after 0700.

We had been up two hours early for a task we were now an hour late for. We were already tired and cranky, and it wasn't just because of the local coppers. We had seen the first media reports of the Delta breach overnight, and had been shocked beyond all expectations to see what was reported. Not only had the situation been resolved peacefully, they said, but it had been resolved by the intervention of an PNG bureaucrat who had somehow entered Delta compound and negotiated an end to the blockade personally!

This was the same public servant that had twice trashed the staff mess and been found wandering the centre shoe-less and high on betelnut. It was obvious where the media had gotten this story from, and the self-serving nature of it was sickening. We had put our safety on the line and this bureaucrat was trying to hijack all our hard work to feather his own political nest. Luckily within a few hours more accurate reports began to emerge. They still didn't really capture the extent of the tension that had been present, but at least they weren't pure fantasy.

The Australian government admitted that a "degree of force" had been used, but reiterated that there were no major injuries amongst ourselves or the transferees. The hunger strikes were continuing in Mike/Foxtrot, but they were petering out. ERT received a personal message from the Abbott office, thanking us for "defeating a major challenge to the government policies".

The transferees fed their own version of events to the media of course, mainly involving brutal and unprovoked attacks by "death-squads" on peacefully protesting and emaciated hunger-strikers, most of whom were also asleep at the time.

The search of Delta went ahead without incident. With most of the troublemakers in Lorengau, those who had returned to the compound were co-operative and just wanted to get on with things. I felt sorry for a lot of them. Many had a lot of their property damaged during the breach and clearance, and a lot of their cigarettes and other belongings had disappeared after the local cleaners had descended upon the compound in the minutes following.

We found the usual stashes of marijuana and home-brewed alcohol, as well as some more makeshift weapons. We found a lot of messed-up pornography – including some involving children – that we passed on to the police. But the most disturbing discovery was the water-bottles filled with petrol. I remembered all those extinguishers that the fire-fighters had been caching in F-Block just before we went in – it had been more than just a precaution.

We later heard that whilst we had been off-island a few weeks before, local cleaners and maintenance staff had been caught bringing fuel into the centre. They had claimed that it was for the lawn-mower, but the fact that it was being carried in water bottles had set off alarm bells, and now our suspicions were confirmed. The local staff were either unaware or unconcerned about the potential life-threatening danger their trading could cause. Hopefully they were fired, but knowing local sensitivities they probably weren't. I was just glad I hadn't copped a Molotov cocktail to the face.

* * *

A state of normality began to return to the MRPC. The hunger strikes in Mike and Foxtrot fizzled out, and IHMS and the other evacuated staff returned to work. Chai was left in the MAA. Even though he had bitten a chunk out of George's leg and had many violent episodes in IHMS that had damaged equipment and required SSAs to pin him to the bed for hours (some soft-touch had not wanted him to be restrained) he had not been handed over with the others.

Partly this was because he wasn't involved in the organised disturbance, and because they knew that if he carried on the way he did with us whilst in PNG custody then he would probably have been beaten to death. Nobody wanted that on their hands. Chai was our problem and he was here to stay, no matter how unhinged and unpredictable he became.

Search warrants were conducted on all the remaining compounds, with much the same results. Apart from that though, ERT were still pretty much confined to F-Block. The transferees were believing their own hype and propaganda about us as a "death-squad" so somebody thought it best we keep a low profile. We were happy to have the downtime. We caught up on our reading and watched a lot of movies.

Soon though, the paper side to such a massive incident began to catch up with us. There was literally hours of CCTV and Go-Pro footage for the investigations cell to sift through, plus statements from everyone that had been involved. Everyone was keen to see those responsible face the full extent of the law, but that all hinged on the charges pressed by PNG authorities. I doubt anybody had any faith in the local constabulary's paper trail, so Wilson was keen to bring as much documentation to the party as possible.

Our investigators were snowed under and working to impossible deadlines. Any SSA who had policing experience and could take a statement was press-ganged into assisting. We all spent hours in the investigations office, going over everything we had seen and done. I wasn't alone in hoping that it wouldn't all be in vain.

* * *

"When are we going back to centre?" The Iranians called out to us, their faces pushed against the fence. "Are you here to take us back?"

We went through this every time we visited the Lorengau prison. The same people that had once sneered and threatened us every time we walked into the compound were now asking for our help, begging to be taken back to the place they had compared to everything from Guantanamo Bay to Auschwitz. Every time we told them the same thing.

"We can't help you any more guys, it is out of our hands."

"But why are we here? We did nothing wrong! We do not understand!"

Still the same tired game. We were their only audience for it however – the PNG wardens didn't care for their complaints, and were likely to let them know in no uncertain terms. Already we had seen a few of the Iranians looking a lot worse-for-wear after breaking the rules of the prison. Apparently, the wardens favoured 2x4's and fan-belts. I could see why the MRPC was fast becoming a fond memory.

We were at the prison for the daily food delivery – one of the jobs command had found for us in-lieu of us not being in the compounds. It turned out that catering was not part of the accommodation package in the PNG prison-system – it was up to an inmate's friends or family to supply them. I don't know where this left an inmate who had neither, but as the transferees were still technically wards of the Australian Government until conviction their culinary upkeep was still our responsibility.

Every day we delivered several dozen hotboxes from the transferee mess to Lorengau prison, where we handed them over to the wardens for distribution. How many of the meals were given to the inmates and how many went home with the wardens we weren't sure. The transferees didn't seem to complain either. It was a big change from back at the MRPC, where they would insult and abuse the local catering staff despite being able to take as much as they wanted.

> "Manus Island is such a small place," I said to Joey. "I wonder how many of the wardens here are probably related to the local staff back at the centre."
>
> "For sure," Joey nodded. "They would have told them exactly how they were back there. They won't be getting any sympathy."

As we were leaving however, we saw something quite astonishing. One of the Iranians had clearly not gotten the difference between prison and the MRPC through his head. He approached one of the wardens we were speaking to and proceeded to ask if they could go on a beach excursion!

You could have heard a pin drop, I fully expected the warden to punch the transferee in the face – but instead he burst out laughing. He had kept a straight face for a second as he processed what he had just been asked. As the transferee walked away, the warden was nearly bowled over in hysterics.

"That was the stupidest thing I ever heard!" he howled.

* * *

A few days later we transitioned to night shift, and things slowed down even more. With no food runs and still confined to F-Block, the next two weeks settled into a grinding rhythm of caffeine abuse and movies. Other SSAs began to laugh at the way we hung around the staff mess looking for new faces to chat with. We were so bored.

I was not the only one much relieved when fly-out day arrived. What had started as by far my most intense rotation had quickly morphed into our most tedious. Despite this, none of us in the ERT would have missed it for the world. That sentiment was best expressed by guys like Alex and Hadrian, who had been through the worst of the riots the previous February.

> "The worst thing about all that was having to go back to work and have them laugh in your face, right after they had literally tried to kill you," Alex said as we boarded the airport bus. "Everybody knew what had gone on and everybody knew that nothing would be done about it. This actually feels like closure for all that back then."

I hoped that justice would come for those sitting in Lorengau prison. Nobody who had been there and seen what we had seen could feel any different. Already bleeding-hearts and asylum-seekers advocates all over the internet were bleating about the inhumanity of it all and calling for their immediate release. After all, these men had done nothing but chant "Freedom". It was funny how they seemed to know so much more about the situation than us, despite being thousands of kilometres away.

As the plane rose above the island and turned in the direction of Port Moresby, I wondered how different things would be for us from now on at the MRPC. Would the result of this showdown and the removal of so much of the bad element usher in a new period of calm? Would the resettlement programme now finally go ahead, and how would that affect the centre?

As always though, Manus Island had other plans.

CHAPTER 18

LIKE IT NEVER HAPPENED

I took an extra week off when I returned to Brisbane for my leave. It had already been pre-planned, but it couldn't have happened at a better time. I enjoyed my extended break, and when I touched back down on Manus I realised that it was about one year to the day now since I had first arrived on this equatorial island. So much had changed, yet so much would stay the same. As soon as I saw the guys on my team, I was to discover just how much the status-quo was determined to remain.

"They're all back in," Alex said, shaking his head.

"What, *all* of them?"

"Yep. Every single one of them."

After six weeks languishing in Lorengau prison, the wardens had apparently had enough and dumped them back at the MRPC. When I found out why, I didn't know whether to laugh or curse. I certainly wasn't surprised though.

"You know that PNG government official that said they would all be jailed and sent to Port Moresby? Turns out that was the old chief immigration officer, the one who told the media he negotiated the Delta siege. It also turns out he didn't have authority to make that claim and that nobody had told the prison they were coming. It took the locals six weeks to realise that nothing was authorised. So now they're all back, and they probably have grounds for a wrongful imprisonment suit as well, even though every single one of them deserved to be there."

It got better though. The rest of the team had gathered to watch Alex deliver the news. I suppose everybody else had the same reaction.

"You know all those statements we spent hours doing? All gone. No paper copies, everything wiped from the system. It's like it never happened. But now they are all back here they have all started lodging their own statements and complaints about what *they* claim happened, and you better be sure that *those* will be investigated."

The transferees were being saved by the PNG legal system – the very system that they had been protesting. But it wasn't saving them through any sort of constitutional action, rather the complete reluctance or inability of the PNG authorities to enforce their own criminal code. As far as they were concerned, the transferees were our problem. Until anything they did directly affected them, they had no interest. In a way, I could understand. But it still didn't make it right.

Rather than sending them straight back into their respective compounds, the transferees returning from Lorengau were housed in a new addition to the MRPC neighbourhood – Charlie compound. The compound had previously been used to house transferees that were leaving via IOM, as those who chose this route were liable for bullying and intimidation from the hard-liners amongst the population.

Any misconception that Charlie was going to be run tough however was quashed as soon as I walked in there. Perhaps in a misguided attempt to placate them, the occupants there were bestowed with even more privileges than were offered to the transferees in the other compounds. It was like they were being rewarded for their behaviour. Sure enough, this soon led to a change in attitudes amongst them.

The fresh perspective they had been given by their stint in Lorengau prison all but evaporated, and they were soon back to be their old rude and entitled selves. They were just as bad, if not worse, than they had been before.

In private, some admitted that they had miscalculated the barricading, and had been shocked by how aggressive our eventual response had been. But others seemed to have developed a swagger about themselves, as if having been in the local jail now made them even harder. We would have plenty of time to experience this spectacle – nearly half the ERT and most of the whiskeys were assigned to look after Charlie, more manpower than was available for any of the other compounds, each of which had ten times the occupants.

It was hard to keep a straight face as the transferees complained about their conditions, some even implying that they had it better in Lorengau, sleeping thirty to a room on a concrete slab. Farrquaat, a snivelling little weasel of an Iranian told us how he and the chief warden had become good friends, and that he had often taken him into town for coffee and lunch!

> "Farrquaat, when we came down to the prison the warden was punching you in the head. What happened to change that relationship?"
>
> "The warden was a good man, much better than any of you!"

It turned out that there was some truth to Farrquaat's story, but like always there was a little more to it. Transfield case workers had begun visiting the prison shortly after we rotated off island, taking over the food deliveries as well as bringing mobile phones for the transferees to call home. Apparently, these phone calls had coincided with various amounts of cash being transferred into wardens' bank accounts. This had in turn coincided with increased privileges and freedoms for some transferees, which apparently included lunch dates.

The most galling aspect of the ringleaders' return however, were the accusations. I had fully expected them to lodge the usual protests of excessive force, and I was not disappointed. As expected, all of them had either been engaged in peaceful protests or sleeping when we had come in, and all of them had been beaten like dogs as they cowered on the ground, begging for their lives. Some of the claims however, just defied all belief.

Monopoly Man, for example, claimed that he had been killed. He claimed that SSAs had choked him to death then revived him using a defibrillator and resumed beating him. Frizzy-haired Sideshow also jumped on the bandwagon, claiming that he had been restrained and beaten when we entered Oscar compound.

It didn't matter that neither of them had been in Oscar at the time and that they had both been in the MAA for a couple of days by then. It didn't matter that neither of them had restraints applied and that their entire stay there had been recorded on CCTV. I guess they figured that nobody would check that. Or maybe they were just so detached from reality that they believed these things had happened. Neither would surprise me.

* * *

Whilst the holiday in Hotel Charlie continued, the resettlement programme had begun and was already showing signs of progress. Molag, an Iranian civil engineer from Mike compound, was the first transferee to be granted a "double-positive" rating by the PNG Department of Immigration and Citizenship and was to be settled in PNG as a refugee. He left the MRPC and moved into the $130 million-dollar transit facility in East Lorengau, where he received a living allowance from the Australian government and went about completing a programme designed to help him adapt to his new life.

It wasn't Australia, but it was better than what he had fled. He said as much to the media when they interviewed him, and told them he was happy to have been successful in his refugee application. Word was he even had interviews lined up for engineering jobs on the mainland once he had completed his integration programme in East Lorengau.

I didn't know Molag, but guys who did said he was a decent guy. He never became involved in any of the trouble the other Iranians seemed to thrive on, which explained why I didn't recognise him. Critics of offshore processing promptly dismissed the story as propaganda, however. Even Wushu weighed in on the topic via social media, claiming that Molag had been a spy for Wilson and the most hated man in the whole of the MRPC. I couldn't speak for the former, but I'm sure there would have been far more deserving contenders for the latter.

* * *

In time, Charlie became less of a hotel and more of a boarding house. Transferees were slowly processed back into the compounds, but not back into the one's they had originally come from. Cheech was moved across the road to Oscar, whilst Monopoly Man, Blackbeard, Ali and most of the Oscar agitators were sent to Foxtrot. Soon the compound was near empty, and the only transferees remaining were the Somali brothers, Heckle and Jeckle.

Heckle and Jeckle refused to move anywhere other than Delta, so for the moment they were staying put. It was ridiculous that after all that had happened they were still able to call the shots like this, but with all the heat from the allegations nobody in control was keen to sign off on the use of force. The decision was made to wait them out, whilst all the while dismantling the compound around them to make staying there less appealing.

The X-Box and TV were the first to go, followed by the board games. All the furniture except their beds were taken out. As soon as the furniture was gone, Heckle and Jeckle lodged complaints and it got brought back straight away. Transferees from Foxtrot and Mike were both brought to Charlie to try and convince them to move in. They were offered visits to both to pick which compound they would prefer, but still they refused. They wanted back into Delta, where the Somalis had influence.

This silly game went on for more than a week, before finally somebody took a gamble. Whilst the brothers were making a visit to the phones at the Green Zone, we packed their bags for them. They emerged from their phone calls to find the team waiting for them and an open gate to Foxtrot. The Somalis went along without so much as an argument. They knew the game was up.

Despite the moving of so many trouble-makers into Foxtrot, the mood in that compound didn't really change. They were quickly ostracised by the other transferees, who had no time for their rubbish. Heckle and Jeckle found out quickly that their sway didn't hold when they demanded their new room-mates move out of their own room to make more space for them. Let's just say, it didn't go well.

The only one of the original agitators that wasn't moved out into the compounds was Captain Jack. I couldn't believe it when I found out why.

* * *

"Double-positive? Really? *Him?*"

When I discovered that Captain Jack had been deemed a refugee by PNG Immigration and Citizenship and moved to the transit centre in East Lorengau, I was completely floored. The "double" meant both recognised as a refugee and deemed suitable for resettlement in PNG society. I couldn't speak for the first positive – there was probably more to his story than rampant drug abuse and pickpocketing – but the second positive was supposed to be based on their behaviour whilst in the MRPC.

We weren't the only ones to be puzzled by this determination – even the other transferees were shocked. Every transferee considered themselves a genuine refugee, but their views on each other's cases were as varied as ours. When I asked one of the other double-positives his opinion on Captain Jack's status, his assessment was blunt.

> "He paid them off. The Papuans are simple and greedy. They would have signed him off as genuine for a packet of cigarettes."

Knowing the level of integrity demonstrated by the chief immigration officer, I didn't doubt this for a second. Money was truly the universal language in PNG, much like everywhere else in the world. That made them easy to manipulate for people like Captain Jack, who like a lot of the Iranians didn't seem to be short of cash. Like everything else, they were making a mockery of the system – as if it wasn't messed up enough already.

Slowly but surely the resettlement process began to gain momentum, and soon over a dozen refugees were living in East Lorengau. But for every refugee that packed his bags for the transit centre, two more remained in their compounds at the MRPC, refusing to take part in the programme.

Some were genuinely concerned about their safety and reception out amongst the Manusian community. Others were just digging in their heels in their belief and perceived entitlement that they should be settled in Australia. There was not much that could be done about the latter – nobody could force them to accept the programme, although winding back of non-essential privileges like internet access and excursions were later introduced to compel them, which led to an inevitable backlash.

To reassure the former, a programme of "sleep-overs" was implemented, whereby double-positives could visit the facility and see what was on offer before making their decision. We went along for the ride – not so much because they were expecting trouble, but more so as a familiar face. We had absolutely no power out there, as those deemed refugees were now considered to be under the full jurisdiction of the PNG authorities. Despite this, the whole facility was still operated and financed by Australia.

It was all a pretty casual affair. We wore plain-clothes the entire time. The facilities at the transit-centre were first-class, better than what both staff and transferees enjoyed back at the MRPC. One of the refugees gave us his assessment of the whole thing, as well as a prediction for its future.

> "It's all good now, but so was Mike compound at the beginning. Once more people come here it will get worse. Once that happens it will be just like Mike, and all the trouble will happen here too."

We mixed with the refugees there in a way that would have been undreamed of back at the centre – all except Captain Jack. The shifty Iranian kept his distance, not just from us but from most of the other refugees. They had pretty much ostracised him – they knew as well as anybody how much trouble he had caused and didn't want any association with him.

Captain Jack wasted no time in ingraining himself into Lorengau society, becoming quite the man-about-town. He drank at the local hotel and soon had several local girlfriends. He even managed to get his hands on a bicycle, which was rumoured to have been a gift from one of them. Who knows what the local men thought of this sleazy

Persian romancing their women, but in true Captain Jack fashion he was also rumoured to have made a visit to the local police station and arranged for protection.

Jackson was the operations manager at East Lorengau. He had left the New Zealand Army as a warrant officer before spending time as a country copper at the wild southern tip of New Zealand's South Island. Jackson was highly respected by local and ex-pat alike, and I suspect by many of the refugees too. He summed up the Captain Jack situation pretty much perfectly.

> "His actions will catch up with him eventually. Out there in the real world he hasn't got a system to hide behind. He'll fuck up, but only *once*."

* * *

We were back in Charlie compound, but this time for a memorial service. The father of an Iraqi transferee had died back in his home country, and transferees from across the centre had joined him in Charlie to show their condolences. Might sound like overkill having ERT present, but as always at the MRPC nothing was as it seemed.

I thought about expressing my condolences to the Iraqi, but in the end decided against it. I didn't know how much he would have appreciated it coming from me, but as I entered the compound I could see that the small and somewhat empty gesture I had just considered making was actually more than what his fellow transferees were doing.

About forty people from across the MRPC had come down for the service, but you could count on one hand the number who were inside with the grieving Iraqi. As the prayer leader offered up his song, most of the mourners were outside, laughing and smoking whilst they socialised with friends from other compounds. I doubted that half of them even *knew* the Iraqi.

"It's just like the Christian prayer meetings," Gene muttered. "They don't even give a shit about that guy in there, they're all just here for themselves. Fucking disrespectful!"

An older transferee who had been inside for the service briefly appeared in the doorway to chastise those milling around outside, but his disgust barely raised an eyebrow. I was surprised that our presence out in the yard hadn't got more attention either, seeing that most of the main players from each of the compounds were mingling all around. This was the main reason we here – these guys rarely got to have such extended face-to-face time with one another, and the intel boys back in control were keen to know who was talking to who.

A Whiskey SSA named Tim was making the rounds, chatting to each of the small groups in Arabic and Farsi. Tim was one of those guys with a natural flair for languages – he had done a Pashtun language course back in the army and had emerged fluent, and picked up Dari by ear whilst deployed in Afghanistan. Since being at the MRPC, he had developed a working proficiency in Arabic, Farsi and Pidgin. This – along with the field intelligence course he had undertaken – made him very adept at following and identifying the goings-on between the transferees, and the insights he shared with us were often fascinating. Tim saw us and made his way over.

"How did his father die?" Hadrian asked.

"Natural causes, I think. Or at least that's what he told me. But one of the transferee Facebook pages is already reporting that he was killed by ISIL. They're already putting a political spin on it, asking why Tony Abbott will send troops to fight Islamic State but not offer refuge to those fleeing them."

"They have to twist everything don't they? They couldn't give a shit about their mate in there grieving his dead father, just what kind of mileage and points they can score out of it for their own situation."

"I'm getting pretty sick of them using ISIL as an excuse," Gene snorted. "If their families are really being attacked, then why aren't these guys back there fighting to protect them? Why are they here expecting Australia to give them a free ride when our mates are over there fighting their war for them? How do these bleeding hearts expect anybody to respect or sympathise with people like that? They're either liars or they're cowards as far as I'm concerned."

"The advocates back home are really pissing me off as well," Tim said. "They act so self-righteous, but they are just using these guys to further their own profiles. Have you seen all these Adopt-a-Refugee letters getting around?"

"Are they something like those Adopt-a-Soldier letters you get from school kids whilst your overseas?"

"Pretty much. A heap of them came in last week, and I was helping some of the guys in Delta to read them. Only one of them was from somebody who sounded like she was genuinely concerned about their situation – it was some little old lady in Tasmania. The rest were all from lawyers and journalists trying to get stories out of them. It was disgusting."

Never let the truth get in the way of a good story. It was an old saying but something that was always adept on Manus Island.

CHAPTER 19

CHANGING WITH THE TIMES

The vultures were still circling, and they all had law degrees. To be fair though, at least these ones had the authority to practice law in PNG. They had turned up too, which was more than what the last guy had done.

Despite their expensive experience with lawyers courtesy of Wushu, many transferees were still keen to challenge their situation in the courts. With the assistance of a group of lawyers flown in from Australia, two separate class actions were being mounted – one against the Australian government for sending them to Manus, and the other against the PNG government for accepting them.

I have no doubt that many folks in the legal community had genuine sympathy for the transferees' plight. I also believe that many were just jumping on the issue for some free publicity.

I would have my first encounter with these noble creatures one morning whilst escorting a number of transferees to their first meetings. It wasn't really an ERT task, but the escort team were understaffed and overworked, so we were happy to lend a hand. The meetings were held outside the MRPC in the office of one of the building contractors, although I'm not sure if that was for the transferees' comfort or for the lawyers. We weren't complaining, as the building contractors had an air-conditioned lounge with pool tables and satellite TV which we could chill out in until they were finished.

We arrived fifteen minutes early with the first plaintiff. He was an Iranian, so we had brought along a Farsi interpreter for him as well. The lawyer arrived fifteen minutes late. Grossly overweight and clearly struggling with the tropical heat, he barely acknowledged us or his client as he barged into the air-conditioned embrace of his temporary office.

When he did emerge, we introduced ourselves and let him know how we were able to assist him whilst we were there.

> "One of us will be waiting here outside the office, the other two will be in the lounge. If there is anything we can help you with, please let us know."

The lawyer looked at the transferee and his interpreter, and then back at us.

> "Why do I only have one interpreter?"

We all glanced at each other, as to see if any of us was missing something the others weren't.

> "Um, because you only have one transferee?"
> "I want a Farsi *and* an Arabic interpreter!"
> "Do you mean you wanted an interpreter who speaks both languages, or two separate people?"
> "WHAT IS YOUR NAME? WHAT ARE ALL YOUR NAMES!? I WILL HAVE WILSON! AND I WILL HAVE ALL OF YOU!"

A few of the boys immediately pulled out their notebook and began jotting down the time and details of the exchange. Huffing and puffing with self-importance and cardiovascular stress, he led the transferee and his interpreter into the office. The interpreter looked embarrassed, but the transferee was grinning from ear to ear and stuck his tongue out at us as he closed the door behind him.

This kind of behaviour carried on for the next few visits. The lawyer was constantly flying off the handle for the most trivial of perceived infractions on our part. Perhaps he was doing it to make himself look like a big man in front of his clients. *Look at the way I push these idiots around – stick with me boys and I'll sort you out.* We also suspected he was being as difficult as possible in order to give the impression that we were not cooperating with him.

We fought back with kindness, which was painful but really all we could do in these circumstances. Despite all his posturing though, he didn't seem to be showing much respect for his own clients. He was universally late for his own appointments, often quite considerably. I spent two awkward hours one afternoon sitting in silence with Blackbeard waiting for the lawyer to return from his extended lunch break.

These timing blow-outs could be partially explained by the fact that he was staying in the $300 a night Harbourside Hotel in Lorengau, which was nearly an hour's drive away. As well as driving in each morning and back again before dark, he was returning there for lunch each day, so it only left two short windows for the interviews per day. I don't know who was covering his accommodation and transport expenses, but it wouldn't have been cheap.

* * *

The first we knew that the PNG Police Mobile Squad had departed the MRPC was when they literally weren't there. The running track we often used took us right past the Police Liaison Office, and often you would see at least one member of the elite paramilitary unit, smoking or napping in a deck chair with their boots undone and their sizable guts spilling out from under their shirts. But this morning the hut was deserted, and their vehicles were gone. The only evidence that they had ever been there were the piles of beer bottles and cigarette butts that littered the area.

We didn't think much of it at first, as we expected a new group to turn up in a few days. The squads rotated every month anyway, and this group had probably just left a few days early. The mobility in their name certainly didn't describe how quick off the mark they were, more the fact that they were moved from province to province every month. This meant that they didn't have time to marry in with the locals and become involved with the tribal system, which was the downfall of effective law enforcement and governance in so much of the country.

The mobile squad's presence on Manus Island had always been financed by the Australian government, and I wasn't surprised to learn that their withdrawal had been about money, or that local stakeholders had been involved. What did surprise me was learning that the Australian government had made a stand against the local businesses' extortion.

Traditionally the mobile squad had been accommodated in the Harbourside Hotel, Lorengau's premier establishment. Luxurious by local standards, it attracted rates of over $300 per person a night whenever the Australian government was footing the bill. Recently though a new hotel named The Paradise had sprung up on the other side of town. The Paradise was owned by the mayor's brother and cost $600 per night. The mobile squad promptly moved in, apparently without consultation to those who would be footing the bill.

The story was that the Australian government, instead of its usual practice of open cheque-book pandering to local landowners, refused to finance this blatant money-grab and the mobile squad were subsequently withdrawn from the island. Their departure was not mourned by the locals. Stories of drunken squad members terrorising the nearby townspeople (even running down children whilst drink-driving) were commonplace. But the biggest thing we noticed about their absence was the gradual increase in vagrants wandering the roads around the facilities.

It was easy to dismiss Manus Island as being in a state of abject poverty, but that's not really true. It was just different to what most Australians (and most likely Iranians) would consider to be a sufficient standard of living. There was no doubt a lot more to the local society than we could see as outsiders looking in, but from what we could gather there had never really been a homelessness problem on the island province until the MRPC had shown up.

We had first learnt about this during our stay at the East Lorengau centre, when we had observed what appeared to be a series of small campfires in the jungle beyond the back fence. The staff there had informed us that they belonged to a group dubbed "The Others" or "The Outsiders" – groups of mainland New Guineans who had come to Manus looking for work.

Word of immense wealth and resources being poured into the province by the Australian government had drawn a significant number of economic migrants to sleepy little Lorengau, in the hope of finding their own fortune. Whilst it was true that many Manusians (the already-wealthy landowners and those with tribal connections) had done quite well from the MRPCs presence, this didn't extend to the majority of the local population, and certainly not to those from across the water.

Unfortunately for the disappointed fortune-seekers, many of them also lacked the means to return home. Thus, camps of homeless men had sprung up in the hills behind the capital, but a few had begun to venture closer to the perceived epi-centre of Manus Island's financial windfall. Without the Mobile Squad prowling the local roads, the vagrants began to seep in. Local security patrols would report them sleeping in shipping containers near the wharf or in the old warehouses and aircraft hangers behind The Swamp. The most recognisable of our new neighbours was one we dubbed Charcoal.

Charcoal was basically the Manus Island version of The Jolly Swagman, complete with dreadlocks, tea-cosy and stonewashed jeans. You would often see him trudging the roads between the RPCs or along the beachfront, or rifling through the mountains of rubbish that the processing centre would generate. He began turning up in so many unexpected places that he was considered a security risk as well as a source of amusement.

The task of marshalling Charcoal fell to our "Wontok-whisperer" Woody. Woody was an ex-New Zealand Army soldier who had spent the last few years running convoys as a private contractor in Iraq. Here on Manus he was the external supervisor, responsible for coordinating the locally employed security guards at The Swamp and controlling access to staff accommodation. It would invariably fall to Woody to shoo Charcoal away from wherever he appeared, and we would often laugh driving away from the centre to see the two of them on the side of the road engaged in some lively conversation.

We began to hear more and more about the trouble the Iranians at East Lorengau were getting themselves into. Our local colleagues would speak about encountering them around town on their days off, and few of the accounts were positive. On the other hand, many of the Tamils and Rohingyas seemed to be doing a lot better, and in some cases married local women and started families.

In another attempt to persuade the reluctant double-positives to move into East Lorengau, daily bus services were made available to take them into town whenever they desired. When the day-trippers returned, they would be subjected to a thorough bag search. This was one of the few search powers we had at the centre, and only applied to their bags (not clothing or person) and only as they were entering the centre.

Every day the transferees would leave with bags full of cigarettes, mobile phones and other taxpayer-provided items and return with bags full of locally-grown marijuana. We would seize the marijuana and pass it on to the local police, who would deal with the matter in their usual method of doing nothing.

The transferees' involvement in the local drug trade wasn't the most unsavoury aspect of their newfound mobility, however. In one of the most unsavoury tasks ever to be assigned to the ERT, teams were assigned to trail one transferee on all his movements outside the MRPC. Suspected to be a paedophile due to the discovery of child pornography in his room following the last riots, ERT members had the unenviable task of ensuring he did not come into any contact with local children whilst at the same time keep enough distance that we could not be accused of harassing or restricting his movement in any way.

Nothing showed how much our time at the centre was changing than the opening of RPC2. Like everything on Manus Island, things seemed to spring up overnight no matter how long the lead-up time was. The jungle that had once stood between the old Bibby wharf and the MRPC was now gone, and in its place a sprawling complex that suggested an organisation that was in for the long haul.

Up until this point nothing at the MRPC seemed to be purpose built. Things were set up from what was available and requisitioned for other purposes when the requirements changed. The now annual riots had shown how perilous it was having most of the control and support services co-located within the boundaries of the centre. Now that problem had been solved, but it signalled a change in direction for our work there. Infrastructure was being put in place to facilitate the eventual handover of responsibilities for the transferees to PNG.

With the opening of RPC2, the original centre as we knew it now became known as RPC1. All the control, admin, intel, investigations, medical and other enabling services were moved into new purpose-built facilities across the road, as were the offices of many of the other stakeholders. The huge corrugated iron hut inside the RPC1 gate that had previously housed them all was converted into storage. A small on-site control element remained in F-Block, but apart from that everyone had moved out.

Where once we had been able to simply walk in to control and speak to anyone about anything we needed, now we had to cross the road, navigate a reception desk and be granted access. The number of people working in there swelled too, easily outnumbering those working the compounds. The relatively small and close-knit crew that had previously existed now seemed to be growing larger and further apart.

The new medical centre was first-class, and easily compared to any small hospital in Australia. Behind them, countless corridors of officers and classrooms led to a large outdoor barbecue area before reaching the new MAA. Unlike the old containers down at The Swamp, this new set-up contained CCTV monitoring and actual cells, although we still didn't have the authority to actually secure anyone inside those cells, but it still hinted at what could be to come.

Whilst nobody would ever complain about the comfort of these new facilities, it all felt sterile and lacked the sense of adventure that had been around the MRPC at the start. With this new-found comfort and sophistication came a growing divide between those who worked the compounds and those who didn't. Many of these run-ins were petty, but it seemed that more and more people who spent their workdays in the corporate-like settings of RPC2 were being allowed to make operational decisions that affected the safety and effectiveness of our teams.

We returned to the island for our latest rotation to discover that all our riot gear had been moved from our former kit room in F-Block to an old container outside the centre. Not only was it outside, it was right up alongside the Oscar compound fence line, meaning that any attempt to retrieve it was done in full view of the transferees and in easy range of rock-lobbing. With some lobbying from Jake and the other teams' leaders, we eventually got our stuff back in F-Block, but the signs of how things were starting to go were worrying.

The pace of refugee determinations by PNG Immigration was gathering momentum. ERT began to spend more time at RPC2 supporting the RSD (Refugee Status Determination) team. We were never privy to the findings and would learn of the result alongside the transferee. We would lurk as discreetly as possible in the corridors, eavesdropping on the meeting between the transferees and PNG Immigration officials and the interpreters passing information between the two. It would be understandable if a negative outcome resulted in a violent reaction from the transferee, but sometimes it was the opposite result that got the most unexpected reaction.

I was never present for a negative result, but the positives always went along the same lines. The PNG Immigration official would declare in a cheery voice:

> "I am happy to inform you that you have been determined to be a refugee by the government of Papua New Guinea. Would you like to accept this finding and begin the resettlement process?"

For every RSD meeting I was present for, the answer from the transferee was always the same – no. Plenty of others were however, as evidenced by the steady stream of residents from the MRPC to East Lorengau. This had been the plan all along, and while the execution had been difficult it seemed to be working. The question would be what would become of those men who refused the offer of resettlement in PNG, and even more contentiously those who were given a negative RSD determination?

We would be finding out first hand sooner than we thought.

Every transferee determined not to be a refugee by PNG Immigration had the right to appeal. Sometimes the determination was reversed, resulting in a resettlement offer. If the appeal process failed however, then that transferee was deemed to be a double-negative. What to do with those people declared double-negative had always been a problem for the future, but now it was here.

Don had taken over as our new Ranger One, having been Ranger Two on one of our opposite teams. A former recon/sniper NCO, Don preferred to be in the compounds with the boys than stuck in the command office back in RPC2. We arrived for night shift that evening and could feel the tension in the air around the compounds. Don ushered us into F-Block to fill us in on the day's events.

> "This morning ICSA served documents on approximately fifty transferees who have received double-negative RSDs. In a nutshell these documents are advising them that they are to prepare for immediate deportation if they do not choose to leave voluntarily via IOM."
>
> "Do they still get the cash if they go with IOM?" I asked.
>
> "According to the document, yes. But as you can imagine the mood in the centre is less-than-serene tonight. We will be keeping ERT out of the compounds for the time-being, until the initial unease blows over and the double-negatives have time to process the information. Hang flex in the crack-den, but be ready to respond if something should blow up."

As we retreated to our "crack-den" as ERT crew room/movie lounge had now been dubbed, we discussed the news and what it could mean for us. With the mobile squad gone, we were easily the heaviest force on the island, despite having the least legal powers. Any forcible evictions from the MRPC would no doubt involve us in some way. The question was would it set off another riot? Just before the door closed, Don yelled out a reminder.

"Enjoy the break tonight guys – Ramadan starts tomorrow!"

I don't think it was deliberate that the deportation news was announced during the Muslim holy month, but it didn't help. The combination of fasters being understandably cranky and non-fasters expecting special treatment had been just as volatile the year before and was bound to lead to the same friction this time around. The added stress of the double-negative situation was like adding fuel to the fire.

During Ramadan, all able Muslims are expected to fast between sun-up and sundown. This pretty much happened naturally at the MRPC however – most transferees slept throughout the day in their air-conditioned accommodation to escape the equatorial heat, and only emerged at night when it was cooler. Evening dinner would become a late breakfast, and breakfast would become a meal before bed. It was a reverse cycle that any night-shift worker can identify with.

The majority of those who did rise during the day and attend the midday lunch were the practicing Muslims, who were required by their faith to pray five times a day. In order to ensure that their caloric needs were still being met, Transfield organised a special midnight dinner service for the fasters throughout the month. This was where the trouble always happened.

You would expect those following the fast to be a little short and irritable by the time midnight rolled around, especially seeing as they had to rise early for morning prayers. Plenty of them skipped the late-night meal and got some extra sleep, so they would have felt the effects much more. But apart from a few complaints about not enough effort being put into making the meals special for the occasion, things were mostly cordial. The problem came from those who weren't fasting but expected to be treated as if they were.

Unlike the open-slather that was the regular meal service, Ramadan was a limited-service affair. Whilst attending diners could still eat as much as they wanted, entry to the meal was restricted to those transferees who had registered for the fast. It was simply an RSVP service to ensure sufficient catering and that those who were fasting could get enough food. But like everything at the MRPC things could never be this simple, and like always the group at the centre of the drama was once again the Iranians.

Every night without fail, angry Iranians would show up at the mess hall demanding entry to the Ramadan meal. The argument between the transferees and the SSAs at the door would invariably follow the same script.

> "Why are you denying me entry to the meal? WHY ARE YOU DENYING ME FOOD?"
>
> "This meal is for fasters only. If you are not registered for the fast you cannot come in. You can register for the fast with your caseworker tomorrow and then you'll be able to come in from then. It's to ensure that the people who need the food most can get enough."

The transferees knew this already, there was no way they didn't. But every calm explanation would be greeted with various Farsi insults and occasionally rants about human rights conventions and other assorted red-herrings.

> "Come on mate, seriously. It's easy, just put your name on

the list. You don't even have to actually *do* the fast, you just need to be catered for, so the fasters don't miss out."

Despite hailing from what was perhaps the world's best known Islamic theocracy, few of the Iranians seemed to actively observe the Muslim faith or show much respect for their fellow transferees who did. Granted many claimed to have converted to Christianity (or Hinduism depending on the day of the week) but it annoyed me to watch them mock the fasters one moment then expect to join their midnight meal the next.

After one such argument with an Iranian I had several identical run-ins with over the preceding weeks, I let my frustration get the better of me. I had humoured this particularly edgy atheist during a previous conversation where he smugly mocked the fasters for praying during the day when they were exposed to sunlight which would feed their bodies through vitamin-E absorption. But now he was getting in my face and I had just had enough. After another spray from him about his human rights being violated, I snapped.

"LISTEN FUCKHEAD, IT IS SIMPLE. YOUR NAME IS NOT ON THE LIST, SO YOU DON'T GO IN. IT'S THE SAME AS IT WAS LAST NIGHT AND IT'S THE SAME AS IT WAS LAST WEEK AND IT'S THE SAME AS IT WAS LAST YEAR. YOU KNOW THIS JUST LIKE YOU KNOW YOU CAN JUST PUT YOUR NAME ON THE LIST AND AVOID THIS WHOLE ARGUMENT EVERY NIGHT BUT NO, YOU JUST HAVE TO ROCK UP AND ACT LIKE A COCKHEAD!"

The Iranian was riled up and went to open his mouth, but I wasn't finished.

"WHAT MAKES YOU EVEN THINK YOU DESERVE THIS? YOU DON'T DO SHIT. THESE GUYS GET UP EARLY AND PRAY FIVE TIMES A DAY AND FAST. YOU DON'T DO SHIT. YOU SLEEP ALL DAY AND THEN BAG THEM OUT WHEN YOU WAKE UP. THEN YOU EXPECT TO EAT THEIR FOOD? WHY DON'T YOU JUST FUCK OFF?"

I fully expected to be reported by the transferee in question, but nothing more came of it. These arguments continued for the rest of our rotation, but I managed to keep my cool for the rest of them. I think my little outburst had let me get some frustrations off my chest. It was a release we all needed.

On occasion a transferee would blow up at being refused entry and throw chairs or assault an SSA, and ERT would take them to the MAA. Others finally decided to play the game and signed up for Ramadan, enjoying the extra food without bothering to get up to pray. Every time I saw that transferee after that he would scowl and make throat-cutting gestures, but never anything more than that.

Despite the tension, we managed to make it through the rest of the rotation without any more word of double-negatives and deportations. Any chance though that we might dodge it altogether were dashed when we returned to the island after our next leave to be told that deportations were indeed going ahead, and they were starting the very next day. The delivery of the message would be carried out by the Royal PNG Constabulary on behalf of ITSA, with support from ERT. The local police would be the lead on this job, pushing home once again that PNG was rapidly gaining primacy in the running of the centre.

With the mobile squad gone the job of delivering the eviction notice fell to the local provincial police. Having grown used to the strong-arm presence of departed paramilitaries and naval police, we were quite shocked when we arrived at a briefing to find what appeared to be a bunch of local school kids in police uniforms. What unsettled us more was what Don told us about the planning session that he had just come from.

Instead of our preferred tactic of calling the soon-to-be deported transferee to an appointment outside the compound and delivering the news free from interference, ICSA had decided they wanted it done right in the compound. With no power to deviate from this plan, we discussed with the teenage police officers the best way to mitigate the risks of things turning into a riot.

> "We will find out where he is in the compound, as discreetly as possible," 'H' explained to the PNG coppers, having been given the job as ERT team leader for the removal. "You guys come straight in, deliver the paperwork from ICSA and advise him that he has to leave with us immediately. We will walk him straight out. No delays. In and out."

'H' was an excellent mentor, and was able to deliver what amounted to an order without it coming across as such. The police just nodded, wide-eyed. They were officially in charge, but clearly, they were in over their heads and appreciated the input. With this set to be the first of many evictions, however, 'H' was clearly not confident that we could pull this process off more than once and have our luck hold out.

> "I reckon we might get away with this once. Once the shock wears off, I'd be surprised if there isn't a riot. I just hope they don't try and do it the same way next time."

ICSA had thankfully picked a relatively easy target for this first eviction. Whilst the transferee was an Iranian from the volatile Oscar compound, he wasn't a known troublemaker. Most of us didn't even recognise him when we were shown his ID photo. The other easy thing, as far as removing him from the country was concerned, is that unlike so many others he had a passport.

It was well known that many of the transferees had destroyed their identification documents when their boats had been intercepted by the RAN. This was apparently encouraged by people smugglers, who were well versed in the tricks of the trade in making it difficult to return someone to their country of origin. When word of deportations had started spreading however, some transferees who hadn't done so on the way in began to make up for lost time. One of the more bizarre cases of this was recounted to me by my old army mate Roger over breakfast that morning.

Roger had been working in the property store for the last few months, responsible for the repository of valuables the transferees had had with them when they arrived. Some of them could have considerable amounts, particularly the Iranians. Transferees were free to retrieve items from the property store at any time, but whilst jewellery and designer clothes were often rotated, a transferee wanting to see his passport was far less common.

> "I thought it was a bit weird that he wanted to see it, but we can't refuse them obviously, so I handed it over. He opened it up and ripped the ID page straight out and shoved it in his mouth. I had to sit there and watch him eat it, then I had to write a report. Seriously, these guys are doing my head in."

Roger assured us however that the inaugural deportee's passport was safe and secure that morning, but it didn't relieve the sense of foreboding we had about the job. H went over the plan again with the police, but things began to unravel as soon as we stepped off. As we made our way along Route Pugwash, we were right in the fishbowl. Both Oscar and Delta compounds had a full view of the unusual sight of ERT and PNG Police walking together. By the time we reached the Oscar gate everyone in the MRPC knew that something was up.

The young coppers had never set foot inside the centre and were clearly quite uncomfortable. By the time we were ready to enter the compound, three of them had decided that they no longer wished to come in with us. This left us with one police officer, a young woman who I can only assume was the senior of the group. The advance team that had gone on ahead to locate the transferee radioed through to tell us that he was sitting on the outdoor gym/TV area – about as deep into the compound as you could get. Ironically it was within spitting distance of the old gate that used to connect F-Block to Oscar, but that gate had become another victim of the bizarre changes that seemed to be going on around the MRPC and was now boarded up.

We found the deportee sitting with friends watching Persian music videos. We hung back as the policewoman approached him, as it had been deemed in the planning group that us standing too close would be intimidating. Nobody had bothered to give this advice to his friends however, as they all jumped to their feet and crowded around. We immediately moved forward, and a weird standover ensued, with the policewoman and deportee in the middle.

Her tone was calm and quiet, and as the deportee nodded along it looked for a moment like things might go smoothly. It wasn't to be.

"Can I go say goodbye to my friends before I leave?" the deportee asked.

The policewoman looked at H, who shook his head as discreetly as possible. A crowd of onlookers was starting to grow around us. The policewoman looked at each of us, and then back at the deportee.

"Yes, okay."

The deportee disappeared in a flash around the side of the accommodation blocks. The crowd didn't disappear however, and soon other transferees were coming forward angrily demanding to know what was going on. The already tense mood was becoming darker.

"I don't think he's coming back," H said.

"He's coming back, alright," Alex said, motioning in the direction the deportee had gone. "But he's bringing a heap of friends."

The deportee had returned, flanked by about two dozen other Iranians. What small avenues of exit we might have had from this isolated corner of the compound were now well and truly closed up. Amir – a long time agitator amongst the Oscar Iranians – stepped forward and declared to the policewoman that the deportee would not be going anywhere. She glanced over at us, as if expecting us to have the answer. We had nothing.

A sickening feeling began to rise in the pit of my stomach. Never had we been blocked in like this before. There was only a handful of us surrounded by a crowd of over a hundred that was growing by the second. I could hear yelling everywhere. The agitation in the crowd was starting to build.

CHAPTER 20

THE BEGINNING OF THE END

We were looking out over the water again, but this time it wasn't the old Bibby wharf or the beach front behind Delta – it was the causeway at Surfers Paradise. I had been looking forward to this night more than I realised – it was the first time I had seen many of the guys in nearly a year.

I wasn't the first to make the decision to leave, nor was I the last. We all knew the gig wasn't forever, and for many different reasons felt it better to leave while we still had the choice. But whilst the money was great and the time off even better, what had made turning up to the airport each month and walking into the centre each shift bearable had been the crew we worked with.

The occasion that called us all together this night was Rob's – not only his 30th birthday but the birth of his first child. Despite all the time the crews had spent together over the years we rarely got together in such big groups to socialise whilst off-island. We always talked about it, but at the end of the day we spent so much time in each other's pockets that we didn't feel the need to in our weeks off. Except for those that had known each other pre-Manus, it was the first time for many of the wives and girlfriends to meet everyone as well. It must have been strange, seeing the men who their worse halves had spent just as many days with over the proceeding few years as them.

As we all caught up, drank way too much beer and discussed what our future plans might entail, we all reflected on the good times we had had on Manus Island. But as the night wore on and we began to reflect on just how angry we had become in those last few months together, Rob said something that summed up the mood at the time perfectly.

"You know things are getting bad when you have to send the whole team to see a shrink."

***

"To be honest, a lot of us are amazed that none have flipped out and bashed any of them yet."

The in-house psychologist was refreshingly blunt. When the ERT had filed into the conference room we didn't know what to expect. Half of us expected a touchy-feely HR session to ram home just how corporate and comfortable things had gotten over the road here at RPC2. The others expected some sort of arse kicking. What we got was a frank discussion and assessment of where the team was mentally. The consensus was angry.

Since the near-disaster of the eviction in Oscar, the double-negative removals had simply disappeared from the agenda. Whatever was going on at the higher-levels was not shared with us, but at the very least it meant no more sketchy jobs under the authority of PNG ITSA. But what it also signalled was the ending of what had appeared to be a genuine exit-strategy to the whole mess.

We had returned to the island after our leave to find that the mood of the place had soured even further since our flight out, despite the prospect of forced-removals now being effectively off the table. The air of volatile unpredictability had now been replaced by one of confident menace. Whilst the stoppage of removals had no doubt been due more to some sort of legal problems than a lack of capacity on the ground, the transferees seemed to have gotten it into their minds that they had scared us off with their show of force in Oscar. The famous MRPC short-memory was back.

As we had walked around the compounds on our first day back, the cockiness shown by the double-negatives and the double-positives unwilling to move to East Lorengau was striking. Where before they would just ignore you or glare from the safety of a group they would now openly challenge and mock us, or spit on the ground as we walked past. They believed that they were untouchable.

They were right.

It had long been a running joke at the MRPC that if a transferee punched an SSA in the face, that the concern would be for the transferee's hand. It had been galling after the riots to have virtually the entire ERT subjected to internal investigations after allegations of rough treatment by the rioter, especially when their own conduct during the period was effectively swept under the rug. But now things were really ramping up a level.

We learnt from our outgoing colleagues that some of the guys had given in to the baiting of the transferees over the proceeding weeks and had been suspended pending investigation. So many in fact, that the call had gone out for off-island team members to fly in on overtime to replace them.

One of the fly-ins was Nick. Nick had escaped his reluctantly-help compound supervisor's job and come across to ERT, and had flown in the week before us to lend a hand. On his first day in the centre, he had intervened when he saw an Iranian abusing local staff in the Oscar mess. The Iranian had simply turned to Nick and spat directly in his face, sending his bile straight into his eyes.

The Iranian was tackled to the ground and moved to the MAA, whilst Nick was taken to medical for assessment. The Iranian made the customary complaints of rough treatment which were subsequently investigated, whilst Nick's attempt to lodge assault charges with the PNG Police amounted to nothing.

The transferee was back in Oscar within 24 hours and was relishing every moment of it. He would make a point of walking past Nick whenever he was in the compound, smiling at him and loudly hacking phlegm onto the ground.

We got our own taste of the new level of provocation a few days later in Foxtrot compound. There was a beach-facing section of trees that ran between the accommodation and shower blocks in that compound, proving a convenient funnel of shade and a sea-breeze that was welcome on the hot equatorial days. Naturally ERT would base our operations there when moving through Foxtrot, but on this day we would have chosen elsewhere.

Alex, Roy and myself were leaning against the shower block wall discussing one of the less serious events that had already befallen our team this rotation – that of Justin being the subject of a written complaint by transferees for farting in the internet room. As we did so, we started to feel what felt like raindrops on our head, despite being under cover.

The laughing from the other side of the wall quickly alerted us to what was going on – transferees under the showers were tossing water on us through the ventilation windows above our heads. We yelled at them in no uncertain terms to stop, but them something a lot thicker, gooier and whiter than water landed on Roy and Alex's head and shoulders.

There was a moment of silence whilst we all registered what had just happened.

"Maybe it's just shampoo?" I offered, having been missed by the offending fluid myself. It wasn't. There was no doubt at all what it was.

We charged into the shower block, greeted by naked and laughing Iranian men pointing at their erect penises.

"You here for more, ERT?"

***

Less than a few hours after they were effectively sexually-assaulted in Foxtrot, Roy, Alex and I were in Delta compound, chasing sea-breeze and shade in a spot wisely away from the shower blocks. The shady spot we found though was already occupied by a caseworker meeting with some transferees, but they were happy to share the space with us.

After her clients had finished up, we began chatting with the caseworker. Things were friendly, and after a while the discussion turned to the current atmosphere within the compounds. We asked her what her thoughts were, hoping to gain some insights of what the transferees might have shared with her.

> "They're just so scared – especially after January. I felt so sorry for the guys when those stormtroopers came in and took them to jail. They hadn't done anything!"

It was a good thing I was wearing sunglasses, or she would have seen my eyes roll out of my head. We were sitting in the exact spot where our colleagues had been set upon and beaten by a violent mob, and many of them still bore the scars. Not that the caseworkers would have seen that, having been evacuated from the centres, if they were even on the island at all. But no doubt the transferees had shared their account of events with her. I wonder if she had any idea that she was sitting with the very stormtroopers that she was lamenting.

> "Were you here for that, back in January?" Alex asked, obviously thinking the same thing.
> "No, but I wish I had been. I could have stopped it. I could have spoken to them…"

We made our excuses to leave, not wanting to play the game after the morning we had. We felt it better to leave the woman in her own denial rather than risk a HR meeting. As we made our way through the maze that was Delta, we came across one of the Transfield art teachers having an animated conversation with an insistent Iranian.

> "These paints are only for people attending the arts classes. If you want to sign up for the classes you are more than welcome, but I can't just give you the paint."
>
> "You are Transfield, you are here to serve us!" the transferee explained. "Why you are acting like Wilson?"

He went quiet when he saw us. Alex was already in a bad mood and didn't mince his words.

> "You're not getting any paint from him, so just fuck off."
>
> "Yeah!" The art teacher suddenly straightened up.
>
> "FUCK OFF!"

We walked out of the compound amazed by what we had just seen. It seemed that we weren't the only ones having our patience tested.

***

Justin didn't hold back when advising the psych about the anger that was building in the team. He was never the sort of guy to be backwards when coming forward.

> "Every day we walk through the compound we are spat at. We are threatened. We are abused. We are challenged to fights. We have guys who are waiting on the results of hepatitis tests and are too scared to kiss their wives

and kids at home. We have two guys that were sexually-assaulted by a cum-throwing scumbag, yet they are the ones that are untouchable here! Nobody upstairs wants to deal with it so they just let it go. And it will keep going like last time and the time before that until it blows up. And next time the locals will be in charge and everybody will FUCKING DIE!"

"Guys are afraid for their jobs," Gene added, his tone more measured than Justin. "None of us fear these guys, but what we fear is losing our jobs if we defend ourselves or our mates, and that is what is happening more and more now. This will just keep getting bigger and bigger until it gives."

"These guys make out like they are the invisible ones, like they are voiceless. But they have a voice and they use it to lie. I've read all sorts of vile shit on the internet – that we sneak into their rooms and molest them at night, that we tie them up and torture them. All these advocates at home peddle this bullshit, they set up crowd-funding campaigns to pay off local police, so they won't be investigated, yet we get questioned every time Justin farts in room!"

That last bit elicited laughter and helped ease the tension that was brewing, but there was still plenty more to get off our chests. There were plenty of decisions being made higher up that were pissing us off as well. Every rotation the training given to ERT was being wound back more and more, to the point that we hadn't touched our shields in weeks. Recertification exercises had been cancelled, and 'H' had eventually quit his job as the ERT training coordinator because everything was getting blocked. He wasn't replaced.

Maybe this was all part of the plan to gradually wind back operations and hand over to the locals, but it seemed like courting disaster. It was as if people up top were forgetting what had happened at the start of the year, or were just quietly hoping it wouldn't happen again.

> "They forget that we saved their arses back in January," Jake said. "But they just tell us not to complain because we get to go to the gym during shift."

We left the session happy to have gotten some things off our chests, but not really thinking anything would change. We left RPC2 to walk back to the compounds, being passed on the way by our former ERT minibus that had long since been sequestered for the double-positives to take on bus trips into town. As it passed us by, Iranians hung out the windows, hooting and jeering at us.

"I hope you guys fucking crash!" Somebody yelled out. I'm not sure who it was.

CHAPTER 21

COMING HOME

Although the transit East Lorengau was the face of the refugee resettlement program, it had to be remembered that settlement in Manus Island itself was never the long-term goal. The small province of fifty thousand residents and limited industry would never be able to support a sudden influx of new permanent residents, as Charcoal and the other vagrants camped out behind the centre showed.

A few might have stayed. We heard stories that a few Rohingya had taken up fishing, married local women and fathered children with them – all without any of the problems that Iranians like Captain Jack had had. But most of the refugees would be expected to move to the mainland, following their transition program at East Lorengau.

Stories began to filter back from the first refugees to head over the water, and it was clear that things hadn't gone according to plan. The first of them, an engineer with a job offer in Port Moresby found that it had fallen through by the time he arrived. Fortunately for him though, he picked up a liaison role with the PNG government agency responsible for resettling the refugees.

The stories of those that headed to PNG's second city of Lae were quite different. A handful had headed there to take up government-funded building apprenticeships. Most quit within a few weeks however, and when they did the PNG government withdrew their financial support and evicted them from their accommodation. After sleeping rough and relying on the charity of locals to survive, some of them returned to Manus and tried to get back in the centre.

One of the men went one step further. He boarded a flight from

Lae to Port Moresby, and then on to Fiji. The problem was that he was later arrested in Fiji with forged travel documents and deported back to PNG.

***

There was other stuff going on behind the scenes that contributed to the air of discontent amongst the teams. We were all aware more than ever that the wrong reaction to transferees' provocation could cost us our jobs, but the truth was that our jobs were not safe anyway. The original contract for operating the MRPC was up for renewal, and Transfield (with Wilson, by default) now had to submit a new tender amongst many competitors.

Our original six-month individual contracts had been extended by another eighteen, but now that had come up for renewal as well. With the tender cut-off date having come and gone with no word either way, we were now on month-to-month extensions and essentially living rotation to rotation. We had all seen how quickly things could turn sour from the old G4S days, and a lot of guys were understandably nervous. I was one of them.

Manus Island had been good to all of us, financially. I was always aware that it was not a long-term career and that it could end at any time, and tried to not become accustomed to the inflated income I had come into. Nevertheless, I had just purchased an apartment, and nobody likes ambiguity when you have a mortgage.

Everyone was always looking at other long-term options, and Manus was great for that. The cashflow and time off helped for planning your next move. But none of those future plans had come together just yet. I wanted things to keep going the way they were. For all my talk of not getting accustomed to the FIFO lifestyle, I was comfortable.

Things at home were changing too. Zoe had always been supportive of me working away, and had put up with a lot of it over the last two years. When we had first gotten together Zoe had been somewhat of a corporate high-flyer and had the social circle to match. I would visit her at her office for lunch on my weeks off, watching the suits come and go and taking in how different our two worlds were. My biggest worry at that time had been how I might keep up with her when Manus ended.

But things had evolved since then. Zoe had never really liked corporate life and really wanted to strike out on her own. She had business ideas of her own incubating in her head and eventually she took the plunge to commit to them full-time. We became involved in the world of the start-ups.

What Zoe was achieving was amazing, but it was always incredibly tough. Anyone who says the life of an entrepreneur is anything but constant hustle and struggle is full of shit. Zoe was in a bubble with only me for support, and that support was not there for three weeks out of six. I missed Zoe painfully whilst I was away, but I could get by on a Skype call a day. She couldn't.

I wanted this gig to run its course. I wanted to see it out to the end. I didn't want to hang up my FIFO boots until I had lined up a dream job at home. Opportunities were popping up here and there, and with the contract uncertain people started to jump before they fell. Several guys were poached by a rival company for the ERT on Christmas Island. It would have been a great opportunity, but the contract required a six-month unbroken stint on the island. Not really an option.

Some guys got jobs in Iraq and Afghanistan. One opportunity came up at the embassy in Kabul, where a new security provider had undercut the existing operator and secured the job of protecting Australia's diplomats there. With the all-important contacts in place from the ex-circuit guys who had retired to Manus, several of the boys secured a spot on the new gig.

Although it was far from a certainty, it was the closest I had ever been to the proverbial holy grail of security contracting, and the closest I was ever likely to be. But with a rotation of nine weeks on with three weeks off, I could never seriously consider it. It would be too unfair on Zoe. She would have put on a brave face, like she always did, but it would have been selfish of me.

The moment I knew I would be leaving before I was ready came one afternoon before nightshift. I had called Zoe on Skype as I always did, and it was clear something wasn't right. Tearfully, she told me she wasn't handling things. The pressure of the business on her was crushing. I felt incredibly guilty. I went to work that night knowing that this would be my last rotation on the island.

Later that night, when it was my team's turn for training, we headed back to our rooms to get changed for the gym. Using this opportunity whilst I was still alert, I sat down on my laptop and began bashing out CVs and cover letters. It was nearly an hour before I appeared in the gym, but I didn't care. My mind had already left the island.

I didn't think this would come back to bite me the way it did. The CCTV cameras that were positioned around our accommodation to deter thieves caught me heading in late, and questions were asked about what I was doing when I was on the clock. ERT had somewhat of a covenant of trust with conducting PT during shift, more so now that so much of our other in-role training had been scaled back. There was talk now that such training time would be cut altogether due to my abuse of the leeway. I felt like I had let the whole team down. Even though the threat wasn't followed through with, it really got me down and made me more determined to leave. I felt like I had lost my team's trust.

I got an email from an employer a few days later offering me an interview. When I met with them in Brisbane they gushed over me and offered me a supervisory role at a government site. I told Zoe when I got home, and she was ecstatic. No more fly-out days. No more crappy Skype calls. No more Manus Island.

I emailed the team and told them the news. They seemed surprised, and offered their congratulations. A few even expressed envy. But I wasn't excited about it. As the day I would have been scheduled to fly back came around, I felt envy that the team were heading off again without me. I decided that I would throw myself into my new job, and really make a go of it.

I hated it from the moment I started. My new job was as a "security-concierge" in charge of three others at a site that housed the headquarters of several government agencies. Little more than a glorified secretary, I had traded the riot squad for activating ID cards and chasing up courier deliveries.

This change had been supposed to help things, but it didn't. I might have been home with Zoe every night, but with long hours and commute I had no life. Sundays 'were miserable, as I had to force myself to get out of bed on a Monday. My income had dropped considerably, yet my living expenses had risen. The pressure Zoe was under didn't ease, and I was in no position to be supportive – although she would say otherwise.

What I hated most though, was that in the back of mind I started to resent her. I resented that I had given up my monthly well-paid adventure in the South Pacific, to work in a place that made me miserable. I love her more than anything in the world, but I felt like I had gotten a raw deal. I felt as if I was back at the very same place I had gone to Manus Island to escape. It was irony at its finest.

***

When news broke that the PNG Supreme Court had ruled the processing centre on Manus Island to be illegal, my first reaction was to laugh. I just assumed that someone had forgotten to pay someone else their bribe that month. But it was the first real sign that the job that was never going to last forever now had an end in sight. A six-month deadline was set for processing to wrap up and for the centre to close. Refugee determinations had long since been completed by ICSA, and those found to be genuine refugees now had the choice of moving to East Lorengau or going home. Remaining at the MRPC with all their cooking, cleaning and earning being done for them was no longer an option because there would not *be* an MRPC. What was going to happen to the double-negatives was less clear.

I caught up with Alex shortly after the news was announced, at the German Club in Woolloongabba. Ironically with the announcement of the centre's imminent closure, Transfield had been awarded a new contract and business was continuing as usual until the closure date. Alex was clearly exhausted when I saw him. Unlike me he had genuinely had enough of the island, having done G4S beforehand and fought through both riots. He told me that a major fight had broken out with transferees in Mike compound and several ERT had been injured, some seriously.

Just a few weeks later, Alex had even more reason to want off the island. I woke to news one morning that there had been a shooting incident at the island. PNG naval personnel had done what amounted to a drive-by shooting, peppering the compounds with un-aimed fire and sending transferees and SSAs alike scrambling for cover. Alex had narrowly avoided taking one of the bullets.

The reasons given were varied. Some claimed it had stemmed from the results of a soccer match between transferees and sailors, whilst others claimed that a local child had been led into the centre by its residents, kicking off a local backlash. The truth was probably a mixture of the two.

When the day finally came that the MRPC was closed for good, there were still a few hundred men living in the centre who refused to relocate to East Lorengau. The Australian and PNG staff packed up and left, heading to the airport for the last time. Locals apparently looted the accommodation and RPC2, getting their hands on whatever remained. The next morning, local tradesmen arrived to start dismantling the fences, turning off the water and electricity while they were at it. The hold-outs still refused to leave, and effectively began squatting in the remains of the decommissioned facilities.

They immediately took to social media, showing the world the horror of their plight. They showed the wells they had been forced to dig in the ground for drinking water – incredibly they had managed to dig them through solid coral rock without an excavator in sight. How they continued to charge the mobile devices they were uploading the videos with was a mystery as well, but I understood nothing on Manus was ever as it seemed.

The squatters began to protest, joined in solidarity by activists in Australia doing all sorts of clever things like lying on train tracks and chaining themselves to doors. It seemed like they were cut from the same cloth. After a few days of this, the PNG authorities moved in and removed the remaining squatters by force and relocated them to the East Lorengau centre. A long chapter in Australia's history of offshore immigration processing was over.